MW00785150

Nietzsche

Nietzsche

The Meaning of Earth

Lucas Murrey

LEHIGH UNIVERSITY PRESS
Bethlehem

Published by Lehigh University Press
Copublished by The Rowman & Littlefield Publishing Group, Inc.
4501 Forbes Boulevard, Suite 200, Lanham, Maryland 20706
www.rowman.com

Unit A, Whitacre Mews, 26-34 Stannary Street, London SE11 4AB

British Library Cataloguing in Publication Information Available

Library of Congress Cataloging-in-Publication Data

Murrey, Lucas.
Nietzsche : the meaning of earth / Lucas Murrey.
pages cm
Includes bibliographical references and index.
ISBN 978-1-61146-154-1 (cloth : alk. paper) -- ISBN 978-1-61146-155-8 (electronic)
1. Nietzsche, Friedrich Wilhelm, 1844-1900. 2. Dionysus (Greek deity) 3. Philosophy of nature. I.
Title.
B3317.M89 2015
193--dc23
2014047068

Printed in the United States of America

To Noam Chomsky and Charles Ferguson,
in the hope of deepening our understanding of the psychic origin of greed.
And to Barbara Bodine, Sérgio Vieira de Mello, and the Iraqi people,
heroines and heroes,
der Sinn der Erde.

Contents

Contents   ix

Acknowledgments

I would like to thank Getty Images for the permission to use the cover picture. I am also especially thankful to my mother, father, sister, and grand-mother—as well as my colleagues and friends—who supported this work.

Preface

In his unpublished preface to *Animal Farm*, George Orwell points out that "unpopular ideas can be silenced, and inconvenient facts kept dark, without the need for any official ban."[1] This occurs not through "government," but the media that inculcates in the people "a general tacit agreement that 'it wouldn't do' to mention that particular fact."[2] Proceeding to the centralization of the press and its mobilization of "daily newspapers," Orwell reminds us that "most of it is owned by wealthy men who have every motive to be dishonest on certain important topics."[3]

This description of the visual and linguistic culture to which we as a species remain captive invites us to consider a few questions. How are we to understand the powerful psychic force that has been harnessed to destroy language and the freedom to see? And in what way does money underlie this unlimited, dirty river of words and pictures that, in turn, instills the social conformity of slavery to individual tyrants?

In no small measure, these are the questions that the following study of Friedrich Nietzsche seeks to answer. As I show, Nietzsche understands individuals in modern time as imprisoned in a distracting, narcissistic image that is violently cut off from nature and community. "And with fifty mirrors around you," Zarathustra says, horror-struck, "you flatter and slander your play of colours!" Further, Nietzsche explicitly connects such visual ghastliness with the no less shocking monetization of humankind, as preeminently exemplified by the modern "city, which steams with the vapour of slaughtered spirit" and which is ruled by isolated tyrants who "jingle with their gold."

This is not to say that such answers are always straightforward. For what does it mean to say that "wealthy men" and women, who, by virtue of their unleashing of the unlimited images in which our everyday lives drown, rule our hyper-visual civilization while they "jingle with their gold"? On the one hand, it is clear that this endless flow of pictures is caught up also in an endless flow of language that knows nothing of the communal spirit of earth. About this Nietzsche leaves little doubt, as when he casts light on the linguistic essence of the city wherein "spirit has here become a verbal game. . . . Loathsome verbal-swill does it vomit!" In fact, it is this "verbal game" from which the centralized press and its "daily newspapers" issue forth: "they make newspapers out of this verbal-swill." "Do you not see the souls hanging like limp, dirty rags?—And they even make newspapers out of these rags!"

But, on the other hand, can we say that Nietzsche identifies the source of the exceptional psychical presence that the moguls of the media willfully appropriate to kill the natural rights of people to see and speak? Although he creatively evokes the Apolline in regard to a "primal desire for appearance," that is, a limitless desire to stabilize "a single world-image," Nietzsche's Dionysian insights are alas neutralized by nineteenth-century strains of nationalism and racism.

In a way, this brings me to the goal of this study, which is to transcend Nietzsche and wonder about our own answers to the questions above. How, for instance, do we understand the origin of the mass psychosis to which our language and style of seeing has succumbed? And in what way has the unlimited essence of the (relatively) new visual media of money been able to indoctrinate, through its control of the media, "a general tacit agreement that 'it wouldn't do' to mention that particular fact"? If the following does not directly answer these urgent questions, one thing remains clear: Examining Nietzsche's search for such answers will surely enrich our own.

L. Murrey
December 7, 2014
Corseaux, Switzerland

NOTES

1. George Orwell, "The Freedom of the Press," *Times Literary Supplement*, 15 September 1972.
2. Ibid.
3. Ibid.

Abbreviations

A The Antichrist
ASC Attempt at Self-Criticism (1886 *Preface to BT*)
BGE Beyond Good and Evil
BT The Birth of Tragedy
CW The Case of Wagner
D Daybreak
EH Ecce Homo
GM On the Genealogy of Morals
GS The Gay Science
HAH Human, All Too Human
KB Kommentar zu den Bänden 1–13
NCW Nietzsche contra Wagner
NF1 Nachgelassene Fragmente 1869–1874
NF2 Nachgelassene Fragmente 1875–1879
NF3 Nachgelassene Fragmente 1880–1882
TI Twilight of the Idols
TL On Truth and Lies in an Extra-moral Sense
UM Untimely Meditations
Z Thus Spoke Zarathustra

Introduction

RISE OF MASS CULTURE AND THE *VISUALIZED CHRONOTOPE*

This work on Friedrich Nietzsche (1844–1900) follows that which I recently devoted to *Hölderlin's Dionysiac Poetry*.[1] In part III of this earlier study I show that Friedrich Hölderlin's songs are unique in (Western) art because they alone retrieve an original sociopolitical experience of space and time (and language) that challenges the lethal visual media of money. Important to this retrieval is *Dionysian seeing*: a literal and metaphorical style of looking that overcomes monetary alienation and reconnects with images of community and nature.[2]

But what makes this earthly form of picturing the cosmos critical is how, in its modern instance, the psychic danger of capitalism in industrial time is brought to light.[3] Hölderlin envisions a money-tyrant who, "to make / A little profit" (v 39–40), reduces nature to that which he can he spy on through a "telescope" (v 51).[4] Like Oedipus, who has "one eye too many," perverse individuals "squander, misuse" (v 46)[5] earth's resources to satisfy their images of individualism.

But as this work also shows, Hölderlin's resurrection of *Dionysian seeing* leans into oblivion. Lack of a mentor—one thinks of Friedrich Schiller, who stood by his "dearest Swabian" as Hölderlin "lived on next to nothing and ate only one meal a day"[6] —gives way to isolation. By 1800, Hölderlin loses contact with Georg Hegel and Christian Neuffer. Although enduring, his relationship with Isaac von Sinclair (who also falls in love with Hölderlin's lifelong muse, Susette Gontard, and who is later accused of treason in Württemberg) represents an ambivalent, tense, and episodic friendship, at best.

In the abyss of Hölderlin's "desolate time" (v 122)[7] is the absence of a timeless love. This is particularly painful because of the isolation to which his Dionysian affections for Diotima (Susette) succumb. Although he preserves his letters from his eternal muse, never once—neither before nor during his forty years of madness—does Hölderlin dare to tell his protestant mother about Susette's existence. And inseparable from the absence of immortal passion is that of his new Dionysus. The tyrant into whom Napoléon degenerates suggests that even revolutionary *patriots* can be no less tyrannical than the (*pater*) king whose stately head they willfully remove. Given such abject poverty and hopelessness, that Hölderlin is able to retrieve with such precision an original Dionysian experience of space and time (what I name the *Dionysiac chronotope*)[8] appears miraculous. All the same, the penniless poet "had no followers of his own."[9] Despite the desperation to which he succumbs, because Hölderlin remains "frozen and benumbed by the winter which surrounds" him, there is no one to whom he can pass "the blazing, gleaming torch"(v 218).[10]

To understand the (industrial) modern light that consumes Hölderlin's Dionysian illumination we must consider, on the one hand, the progress of technology in the eighteenth century. Although the poet is inseparable from idyllic southwest German (and French) landscapes, already during his earliest songs humankind is unlocking a new form of energy capture. Suddenly Western civilization has access to what seems like an unlimited amount of steam and electric power.[11] Throughout the remainder of Hölderlin's life, the speed of technological progress not only continues, but increases its velocity. Humphrey Davis's hideous mass of Voltaic piles (and sulfurous fumes) in 1808 is followed by Hans Ørsted's (accidental) discovery of electromagnetism in 1820 and Michael Faraday's transformation of this (magical) phenomenon into movement one year later in 1821. In a little over two decades after Hölderlin's death on June 7, 1843, James Maxwell formulates the first theory of wireless communication in his *Dynamical Theory of the Electromagnetic Field* from 1865.

But to understand this "desolate time"—the discovery of natural laws are in themselves not necessarily bad—consumes the epiphany of Hölderlin's "[c]horus-leader of stars" (v 1196),[12] we must reflect not only on the rapid progress of technology, but also that upon which these physical revelations unconsciously rest, namely the concentration of money that is inseparable from such modern advancement. Still today we continue to content ourselves with the familiar (and simplistic) view that advances in technology bring the world together and, therefore, lead to a democratic, even utopian state. Ever since this time the modern individual who dares embrace such (breakneck) technological change is often pictured as adventurous, exciting and a model for us all. One recalls Phileas Fogg from Jules Verne's *Around the World in*

Eighty Days from 1873: an unreal, that is, abstract picture of a person who appears, significantly, at the height of the British Empire.

Before we celebrate this optimistic image of progress and democracy we have to consider how the technological steps forward that Western civilization claims are invariably appropriated by its masters who seek first "to make / A little profit" (v 39–40), even if (in fact, especially if) this means more steps backward for people and nature. For what has defined modern life thus far has not been the communal magic of phenomena that science can inspire, but, instead, what these natural phenomena can do to help already wealthy individuals increase their wealth. Consider the historical time when the Western belief that nature and people are essentially mechanistic—one thinks of Julian Offray de La Mettrie's *L'homme machine*[13] from 1748 and the *automata* of Jacques de Vaucanson (1709–1782)—undergoes a geographic shift. Britain's unique coal resources and incentives for engineers and entrepreneurs to develop new forms of technology change the businessman from Liverpool (who has been selling boatloads of textiles and guns for slaves in Africa)[14] into a master of the new mechanical time. This leads also to what I have noted in my earlier study: the iron umbilical cord (Stephenson's *Rocket*) that is set between Liverpool and Manchester already in 1829.[15] And as we shall see in the next chapter, it is no accident that Nietzsche, the first (self-proclaimed) Dionysian philosopher (and who follows in Hölderlin's footsteps in ways that even he could never imagine), understands his philosophical exploration of community and earth as a part of a new "struggle" against "English-mechanistic world-dumbing," *im Kampf mit der englisch-mechanistischen Welt-Vertölpelung.*[16]

The unlocking of industrial technology is first and foremost a leap in energy capture. One calorie consumed while mining coal yields fifty. The application of this energy explosion to agriculture leads to one of the most radical transformations that our species has undergone: *The emergence of exponential population growth.* All of a sudden we humans are taller and heavier, we live longer and, relative to before, we essentially eliminate infant mortality. Our familiar *more-of-everything* culture is founded on the increasing mechanization of everyday existence (itself a consequence of unlocking and consuming this new style of energy capture). By 1830 almost anything made by hand can be made faster by a machine. Together these peculiar forces allow England to invent the first high-production economy (and mass consumer culture). No later than 1850, less than seven years after Hölderlin's death, Britain bestrides the world like a Titan, "striving," as Nietzsche says, "for *English* happiness."[17] Given the disconnected spirit of limitlessness that is peculiar to money and that such mass consumption can only reinforce, this means—to continue in the language of Nietzsche—"happiness of the greatest number."[18] This is something to which I shall return.

But for now, let us be somewhat clearer about the kind of numeric ecstasy this implies. Capitalism's internal dynamic of necessary and unlimited self-expansion produces, in a relatively brief amount of time, a (brave) new world of industry that knows nothing of (self-)regulation. Consider the industries to which steam power has leaped by 1870. Already Britain's engines are generating four million horsepower, equivalent to the labor of forty million men. This concentrates the estrangement of humans from nature and one another. The poverty upon which modern money-tyrants, to whom Nietzsche refers when he speaks of "these ponderous herd animals with bad consciences (who commit themselves to promoting egoism as an issue of general welfare),"[19] leads to an unprecedented wave of urbanization. One recalls Karl Marx's description of the *Scottish Enclosure Acts* that began in the eighteenth century and uprooted countless communities that, after centuries of living on the land, have to flee to London in search of slave wages.[20] Tragic losses of earth and communality pave the way, literally, to the absorption of more than half of the world's population into cities. The effect of this cataclysmic change pulsates today in Tokyo, Mexico City, Mumbai, New York, and Sao Paolo, to mention just a few.

To understand the lightning (technological and monetary) "progress" that devours Hölderlin's *Dionysiac chronotope*, we have to look directly at the egoism of nineteenth century "earthly masters" (to use a sinister phrase from Paul in the New Testament) and the masses of new "[s]laves" that these industrial moguls demand: a catastrophic loss of fairness, justice, and feel for the sacred, all of which are now sacrificed to the supposed inevitability of quantifiable competition. We have mentioned the emergence of the prototype of our "self-destructive culture of the unlimited."[21] Given the fashionable aesthetics of the time, it is to be expected that contemporary reports—the *media control* of the early industrial era—seek to absorb this misfortune into hyper-abstract (that is, sociopolitically ineffectual) intellectual categories. Particularly popular is the still modish concept of the *sublime*: "the vast bellows that give those roaring blasts [from the furnaces, forges, &c.] make the whole edifice horridly sublime."[22] Here *horrid* is—somehow?—not really horrid.

Nevertheless, a few commentators are less romantic when confronting "the lethally limiting unlimitedness"[23] of money and the social practices that it generates:

> All fixed, rusted relations, with their train of ancient, venerable imaginations and world-views are swept away, all new-formed ones become antiquated before they can fossilise. All that is solid melts into the air, all that is holy is profaned, and humans are at last compelled to face with sober eyes their real conditions of life and their relations with their kind.[24]

Consider also the "half-frightful scene" of "the iron and coal works"[25] in Birmingham from the summer of 1824:

> A space 30 sq. miles . . . covered over with furnaces, rolling-mills, steam-engines and sooty men. A dense cloud of pestilential smoke hangs over it forever, blackening even the grain that grows upon it; and at night the whole region burns like a volcano spitting fire from a thousand tubes of brick. I thought of the price we had to pay for our vaunted supremacy in the manufacture of iron. But oh how wretched hundred and fifty thousand mortals who grind out their destiny there! In the coal-mines they were literally naked, many of them, all but trousers; black as ravens; plashing about among dripping caverns, or scrambling amid heaps of broken mineral; and thirsting unquenchably.[26]

This grisly scene recalls Hölderlin's critique of "despicable gold," *schnödem Gold*, and the modern individuals who selfishly "squande[r], misus[e]" (v 46) the "powers" (v 46) of nature.[27] In particular, it evokes the image of tragic isolation from *The Archipelago* where,

> [e]ach individual is nailed alone
> To his own work, in the noise of his workplace
> Listening only to himself and imprisoned in a labour of madness,
> With an aggressive hand, restless, but always and forever
> Bringing forth nothing, like the Furies, from the toil of his hands. (v 242–46)

But as we have seen, Hölderlin's poetry retrieves not only Greek tragedy to question the unlimited "machine process"[28] of "a clever race" (v 48)[29] of money-tyrants in the present, but also Greece's warnings about the mortal danger of the eyes in myth, cult, and theater. Semele, who is linked (directly) to Dionysus and (indirectly) to Persephone and Narcissus (and even to Oedipus, who as a tragic hero and tyrant is related to Kreon and Pentheus), models the new mortal threat of seeing that accompanies a *visualized* space-time of money no longer in balance with nature.[30] Hölderlin adapts the early Hellenic response to this peril to absorb the (unlimited) abstractions of *monetized* eyes that selfishly appropriate modern visual media such as the "telescope[s]" (v 51) into the (unlimited) horror of mystic initiation.[31] Consider Hyperion's criticism of the modern man who, "when he reflects," degenerates into "a beggar" like the wandering, homeless Oedipus.[32]

Understanding the visual unconscious of money and technology that swallow Hölderlin's *Dionysiac chronotope* whole is thus to understand those who support the perverse, hyper-abstract thinking to which they are tied. The explosion of energy discussed above is expressed in regard to a (limitless) homogenization of space and time. A train cutting through a rural landscape is the modern extension of "the paradox of an unlimited abstract territoriality" that existed already in the imagination of early historic Greece, one that encompasses not only "all geographic space," but also, "beyond that, the whole cosmos."[33] This means a deepening of the *visualized chronotope*[34] against which Hölderlin's poetry (unconsciously) struggles. The hyper-abstractions of Greek philosophy, medieval Christianity, the *Renaissance*, the Enlightenment, and Romanticism now coalesce into "the homogenised sensibility of our hyper-monetised, atomised, and self-destructive culture of the unlimited."[35]

Important is not simply the history of a mass population ruled by a concentration of the new visual spirit of money, but also the uneasy physical (and psychical) symptoms that haunt this era. Consider the spatialized time that structures a train station—the *modern experience* that a wealthy, urban gentleman like Phileas Fogg knows as if intuitively without having to consult his watch because he has internalized the concept of temporality as a series of static (Aristotelian) images.[36] Consider also the moving picture of the landscape seen through a glass window: an endless succession of places with which the individual in the iron compartment has no relation. And consider finally the wages paid by hours and minutes after an individual worker "clocks in."

This implicit collapse of the primal, incalculable experience of space and time in the nineteenth century implies further the vanishing of nonvisual experiences: the smell of a landscape, the natural sounds of human labor (now in competition with the whizzing noise of automated machines), or the nearness of an embrace (who the person embracing does not see) are all suddenly (tragically) distant. When we think of what is lost, it is clear that Marx's description of "[t]he *forming* of the five senses" in 1844 as "a labour of the whole of world-history"[37] can be understood as a gesture to the history of this physical/psychical perversion. Our relation to nature and ourselves, as Marx and Hölderlin feared, "melts into the air."

But the victory of the *visualized chronotope* over a Dionysian image of earth and community has still to be explored. In contrast to the magical picture of Hölderlin's "[c]horus-leader of stars" from around 1802, the nineteenth century produces the terrifying image of a "whole region [that] burns like a volcano spitting fire from a thousand tubes of brick." The light that emerges from burning fossil fuels (most of which are at least sixty million years old—that is, long before we humans and our five senses, including our eyes, evolved) is not simply the familiar opposite of Dionysian light and seeing, but the beginning of an altogether new world-historical lightlessness. Black iron, black coal, black smoke, and black houses, let us not forget, create the Victorian costume: black funerals and top hats—and even the name *Black Country*. Demeter's gift to humankind in the form of a luminous epiphany of corn and mystical "light," $\varphi\tilde{\omega}\varsigma$[38] —to which Hölderlin refers when he sings of a "flowering land where upon sunny plains/Noble corn and fruit ripens" (v 263–64),[39] yields to "[a] dense cloud of pestilential smoke [that] hangs over [the earth] forever, blackening even the grain that grows upon it." This reminds one of the (spiritual and physical) darkness that accompanies the now ever-present horrors of the industrial accident: dismembered bodies and eyes that the manmade (mechanized) thunder of the modern train crash invites.

This brings us closer to that which, more than anything else, enables the darkening of Hölderlin's Dionysian light: the emergence of the visual spirit of nineteenth-century mass consumer culture. We have noted how science tends to be absorbed into the *monetized chronotope*.[40] Instead of exploring the enchantment of phenomena like steam, electricity, and electromagnetism, Western masters have been exclusively interested in what these earthly phenomena can do to for their individualism, in particular how they can master nature to make more money. Here I extend this argument to the *visualized chronotope*. This comes into focus when we recall the magical colors that filled Heinrich Geißler's glass tubes in the 1850s. Although enchanting, the visual realm of science and magic is foremost a (profitable) distraction. In fact, so great is the way that the visual impulse in humankind is suddenly exploited, it is tempting to think that we as a species suddenly succumbed to the fatal attraction of our own image in a mirror. For Nietzsche, the English problem he identifies is greater than England herself: "for I am already touching upon something *serious* to me," he writes, "on the 'European problem,' as I understand it, on the breeding of a new ruling caste for Europe."[41]

As Richard Seaford suggests, the internal dynamic of necessary and unlimited self-expansion that belongs to capitalism produces values that are different in kind from those of previous eras.[42] Perhaps most terrifying of these new values is the lethal visual culture that accompanies (and reinforces) money. In my previous work, I have touched upon the deep history of the desire to fix an image, for instance, when Alberti seeks mathematically informed pictures.[43] During Hölderlin's lifetime, the old obsession with the camera obscura gives rise to the first photograph in 1825, the patenting of the zoetrope in 1834 by a British mathematician, and the first lucrative photographic processes in 1837 and 1841. Soon after, the photographic magic lantern (1850) and the first color photograph (1861) are invented.

Like Hölderlin, Nietzsche's attraction to Dionysian light coincides with the rise of this modern visual culture. The sociopolitical significance of photography is unleashed just after 1871 when it is appropriated by the French State for criminal identification following the Paris Commune.[44] Experiments in the photography of motion (1873), commercially successful graphic prints, including halftone photographs in New York City (1880), the patenting of the first film in roll form (1884), the first electromechanical TV scanning system (1884), the manufacturing of flexible transparent film (1889), and the invention of the Kinetoscope (1889) all occur while Nietzsche, who aggressively abandons the progress of such visual media, is busy bringing forth an (oppositional) Dionysian style of seeing.

It is thus not only the *monetized chronotope*, but the *visualized chronotope* of the last two hundred years to which Hölderlin's poetry succumbs—
and this means also the lightless abyss wherein our next earthly and communal hero first stumbles across an authentic image. But perhaps most frighten-
ing is how *visualized thought* exacerbates the "diseased mind" (v 1015) of
the intellectual money-tyrant. As I have shown, there is a mental illness that
reinforces the hyper-abstract concept of the *sublime*. Edmund Burke bizarre-
ly claims that all humans "have a degree of delight, and that no small one, in
the real misfortunes and pains of others."[45] The wealthy Whig of the late
eighteenth century proceeds: "there is no spectacle we so eagerly pursue as
that of some uncommon and grievous calamity."[46]

Burke's psychosis is similar to that of the tyrants of the Greek stage such
as Pentheus, who in Euripides's *Bacchae* wants to cut off the head of the new
magician (Dionysus) who has come to his city—Pentheus, who sees the
demigod of earthly light bound in a dark cell and threatens to imprison
Dionysus's maenads, upon whose image he desires to secretly spy (in exchange for a large sum of gold).[47]

Hyper-abstractions like the *sublime* tend to legitimate the inhumanity of a
monetized-visualized cosmos wherein individual rulers have no responsibil-
ity to peoples and environments. Burke's perverse reflection on seeing is
followed by descriptions of "vast bellows that give those roaring blasts [from
the furnaces, forges, &c.] make the whole edifice horridly *sublime*."[48] Such
devious attempts to repress this abyss continue in the clever, but finally
ignorant musings of many nineteenth-century intellectuals. Five years before
Hölderlin's death the English literary critic William Hazlitt formulates the
following (grotesque) rhetorical question:

> Why do we go to see tragedies in general? Why do we always read the
> accounts in the newspapers of dreadful fires and shocking murders? Why do
> so many persons frequent trials and executions, or why do the lower classes
> almost universally take delight in barbarous sports and cruelty to animals, but
> because there is a natural tendency in the mind to strong excitement, a desire to
> have its faculties roused and stimulated to the utmost?[49]

Most of us are unable to accept the idea that "ungovernable violence . . .
and a restless love of mischief,"[50] in particular an enjoyment of the images of
the suffering other, are natural. Among those who, in contrast to Burke and
Hazlitt, sense the visual tragedy that underlies industrialization (when "all
that is holy is profaned") is the French poet Charles Baudelaire. Baudelaire
presciently foresees the impending symptoms of modern visual media:

> A vengeful God has granted the wishes of this multitude. Daguerre was his
> Messiah. And now the public says to itself: "Since photography gives us every
> guarantee of exactitude that we could desire (they really believe that, the

idiots!), then photography and art are the same thing." From that moment on our squalid society rushes, Narcissus to a man, to gaze at its trivial image on a scrap of metal.[51]

As we shall see, among those whose Dionysian voice arises to resist the *visualized chronotope* that spirals out of England is Nietzsche: "What is lacking in England, and what has always been missing," he declares, is "a real *power* of spirituality, a real *profundity* of spiritual reflection, in short, a philosophy."[52]

EMERGENCE OF UNLIMITED LANGUAGE

Part II of this work shows that Nietzsche's retrieval of Dionysian Greece is significantly more infected by nationalism than Hölderlin's adaptation of Hellenic earth and co-being.[53] Nevertheless, Nietzsche's pointed criticisms of England are not only nationalist in tone. Among other things, philosophy and language are, for him, inseparable. When Nietzsche declares that "[t]hese Englishmen are no race of philosophers,"[54] we are invited to consider the thoughtless transformation to which language succumbs in the nineteenth century. This means the rapid extension (and homogenization) of the English language across the entire planet.

Although the number of native Mandarin Chinese speakers is well over two times that of native English speakers, when one counts the number of persons who also speak second languages, English outnumbers Chinese by more than one-third. Almost 30 percent of the seven billion (plus) persons populating earth speak English whereas 20 percent speak Chinese—the closest second, incidentally, of the other approximately 6,500 languages in existence. Like Hölderlin who warns us about *monetized* (and homogenized) "names" (v 52) that emerge alongside the reduction of the cosmos to images seen through visual media like the modern "telescope" (v 51), Nietzsche senses the danger of a *visualized language* that knows no earthly or communal limit.[55] In this section, we briefly turn to the deeper reason why the heart of Hölderlin's poetry (*Dionysiac language*)[56] is lost during the arc of the nineteenth century, that is, during the emergence of an *unlimited language* of technology, money, and visual culture.

This is not to say that the progress of experiencing (and thinking about) language during industrialization is exclusively negative. The transition from Gutenberg bibles of the fifteenth century to newspapers and journals of the eighteenth century—and the literacy explosion in England and elsewhere in Europe that soon follow (again, due to industrial energy and population increase) is significantly caught up, if only in part, in a story of sociopolitical liberation. The steam press of 1810 and rotary drum printing of 1843—one might also include Morse Code of the 1840s and the transatlantic telegraph cable of the 1860s—tend to be thought of as making the world a smaller, more democratic (and utopian) place. After all, humans who can communicate better can better establish their individual freedoms. The *Freedom's Journal*, the first African American newspaper from 1827, is indeed a powerful sociopolitical awakening.

But this optimistic story masks a deeper one of money and, in particular, the secret story of a lethal language of individualism. For it is not the (ancient) powers of steam and writing that suddenly come together in 1810, but instead a *patent* (for the steam press) that ensures that all money made by this machine shall go to one individual and he alone. The same can be said about the rotary drum press, which is patented in 1847. Perhaps most illustrative of how Western civilization tends to be more attracted to what earthly phenomena such as steam, electricity, and electromagnetism can do for individuals seeking to make more money—than what the communal and earthly magic of these events can inspire—is the transatlantic telegraph cable that has its origin in British engineers and American businessmen of the mid-nineteenth century. Although never mentioned, there is no record that these individuals had any significant interest in the improvement of humankind.

Belonging to this history is a new *monetized* media control, as witnessed in that which underlies the Crimean war of 1853–1856. This means the first instrumental use of a new modern complex of journalism, railways, and electric telegraphs to sway public opinion. As we shall see, Nietzsche is acutely aware of the difference between the *Dionysiac language* he seeks to resurrect and the increasing subordination of language to "the homogenized sensibility" of the machine. As if a mirror reflection of the visual industry that haunts the dark philosopher, there is also a corresponding media industry that (industriously) contrasts the chthonic spirit of Nietzsche's Hellenic language. One thinks of the typewriter (1867), the patenting of the five-unit telegraph (1876), the telephone (1876), the phonograph (1877), the linotype (1884) the Nipkow disk (1884), and—last but not least—the invention of the literary agent (1888) just when Nietzsche's vanity publishing comes to an abrupt, tragic halt.

On the one hand, the "mysterious and terrifying power, the unlimited isolating passion for individual gain, more powerful even than the instinct for self-preservation" that brutally reduces language to visual media (for profit) concentrates what we may call a style of word-instrumentalization that emerges already in early historic Greece.[57] On the other hand, how we tend to think of language, in particular how higher forms of research and education formulate an understanding of written and oral communication at this time, becomes more disconnected from earth and community. Nietzsche reminds us that most intellectuals of this century (including Burke and Hazlitt) imply that the language of humankind is secretly the language of the monetized (English) ruling class: abstract, unlimited, and visually aggressive.

But a few people with the "real *power* of spirituality" confront the unhappiness that haunts the time when language, like everything else, "melts into the air." Consider Baudelaire's celebration of the picture of the past to which the new visual culture and language of modern time lead:

> Some democratic writer ought to have seen here [in regard to the emergence of photography] a cheap method for disseminating a loathing for history and for painting among the people. [58]

For the purposes of our story, we now turn to what is arguably the most significant (and threatening) enhancement of Hölderlin's *Dionysiac language*. In his own way (and historical context), Nietzsche senses the power of Hellenic poetry to transcend the restless images and linguistic perversions of the modern money-tyrant "moving this way and that"—his description of "Bentham's footsteps," we should note, is uncanny in its echo of Pentheus in *Bacchae*, who is described as running "feverishly this way and that" (v 625) [59] —and gestures to a new experience of language.

PREVIOUS TREATMENTS

As I shall show in my forthcoming work *Fin-de-siècle Germany and the Trauma of the Great War* (2016), the reception of Nietzsche's philosophy already in the 1890s up until the rise of Hitler's Germany in 1933, in particular with regard to those individuals orbiting Stefan George's *Geheimes Deutschland*, is fundamentally flawed. For all its creative impulses, Nietzsche's connection to Dionysian Greece and its sociopolitics—to say nothing of its intuitive critique of money as an ancient visual media—tends to be neutralized by nationalism and racism. To make matters worse, Nietzsche himself often provides models for individuals to elaborate illusions of individual, nationalistic, and even racial superiority. And as we should expect, scholarship on Nietzsche during Nazism is unacceptable. This leaves Nietzschean scholarship from 1945 until the present, and this means the German-American philosopher and translator Walter Kaufmann, who seeks to rescue Nietzsche's tarnished reputation after 1945. This mission begins with Kaufmann's 1950 publication of *Nietzsche: Philosopher, Psychologist, Antichrist* and gives way to the many Nietzsche scholars since 1950s who either modify or criticize Kaufmann's salvation.

What is astonishing about this secondary literature, however, is that despite its apparent shifts in historical perspective there is at its core something that is radically homogenized. Even in regard to the limited subject of the following study there seems to be a void of variation. This is not to say that no one has treated Nietzsche's relationship with the Dionysian and earthly, nor the sense of a Dionysian community. The problem of Nietzsche's relationship with democracy and the extent and nature of his affinity with National Socialism have also been the focus of several studies. Scholars today would doubtlessly point to Ferdinand Tönnies's *Community and Society* from 1887, Ludwig Klages's *Nietzsche's Psychological Achievements* from 1926, Georg Lukács's *Destruction of Reason* from 1954, as well as Henning Ottmann's *Nietzsche's Philosophy and Politics* from 1999 and Domenico Losurdo's *Nietzsche, the Aristocratic Rebel* from 2009. A contrasting view of the approach taken here can be found, furthermore, in Martine Prange's recent study, *Nietzsche, Wagner, Europe* from 2013.

But to understand what follows in regard to these past explorations would be a diversion. My analysis of Nietzsche is something that these previous perspectives could hardly imagine. This has nothing to do with a private need to create an original and bold work that sets itself firmly against the critical consensus that has built up around Nietzsche's work (as has been suggested)—nor with a desire to confirm a more popular unease—indeed, notoriety—associated with Nietzschean thought. It is true, I confess, that what follows is (implicitly) opposed to Kaufmann. But this is not in a way that is similar to the critique of Kaufmann that has been articulated in a number of postmodern critics over the past few decades. For those who make it to the end of this work, it shall become clear that Nietzsche's philosophy (tragically) conceals its own undiscovered potential. And although this story, to the extent that it overturns an existing critical consensus, may appeal to specialists, it was written no less for the non-specialist. What does tragic concealment and undiscovered potential mean for us all?

Nietzsche's significance also as a forerunner of Nazism has faded among recent scholars. But these are the very same scholars who, like their predecessors, fail to link Nietzsche's nationalism to his reception of Hölderlin and Dionysian Greece—and who fail to read the works of Nietzsche's middle/late period, for instance *On the Genealogy of Morals*, in light of his earlier work, *The Birth of Tragedy*. But even this hardly touches upon the deeper, more urgent, and even mysterious issue.

To introduce that which shall doubtlessly be difficult for (Nietzschean) scholars who have made the fatal mistake of ignoring history, I should stress that the following work is founded upon an exploration of two parallel historical processes both of which I have already explored—and both of which, despite any attempts to repress the reality of these phenomena with intellectual hyper-abstractions, are not going away: the *monetization* and *visualization* of our cosmos.

To be clear so that the reader (specialist and non-specialist alike) has the freedom to think about this little understood history,[60] I would like to introduce a few of the difficult, but necessary (and liberating) leaps of thought that this work, in contrast to every other study of Nietzsche that has existed, requires. In this text I repeat the Seafordian insight discussed in my previous book on Hölderlin and his relation to Dionysian Greece (5.2):[61] Philosophy emerges from the unlimitedness of money that creates an unconscious imagination that, in turn, sees the universe as ruled by an abstract, singular, and unlimited substance. Although (or perhaps because it is) exceptional, this understanding will be difficult for individuals unacquainted with the ancient mysteries of Greece and the earthly, communal spirit of tragedy.

How does philosophy emerge from money? The visual media of coinage (perhaps to pay mercenaries) is invented in early historic Greece during the seventh century B.C.E. (and quickly spreads thereafter).[62] But why early historic Greece? Because Homer invents the visual media of (alphabetic) writing just before—around 800 B.C.E.—and this peculiarly prepares the prehistoric Greeks to transition into the first ever *monetized* and *visualized* historical society.[63] And this may well lead one to wonder in what way this is relevant to the question above. Because, as all philosophers (should) know, precisely while Solon is searching for a *térma* (limit) in wealth in the sixth century B.C.E., Pythagoras invents the word "philosophy."[64]

The linguistic invention (of philosophy) is not only predicated upon the *visualizing* media of alphabetic writing. It is also, as Seaford trenchantly points out, the product of a *monetized* unconscious that, in turn, *sees* the cosmos anew as ruled by an abstract, singular, and unlimited substance. This doubtlessly needs a little explaining. For why is this so? Because money, like writing, is abstract, singular, and unlimited—and these peculiar (and potentially lethal) qualities impress themselves profoundly onto the historic imagination of humankind. In fact, money imprints itself on the soul of humankind with such velocity that, after this transformation, it is almost impossible, because of its (limitless) permeation in human life, to retrieve even the reality of its cataclysmic birth: the fact of the historic emergence of writing and money and what they together mean.

In this work I continue with the idea that Nietzsche, like Hölderlin, *adapts the adaption* of Dionysus's epiphany as a magical light in tragedy, as when the god appears to his mystic chorus in *Bacchae* and raises it up from its isolation and darkness. Because money emerges in Greece, only those who isolate themselves from history will find it anachronistic to point out the fact that the Dionysian spirit of Greece confronts money. As I shall stress throughout the text—and repeat in the coda—Nietzsche follows Hölderlin in his illumination of the Dionysian struggle with a monetized style of seeing (as embodied, for instance, by Pentheus) where images have meaning only insofar as they are rooted in a (self-isolating) desire for profit.

Furthermore, I shall also make reference to what Seaford calls a cosmic (vertical) axis. Although this phrase may seem elusive, its meaning, which I also develop in my Hölderlin book, is clear. A cosmic (vertical) axis is a reciprocal relationship between mortals and immortals rooted in a particular place. Through the mystic reenactment of its mythic epiphany on stage, the *polis* harnesses a sociopolitical potential to redeem cosmological confusion that arises from the visual media of money. This is clear in the contrast between the redemptive lightning and thunder to which the blind, wandering Oedipus succumbs and the horrific vision to which the tragic burial of the living (Antigone) coupled with the tragic refusal to bury the dead (Polynices) leads. In tragedy, the Greeks seek to actualize the sociopolitical power of art to overcome the lethal *monetized* and *visualized* spirits of tyrants such as Kreon. It is the image and language of the rebirth of this cosmic (vertical) axis—following monetary and visual destruction—that Nietzsche, in a time of rapid industrialization, cleverly seeks. And it is this modern German philosophical retrieval that is relevant to our (hyper-monetized) *Digital Revolution* today.

SUMMARY

In part I, I focus on two fundamental gestures in Nietzsche's philosophy: Firstly, his retrieval of the tragic play and secondly, his adaption of ancient tragedy to absorb and transform our *monetized* and *visualized* civilization in the present. Chapter one describes the dual origin of the style of seeing that accompanies money both in the Near East and Greece, as well as its descent from early historic time into the nineteenth century. Chapter two treats Nietzsche's analysis of myth, ritual, and the opening out of both in tragedy to battle *monetized* and *visualized chronotopes*. Chapters three, four, and five illuminate the application of this retrieval in the genesis of Nietzsche's own (modern) myth of *Zarathustra*.

The neutralizing of Nietzsche's *Dionysian chronotope* by his *proto-National Socialism* is the theme of part II. Chapters six and seven describe the nationalism (and racism) that plague Nietzsche's early work, chapter eight their (intensified) return in his later writings, and chapter nine the historical context in which this spatio-temporal (and linguistic) psychosis emerges. Chapter ten suggests that despite Nietzsche's criticisms of Christianity, his (anti-Semitic) racism betrays its continued presence in his thought.

Although the conclusion begins by noting Nietzsche's nuanced relationship to Herakleitos, early historic Greece, and tragedy, it focuses finally on the absorption of his Dionysian thinking into a style of (unlimited) battling, self-glorification, and self-isolation peculiar to Herakleitean hyper-abstractions. In a coda I suggest that, because of this concealment, that which makes Nietzschean philosophy *good*, has still to be discovered.

NOTES

1. Lucas Murrey, *Hölderlin's Dionysiac Poetry: The Terrifying-Exciting Mysteries* (Heidelberg, New York, Dordrecht, London: Springer, 2015).

2. Ibid., chapters 7–11.

3. Ibid., 7–9.

4. Friedrich Hölderlin, *Sämtliche Werke und Briefe*, hg. Jochen Schimdt, Bd. 1, *Gedichte* (Frankfurt am Main: Deutscher Klassiker Verlag, 1992) 306–07. Cited in Murrey, *Hölderlin's Dionysiac Poetry*, chapter 8.

5. Cited in Murrey, *Hölderlin's Dionysiac Poetry*, 9.2, 8.

6. Cited in Eliza Butler, *The Tyranny of Greece over Germany: A Study of the Influence Exercised by Greek Art and Poetry over the Great German Writers of the Eighteenth, Nineteenth and Twentieth Centuries* (Cambridge: Cambridge University Press, 1958), 213. Murrey, *Hölderlin's Dionysiac Poetry*, 6.2.

7. Cited in Murrey, *Hölderlin's Dionysiac Poetry*, 8.

8. Ibid., 1.

9. Butler, *Tyranny of Greece over Germany*, 238.

10. Cited in Butler, *Tyranny of Greece over Germany*, 215; cited in Murrey, *Hölderlin's Dionysiac Poetry*, 9.1.

11. Murrey, *Hölderlin's Dionysiac Poetry*, 6.1, 7.1.

12. Cited in Murrey, *Hölderlin's Dionysiac Poetry*, 6.1.

13. Ibid.

14. Ibid.

15. Ibid., 9.2.

16. BGE, in *Friedrich Nietzsche, Kritische Studienausgabe*, ed. Giorgio Colli and Mazzino Montinari , vol. 5, *Jenseits von Gut und Böse, Zur Genealogie der Moral* (Berlin: de Gruyter, 1999), 195. All translations are mine, unless otherwise noted.

17. BGE in *Nietzsche, Kritische Studienausgabe*, vol. 5, 164.

18. Murrey, *Hölderlin's Dionysiac Poetry*, 3.1–2. BGE in *Nietzsche, Kritische Studienausgabe*, 164.

19. Ibid.

20. See the subsection *Expropriation des Landvolkes von Grund und Boden*, in Karl Marx and Friedrich Engels, *Werke*, vol. 23, *Das Kapital: Kritik der politischen Ökonomie*, Erster Band, *Buch I: Der Produktionsprozeß des Kapitals* (Berlin: Dietz Verlag, 1983), 744–60.

21. Murrey, *Hölderlin's Dionysiac Poetry*, 6.1.

22. Ibid., 14.

23. Richard Seaford, *Ancient Greece and Global Warming: The Benefits of a Classical Education, or: Learn from the Past to Live in the Present* (Exeter: Credo Press, 2011).

24. Karl Marx and Friedrich Engels, *Manifest der Kommunistischen Partei* (Stuttgart: Reclam, 1989), 22–23.

25. Thomas Carlyle, *The Letters of Thomas Carlyle to his Brother Alexander with Related Family Letters* (Cambridge: Belknap Press, 1968), 177.

26. Ibid., 177–78.

27. Cited in Murrey, *Hölderlin's Dionysiac Poetry*, 8.

28. Ibid., 7.1.

29. Ibid., 8.

30. Murrey, *Hölderlin's Dionysiac Poetry*, 2–3, 7, 9.

31. Ibid., 9.1.

32. Cited in Murrey, *Hölderlin's Dionysiac Poetry*, 7.1.

33. Ibid., 3.1.

34. For a discussion of the original, ancient *visualized chronotope*, see Murrey, *Hölderlin's Dionysiac Poetry*, 3.

35. Seaford, *Ancient Greece and Global Warming*.

36. Aristotle's understanding of time as a series of static images is significantly related to his monetized (that is, philosophical) unconscious. See Murrey, *Hölderlin's Dionysiac Poetry*, 5.

37. Karl Marx, *Ökonomisch-philosophische Manuskripte, Heft III*, 3 (Frankfurt am Main: Suhrkamp, 2009), 123.

38. Murrey, *Hölderlin's Dionysiac Poetry*, 2.3.

39. Cited in Murrey, *Hölderlin's Dionysiac Poetry*, 5.3.

40. For a discussion of Seaford's account of the original, ancient *monetized chronotope*, see Murrey, *Hölderlin's Dionysiac Poetry*, 2.3.

41. BGE in *Nietzsche, Kritische Studienausgabe*, 195.

42. Seaford, *Ancient Greece and Global Warming*.

43. Murrey, *Hölderlin's Dionysiac Poetry*, 6.1.

44. See G. Doy, "The Camera against the Paris Commune," in *Photography/Politics: One*, ed. V. Burgin et al. (London: Photography Workshop, 1979) 13–26; Donald English, *Political Uses of Photography in the Third French Republic 1871–1914* (Ann Arbor, MI: UMI Research Press, 1984); Alisa Luxenberg, "Creating Desastres: Andrieu's Photography of Urban Ruins in the Paris of 1871," *Art Bulletin* 80, no. 1 (1998).

45. Murrey, *Hölderlin's Dionysiac Poetry*, 14.

46. Ibid.

47. Ibid., 2–4.

48. Ibid., 14.

49. William Hazlitt, *Characters of Shakespeare's Plays*, 3rd ed. (London: John Templeman, 1838), 54. That this unfortunate passage is an embarrassment to those who heroize Hazlitt is suggested in how it is often willfully repressed. See, for instance, *The Selected Writings of William Hazlitt*, ed. Duncan Wu, introduction by Tom Paulin, vol. 1, *An Essay on the Principles of Human Action, Characters of Shakespeare's Plays* (London: Pickering & Chatto, 1998) 118.

50. Hazlitt, *Characters of Shakespeare's Plays*, 27.

51. Charles Baudelaire, *Revue Française*, Paris, June 10–July 20 (1859) in *Charles Baudelaire, The Mirror of Art*, trans. Jonathan Mayne (Garden City, New York: Doubleday Anchor Books, 1956), 230. This is not to say that Baudelaire does not see photography, when it is free of the homogenizing forces of money, as having dynamic sociopolitical potential.

52. BGE in *Nietzsche, Kritische Studienausgabe*, 195.

53. Murrey, *Hölderlin's Dionysiac Poetry*, 12.

54. BGE in *Nietzsche, Kritische Studienausgabe*, 195.

55. Cited in Murrey, *Hölderlin's Dionysiac Poetry*, 8. For a discussion of the original, ancient *visualized language*, see chapter 4.

56. Ibid., 4.2.

57. Seaford, *Ancient Greece and Global Warming*. Murrey, *Hölderlin's Dionysiac Poetry*, 5.1.

58. Baudelaire, *Revue Française*, in *Charles Baudelaire*, Mayne 230.

59. BGE in *Nietzsche, Kritische Studienausgabe*, 164. Cited in Murrey, *Hölderlin's Dionysiac Poetry*, 4.2.

60. Because this history—although it has always been in the air and, thanks to Seaford, since 2004 has been placed squarely before us—has never been taught (neither in secondary nor "higher" forms of education), the non-specialist may well be intellectually superior to the specialist in understanding this work.

61. In fact, the thesis that follows has been put forth by Seaford (at least implicitly) since the late 1990s. See Richard Seaford, "Tragic Money," *JHS* 119–39. For its (explicit) argument, see Richard Seaford, "Monetisation and the Genesis of Philosophy," *Ordia Prima* (2004): 2. The main work is Richard Seaford, *Money and the Early Greek Mind* (Cambridge: Cambridge University Press, 2004).

62. Murrey, *Hölderlin's Dionysiac Poetry*, 3.1.

63. For our purposes *alphabetic writing* such as the letters on this page is *writing*. It is in this style of text that those who disagree with the facts of history, for instance philosophers who specialize in Nietzsche, will (unconsciously) voice their discontents. In regard to the visual transition I mention above, although I have proposed this thesis since at least 2008 (while still a PhD student at Yale University), I shall continue its elaboration in forthcoming talks and books.

64. Murrey, *Hölderlin's Dionysiac Poetry*, 5.2.

I

Dionysian Philosophy

Chapter One

Evil Eye

"THE POISONOUS EYE OF *RESSENTIMENT*"

Given Nietzsche's critique of English (and European, that is, Western) industrialization (1), it is to be expected that, like Hölderlin, he is especially discontent with the *monetization* (and *visualization*) of his own culture and language. In 1838 Louis Daguerre declares that "[t]he daguerreotype is not merely an instrument which serves to draw nature . . . , [but that it] gives her the power to reproduce herself."[1] Soon after Daguerre's declaration, Germany gives herself a railway system and feverishly looks forward to the "blood and iron" of the *Norddeutsche Reich*.[2] For Ludwig Feuerbach in 1843 this is a peculiar time that "prefers the image to the thing, the copy to the original, the imagination to reality, [and] appearance to essence."[3] Nietzsche is significantly discontent with the peculiar visual spirit that haunts this homogenization of space, time, and language. One recalls the typewriter that he quickly abandons to the basement of his rural home in Sils-Maria, Switzerland.

But for reasons that shall become clear in chapter three, it is not so much a conscious, but an unconscious attraction to the *Dionysiac chronotope* and *language* that gives Nietzsche his place in Hölderlin's story. Although he celebrates *Hyperion* and plans to write his own *Empedokles*—and this after the fifteen-year-old youth proclaims the unknown Hölderlin to be his "favourite poet," *Lieblingsdichter*—Nietzsche appears to be unaware of the Hellenic depths lurking in the songs of his countryman. Never once does he mention Hölderlin's Sophocles translations.[4]

To understand this narrow, if inspired, relation to Hölderlin, we have to understand the narrowing intellectual forces against which Nietzsche's interest in Greece grows. On the one hand, emerging disciplines such as literary science (that should have absorbed Hölderlin's *Dionysiac language*) tend to

3

compartmentalize and isolate themselves in hyper-abstractions disconnected from sociopolitics. One thinks of August Schlegel's Viennese lectures *On Dramatic Art and Literature* from 1809–1811. On the other hand, older disciplines such as philosophy also suffer the egoism that accompanies this new money-visual culture.

> In Germany after 1830, for example, reactionary forces purges the Young Hegelians—including such able thinkers as Ludwig Feuerbach, Karl Marx, Max Stirner, and David Strauss—from academic positions.[5]

"This helped consign the country's universities," John McCumber proceeds,

> to a generation and more of the kind of egoistic charlatanry described by Lewis White Beck: "[m]en entered and left the [Neo-Kantian] movement as if it was a church or political party; members of one school blocked the appointments and promotions of members of the others."[6]

But the vacuum of thought that accompanies philosophy in the nineteenth century, in particular Kantian-inspired philosophy, leads to something new—something that not even the musical genius of Wagner, who "to the close of the *Eumenides* . . . remained in a state of ecstasy"[7] could imagine. In contrast to the traditional lens of Christianity (and early to mid-nineteenth-century science), Nietzsche's exploration of Dionysus' magic acquires an unprecedented historical, perhaps even biological power. Charles Darwin's *On the Origin of Species* from 1859—which appears just before the young German composes his early essay "Fate and History" in 1862—is soon followed by Heinrich Schliemann, who in 1868 "first set foot on the plain of Troy during his trial trip for a voyage of discovery which was to lay bare the civilisation of ancient Greece."[8]

This is not to say that Nietzsche's excavation of Dionysus is exclusively what we might call bio-archaeological in nature. In fact, a better word may be something like historio-linguistic. Let us reconsider Friedrich Ritschl's (in)famous recommendation for his young graduate student in the early 1870s: "I prophesy that (Nietzsche) will one day stand in the front rank of German philology."[9] For reasons that shall become clear in the coda, Ritschl's word is premature. Nevertheless, it is the emerging discipline of language and love of its ancient history that facilitates Nietzsche's real contribution to thinking, namely his use of the language of the ancient antithesis of Dionysus and Apollo in modern time.[10] Through this linguistic style of thought, the Dionysian philosopher not only (consciously) enriches his personal, if narrow passion for Hölderlin's poems, but also (unconsciously) the historic heart of Hölderlinian poetry—this means, in essence, what Hölderlin discovered about ancient art and language that is relevant to us today.

But to understand Nietzsche's deepening of the history of Hölderlin's *Dionysiac chronotope*, we first have to understand his critique of a *visualized* space-time. Although similar to Hölderlin, Nietzsche's analysis is historical (even prehistorical) in ways that transcend Hölderlin. On the one hand, there is the non-Western, early historic "poisonous eye of *ressentiment*," *das Giftauge des Ressentiment*, that Nietzsche associates with a Semitic "*slave revolt in morality*." [11] This perversion of seeing thus emerges after the conquest of the Jewish ruling class and their removal from Jerusalem to Babylon during the middle of the sixth century (586–538) B.C.E. [12]

Critical to this communal trauma is the loss of an earthly spirit that binds individuals to one another. One thinks of Moses planting a vineyard in the Bronze Age around 1400 B.C.E., King David composing psalms in the eleventh and tenth centuries and Elijah's rituals of wine and fire in grottos in the ninth century. [13] The sudden absence of this natural spirit transforms the "[t]he Jews [into] that priestly nation of *ressentiment par excellence*": "*no longer* united with Israel," the sacred presence of nature, that is, "the seasons of the year and all the happiness that accompany domesticating animals and farming" and "above all rain," is "*denaturalized*." [14] Now the earth

> becomes an instrument in the hands of priestly agitators whose entire happiness is henceforth interpreted as a loan, whose unhappiness becomes a punishment for the "sin" of disobeying God. [15]

And as "the natural concepts of 'cause' and 'effect' are turned upside-down," this perverse "*anti-natural* causality" of the tribe leads, in turn, to a loss of strength. Nietzsche sees this "abstract opposition to life" as a "fundamental deterioration of fantasy" and names it an "'evil eye' ['böser Blick']" for all things." [16]

The experience of alienated seeing that accompanies this "*slave revolt in morality*"—"the poisonous eye of *ressentiment*," the "evil eye" (elsewhere Nietzsche speaks of "treacherous eyes," *verrätersich[e] Augen*)—implicitly gestures to the emergence of money. [17] This is important because here we witness a critical instance of *visualized* and *monetized chronotopes* coalescing about one another. The "loan" of "happiness" that, "in the hands of priestly agitators," individuals can accumulate without limit (and thus position themselves alongside the one true God over other mortals) significantly betrays the internal, vengeful spirit of money (and a destructive style of seeing) that knows nothing of earth and community. We can discern an echo of this "abstract" monetary-visual vengeance—what may also be referred to as a monetized-visualized "opposition to life"—in the historical instant that Nietzsche identifies when "the prophets melted (concepts such as) 'rich,' 'godless,' 'world,' 'violent,' 'sensual' into one and (thus) for the first time *coined* [gemünzt] the word 'world' as a term of opprobrium." [18]

But that this dangerous experience of space and time is caught up in the *monetized chronotope* is still clearer, if implicitly, when we consider the linguistic *ressentiment* upon which it rests. To understand this style of language, however, we have to first consider the uprooting of sacred names from Israel (that is, the loosening up of the ancient identity of the Jews), that coincides with the emergence of a resentful slave mentality in Babylon.

On the one hand, there is a religious crisis of language present in the competing names for God: Yahweh (a volcano spirit from the Sinai) and Elohim (Semitic for "gods") in Genesis.[19] On the other hand, there is the spirit of murder to which "the chosen people among peoples"[20] succumb. When "by the rivers of Babylon [the Jews] cannot sing God's song in a foreign land," some homeless Jews internalize the genocidal spirit of their Assyrian aggressors. "That person will do to you what you did to us," declares the infamous Psalm: "He will be very happy then! / He will catch your children and hit them with a rock."[21] One thinks of the slow-motion Israeli genocide of Palestinians today.

Reinforcing "the *ressentiment* of such creatures for whom the actual reaction, deed fails, who hold themselves together only by way of an imaginary vengeance without compensation," is a *monetized* method of "effect[ing] satisfaction on its enemies."[22] This is suggested in the money-changer's text (written in West Semitic Aramaic on the walls at Belshazzar's feast) in the biblical story of Daniel. For the Jewish prophet whose world has collapsed, the new visual media of money offers a secret language of violence toward the non-Jewish other. The ambiguous signs of text, as Daniel reveals, secretly say that "God has numbered your kingdom."[23] Although Nietzsche does not mention the story of Daniel in his analysis of the communal trauma that the early historic Jews suffer, when he speaks of the "nihilism and signs of a despairing, mortally wearied soul," it is clear that the *visualized* language of this tribe's "mortally wearied soul" may well include, even reinforce, a *monetized language*[24] that is potentially hostile to locality and others.

"MACHINIST AND DECORATIVE ARTIST"

But there is another visual perversion in history—still more lethal—to which Nietzsche gestures. To understand this second source of "two millennia of hostility toward nature and damage to human being" we turn from the ancient Near East to the ancient Mediterranean, in particular to that which disrupts "the Dionysian capacity"[25] of the early historic Greeks.

At first, the prehistoric intermingling of Dionysus and Apollo gives rise to a concentrated "essence of Apolline art"[26] in the early historic time. This we see in the appearance of the sculptor and epic poet who are "sunk[en] in pure gazing at pictures."[27] Nietzsche invites us to consider Homer's uncanny power to evoke a frozen "picture of the angry Achilles."[28] But when one also considers "the linguistic difference" that separates "Homer and Pindar"—similar to Hölderlin, Nietzsche is attracted to the "orgiastic" spirit of Pindaric song—it is clear that Dionysus's "tragic myth," in particular its "most intimate relationship between music and myth" makes its historic epiphany to enhance "the weaker degrees of Apolline art."[29]

In the next chapter we discuss the "Apolline illusion" wherein "the Dionysian" appears *as if* it "is really in the service of the Apolline."[30] The confrontation of "this immense contrast"[31] —the heavenly light and language of Apollo opposing the earthly light and language of Dionysus—culminates in *The Birth of Tragedy out of the Spirit of Music.*

Nevertheless, this "most profound revelation of Hellenic genius"[32] succumbs to a historical tragedy that, in contrast to that which emerges in the Near East, is internal to Western civilization. To be sure, "Greek art and especially Greek tragedy delayed" its "suicide," "above all [its] destruction of myth."[33] Implicitly referring to the religious crisis that Greece suffers during the emergence of money, Nietzsche directs our attention to the danger of "[t]he bourgeois mediocrity into which Euripides place[s] all his political hopes."[34] Tragedy's tragic transition into consumerism is also a transition into reassuring visualizations *and mechanizations*: "now the transcendental redemption of justice in Aeschylus is denigrated into the flat and impertinent principle of 'poetic justice' with its customary *deux ex machine.*"[35]

At the center of this perversion is the loss of *Dionysiac language.* The earthly and communal chorus, "the Dionysian basis of tragedy already begins to disintegrate"[36] with Sophocles, who privileges the image of the isolated, individual actor.

While apprehensive about a visual and mechanistic consumer culture, Nietzsche is likewise concerned about a hyper-abstract philosophy—one that even quickens "the death of tragedy."[37] Shocked by the absence of "tragic wisdom," for whose "signs even among the great Greeks of philosophy—those belonging to the two centuries before Socrates" he searches in vain, classical Greek philosophy, in particular the unnatural thinking of "Socrates," is identified "as the instrument of Hellenic dissolution, as a typical decadent. 'Reasonableness' versus instinct."[38] The emergence of Plato's "*theoretical man*" who replaces myth with "a *deux ex machine* of its own, namely the god of machines . . . in the service of higher egoism" leads to an "abstract state" governed by "abstract laws," abstract "morals" and an abstract form of "education."[39] Nietzsche further points to Aristotle's misunderstanding of the tragic chorus.[40] And this, the "life-consuming nature of Socratic optimism,"[41] gives way finally to a world-historical loss that knows no geographic limit. "With the death of Greek tragedy," Nietzsche writes, "a monstrous, deep sense of emptiness arose everywhere."[42]

Among the "ethical consequences" of this "break with the unconscious metaphysics of [an] earlier existence"—that is, with the rise of new need "to live uprooted from native soil"—is an intermingling of Western civilization with what is (recklessly) called a "vague oriental superstition."[43] The impossibility of "transplanting a foreign myth"—into which Dionysus is denigrated—in a *monetized* and *visualized* society that has "no fixed and sacred primal place" and which facilitates the loss of Dionysian rulers sprung from the earth—*autóchthonas* (the "counter-Alexanders")—leads to a slave-devouring "Alexandrian culture."[44]

Moreover, the tie of the *visualized chronotope* to "idyllic seductions, in its Alexandrian arts of adulation" and "the empty and distracting tendency to delectation" witnesses a concentration of *visualized language*: "the Alexandrian man is finally a librarian and corrector of proofs, and wretchedly goes blind from the dust of books and printer's errors."[45] All of this prepares the way for the splintering emergence of Western Christians.[46]

But the transition from "Plato's philosophy" to "the vampire of imperium Romanum"[47] and the time after focuses the "bourgeois mediocrity" and "higher egoism" that follows the classical time of Greece. Insofar as the crusades are nothing more than "an elevated form of piracy," the "profoundly nihilistic" spirit of Christianity not only severs the original bond between Western civilization and Dionysian art, but also its link even to "the weaker degrees of Apolline art": "neither Apolline nor Dionysian," the "kingdom . . . not of this world" whose "physiological evilness" alienates nature and community produces the first hyper-abstract modern image of Greece: "the reawakening of the Alexandro-Roman antiquity in the fifteenth century."[48] In particular, the rebirth of "old Greek music" through the "stilo rappresentativo" and "the ineffably *sublime* and sacred music of the Palestrina" creates a "theoretical person, . . . the critical layman" who, because he "is unable to behold a vision[,] forces the machinist and decorative artist into his service."[49]

The culture and art that emerges in the time of Galileo's "spyglass" (courtesy of the Banco dei Medici)—the same new visual technology through which the modern "philosopher" and "mathematician" reads the "grand book" of "the universe (which stands continually open to our gaze")—is finally a "depotentiation of appearance as appearance."[50] Nietzsche identifies the underlying Greco/Judeo-Christian denigration of music (and the voice) during the emergence of modern text:

> It was the rightful demand of unmusical listeners that one must above all understand the words: so that a rebirth of music is only to be expected if some style of song was discovered through which the word of text tyrannises the counter point as a master lords over a servant. For, just as the [Platonic-Judeo-

Christian] soul is more noble than the body, words are more noble than the accompanying harmonic system.[51]

Similar to Hölderlin, who warns us of the (blind Oedipus-like) "beggar" into which the isolated individual degenerates "when he reflects," Nietzsche goes on to resist the enlightened (isolated) ego of "Descartes"—the modern correlate to the Socratic "theoretical man"—and this includes the Christianized, mechanized spirit of his "empirical world."[52]

No less dangerous to community and nature—precisely that which "a wise man does not understand" (v 22)—is Kant's hyper-abstract thought, which, because it separates the world "into a 'true' and a 'seeming' one," is first and foremost a "theological success."[53] This critique of the *visualized chronotope* and *language* as they descend from their Western (Greek) and non-Western (Semitic) sources into concentrated forms in modern time culminates in Nietzsche's criticism of romantics who struggle against the Socratic underpinnings of the *Enlightenment*: "The wakers-of-the-dead" with whom he (having associated himself)[54] may well have included Hölderlin.

But as we have seen in the introduction, Nietzsche's analysis of hyper-abstract space, time, and language extends beyond *Romanticism* to the nineteenth century. Like Hölderlin, who warns us to not forget "that more than a machine process, that a spirit, a god, is in the world" and admonishes us to beware of a "clever race" of scientific, industrial capitalists who reduce nature to images with modern visual technology, as when they peer through "[t]he telescope . . . and coun[t] and / Nam[e] the stars of heaven with names" (v 51–52), Nietzsche warns us of "the problem of science."[55]

The emergence in the nineteenth century of "a never-before-heard-of form of being [Daseinsform], the type of the theoretical human"[56] reduces the cosmos still further to that which is visible and calculable for profit. This abstract image of nature, in turn, is projected back onto reality. No longer "thinking of being to recognize" its natural, communal mystery, "but instead to correct it,"[57] modern monetized individuals relate to nature only insofar as this relation corresponds to an abstract and isolated (visualized) ego. We have mentioned Nietzsche's distaste for "the homogenized sensibility" of modern (visual) media (oftentimes also linguistic) such as the telegraph, telephone, and typewriter.

At the core of the *visualized chronotope*, in which "[o]ur entire modern world is entangled . . . labouring in the service of science,"[58] is an abstract, *visualized language*. "The transformation of neural stimuli in sounds" that echo the locality of earth—Nietzsche calls attention to "[t]he various languages that exist alongside one another"—becomes subservient to the (anti-Apolline) illusion that our alphabetic texts and spoken words are adequate representations of reality.[59] This false picture of language is reinforced by philosophers such as Kant, Hegel, John Mill, Soren Kierkegaard, Arthur

Schopenhauer—to give just a few examples—all of whom who are, like philosophers today, ignorant of the history of writing.[60]

Critical is the melancholy that haunts "abstract humans, unaccompanied by myths."[61] As they "cling" to Christianity with their "'moralising' and humanising" progressive secularization (through the burial of the Judeo-Christian God) introduces a time that "is condemned to exhaust all possibilities and to nourish itself wretchedly on all other cultures."[62]

For Nietzsche, the modern imperialist "consuming desire for knowledge" of "the myth-less man . . . eternally hungry [and who] digs and grubs for roots . . . even among the remotest antiquities"[63] is reflected in the emergence of an imperial mass consumer culture. Our proto-"self-destructive culture of the unlimited" thus gives rise to nationalistic slogans ("'Deutschland, Deutschland über alles'") that reinforce devious ideals that, in truth, exploit the poor, like the "'dignity of labour.'"[64] In particular, it is the money-driven media culture as embodied in a new degenerate "speaking-style"—for instance, in that of the mainstream "'journalist,' the paper slave of the day"—and the false picture of education that such double-speak complements[65] with which Nietzsche is concerned. The language of modern time is understood significantly through a metaphor of degenerate "coins."[66]

But what is most harmful about the present is that to which the ancient *visualized chronotope*—"the poisonous eye of *ressentiment*"—what we might also call the *unhinged "Apolline illusion"*—leads. In our new time of modern technology, capital, and media control, that is, during the emergence of the "higher egoism" into which these forms degenerate, the power of art to inspire coherence between humans and nature is neutralized by "hallucination[s]" and "gestures" that know nothing of Dionysian "tones."[67]

Spaces, times, and languages that echo the "healthful soil of earth"[68] abruptly disappear following industrialization. This means that a new "homeless wandering about"—elsewhere Nietzsche speaks of "the primal suffering of modern culture"—is a symptom of the degeneration of "authentic art" into "superficial entertainment."[69] This is exemplified with striking clarity in the "musician-problem of Wagner."[70] Wagner's visual phantasmagoria reminds us—not without irony—that "the loss of myth . . . the loss of the mythic home, of the mythic womb" is, in essence, the loss of "music."[71] Now,

> an inauthentic aesthetics, inspired by a misled and degenerate art, has, by virtue of the concept of beauty prevailing in the world of visual arts, accustomed itself to demand that music be an effect similar to that of works in the visual arts, namely the excitation of delight in beautiful forms.[72]

No longer appearing from invisible "sounds" rooted in earth's darkness below, the image of the modern world is constrained to inauthentic "gestures" that have lost their organic relation to the body—"especially the mus-

cle sensations [that] have been immobilised."[73] Nietzsche goes on to relate
his theory of sensual *decadence* to language. Individual "words" that (unconsciously) reflect and reinforce the "egoism" of the media industry "leap out
of the sentence in which they belong . . . and obscure the sense of the whole
page, and the page in its turn gains strength at the cost of the whole."[74] At the
heart of this linguistic tragedy is the death (of the communal originality) of
sound: "the fate of music" that modern humans "suffer . . . like an open
wound."[75] This loss of myth and music paralyzes the "world-transfiguring"
power of "music": The new Wagnerian "decadence-music" is thus unleashed
to consume "the flutes of Dionysus"[76] without limit.

NOTES

1. This is from a notice that Daguerre circulated to attract investors to support his new
(visual tech.) business. Cited in Susan Sontag, *On Photography* (London: Penguin, 1977), 188.
2. See Wolfgang Schivelbusch, *Geschichte der Eisenbahnreise: Zur Industrialisierung von
Raum und Zeit im 19. Jahrhundert* (München: Wilhelm Fink, 1989).
3. Ludwig Feuerbach, "Vorrede zum zweiten Auflage," in *Das Wesen des Christintums*
(Stuttgart: Reclam, 1978), 26.
4. Friedrich Nietzsche, *Schulaufsatz des fünfzehnjährigen Nietzsche über Hölderlin*, "Brief
an meinen Freund, in dem ich ihm meinen Lieblingsdichter zum Lesen empfehle," 19.10.1861,
in *Dichter über Hölderlin*, hg. Jochen Schmidt (Frankfurt: Insel Verlag 1969), 109. Nietzsche
never mentions them and they seem to have not been present in the library at the Landesschule
Pforta.
5. John McCumber, *Time in the Ditch: American Philosophy and the McCarthy Era*
(Evanston, IL: Northwestern Press, 2001), xvi.
6. Ibid.
7. Lucas Murrey, *Hölderlin's Dionysiac Poetry: The Terrifying-Exciting Mysteries* (Heidelberg, New York, Dordrecht, London: Springer, 2015), chapter 6, section 1 (6.1). Cited in
Murrey, *Hölderlin's Dionysiac Poetry*, 6.2.
8. See Nietzsche's "Fatum und Geschichte," in *Friedrich Nietzsche, Kritische Studienausgabe*, ed. Giorgio Colli and Mazzino Montinari, vol. 1.1, *Jugendschriften—Nachgelassene
Aufzeichnungen Anfang 1852/Sommer 1858* (Berlin: de Gruyter, 1995). Eliza Butler, *The Tyranny of Greece over Germany: A Study of the Influence Exercised by Greek Art and Poetry
over the Great German Writers of the Eighteenth, Nineteenth and Twentieth Centuries* (Cambridge: Cambridge University Press, 1958), 304.
9. Cited in Walter Kaufmann, *The Portable Nietzsche* (New York: Viking, 1982), 7.
10. As Seaford points out, in the second century A.D. "Plutarch contrasted the music of
Dionysus with that of Apollo, and extended the contrast to a more general one between the
'uniformity, orderliness, and unmixed seriousness' of Apollo as depicted by artists and a
'certain mixed playfulness, aggressiveness, seriousness, and frenzy' in their depictions of Dionysus (Moralia 389b)." Richard Seaford, *Dionysus* (London and New York: Routledge, 2006),
143. Seaford further reminds us that[t]he Apolline and the Dionysiac were elaborated as
contrasting ideal types of beauty by the art historian Winckelmann (1717–1768), as contrasting
creative principles by the philosopher [and roommate to Hölderlin] Schelling (1775–1854), and
by the jurist and anthropologist [Johann] Bachofen (1815–1887) as contrasting principles that
include sexuality, gender, spirituality, and social organisation. Bachofen maintained that
whereas politics creates barriers between individuals, Dionysus removes them and 'leads
everything back to unity' (Discourse Concerning the Tomb Symbolism of the Ancients, 1859).
Ibid.
11. GM, in *Nietzsche, Kritische Studienausgabe*, vol. 5, *Jenseits von Gut und Böse, Zur
Genealogie der Moral* (Berlin: de Gruyter, 1999), 274. BGE, in *Nietzsche, Kritische Studie-*

nausgabe, vol. 5, 116–17. See also GM, ibid., 267–68 and 270. Although Nietzsche's rhetoric is oftentimes proto-National Socialist—an important issue that is treated in part II of this study—here we explore first the extent to which he offers a potentially insightful (and nonracist) history of the origins of modern Judaism.

12. Barry Powell, "The Philologist's Homer," in *Homer: Blackwell Introductions to the Classical World* (Malden, MA: Blackwell Publishing, 2004), 18.

13. Consider Nietzsche's Dionysian description of the "critic and satyr-like [Satyriker] Isaiah." AC, in *Friedrich Nietzsche, Kritische Studienausgabe*, ed. Giorgio Colli and Mazzino Montinari, vol. 6, *Der Fall Wagner, Götzen-Dämmerung, Der Antichrist, Ecce homo, Dionysos-Dithyramben, Nietzsche contra Wagner* (Berlin: de Gruyter, 1999), 193.

14. GM, in *Nietzsche, Kritische Studienausgabe*, vol. 5, 286. AC, in *Nietzsche, Kritische Studienausgabe*, vol. 6, 193–94.

15. Ibid.

16. Ibid.

17. BGE, in *Nietzsche, Kritische Studienausgabe*, vol. 5, 233. Murrey, *Hölderlin's Dionysiac Poetry*, 3.1.

18. BGE, in *Nietzsche, Kritische Studienausgabe*, vol. 5, 117. Emphasis added. "gemünzt" can also mean "minted."

19. Powell, "The Philologist's Homer," in *Homer*, 18.

20. BGE, in *Nietzsche, Kritische Studienausgabe*, vol. 5, 116.

21. Psalm 137.

22. GM, in *Nietzsche, Kritische Studienausgabe*, vol. 5, 270, 267.

23. 5.25–26. See also Barry Powell's "Homer and Writing," in *A New Companion to Homer*, ed. Ian Morris and Barry Powell (New York, Köln: Brill, 1997), 11–12. That the book of Daniel is produced (mainly or entirely) in the second century B.C.E., that is, at a time when Judaea is already part of the Hellenistic world—and this means pervaded by coined money (Seaford)—also suggests that money's abstract and visual essence enables individuals such as some uprooted Jews to visualize the destruction of the (non-Jewish) other.

24. BGE, in *Nietzsche, Kritische Studienausgabe*, vol. 5, 23. For a discussion of the original, ancient monetized language, see Murrey, *Hölderlin's Dionysiac Poetry*, 4.

25. EH, in *Nietzsche, Kritische Studienausgabe*, vol. 6, 313. BT, in *Friedrich Nietzsche, Kritische Studienausgabe*, ed. Giorgio Colli and Mazzino Montinari, vol. 1, *Die Geburt der Tragödie, Unzeitgemäße Betrachtungen I–IV, Nachgelassene Schriften 1870–1873* (Berlin: de Gruyter, 1999), 153.

26. Murrey, *Hölderlin's Dionysiac Poetry*, 3.2. BT, in *Nietzsche, Kritische Studienausgabe*, vol. 1, 140.

27. Ibid., 44.

28. Ibid.

29. Ibid., 49. Given that his translations of Pindar (and *Bacchae*) are not discovered until 1909, Hölderlin's interest in Pindaric song (and Euripides' tragedy) is something about which Nietzsche could never have known. For the visual style of the Apolline (Homeric) artist and the contrast between him or her and the Dionysian artist, see also 44, 48–50. Murrey, *Hölderlin's Dionysiac Poetry*, 7.2, 10.2. BT, in *Nietzsche, Kritische Studienausgabe*, vol. 1, 153, 150.

30. Ibid., 137.

31. Ibid., 104.

32. Ibid.

33. Ibid., 75, 148.

34. Murrey, *Hölderlin's Dionysiac Poetry*, 3.1. BT, in *Nietzsche, Kritische Studienausgabe*, vol. 1, 77.

35. Ibid., 95. See also 114.

36. Ibid., 95.

37. Ibid.

38. EH, in *Nietzsche, Kritische Studienausgabe*, vol. 6, 312, 310. See also BT, in *Nietzsche, Kritische Studienausgabe*, vol. 1, 89–91, 95, 117, 126–27, 146.

39. BT, in *Nietzsche, Kritische Studienausgabe*, vol. 1, 115 , 145.

40. Ibid., 95. See also EH, in *Nietzsche, Kritische Studienausgabe*, vol. 6, 312.

41. BT, in *Nietzsche, Kritische Studienausgabe*, vol. 1, 153.
42. Ibid., 75.
43. Ibid., 148.
44. Ibid., 149. Murrey, *Hölderlin's Dionysiac Poetry*, 5.2. BT, in *Nietzsche, Kritische Studienausgabe*, vol. 1, 146. Demosthenes, *Against Neaeras*, 74, in Demosthenes, *Orationes*, ed. Michael Rennie, vol. 3 (New York: Oxford University Press, 1991), 317 (1369). EH, in *Nietzsche, Kritische Studienausgabe*, vol. 6, 314. BT, in *Nietzsche, Kritische Studienausgabe*, vol. 1, 117. See also 17, 110–111, 115.
45. Ibid., 126, 120.
46. AC, in *Nietzsche, Kritische Studienausgabe*, vol. 6, 192. See also GM, in *Nietzsche, Kritische Studienausgabe*, vol. 5, 267. See also sections 44 and 51, 218–21, 230–32, respectively.
47. EH, in *Nietzsche, Kritische Studienausgabe*, vol. 6, 311. Murrey, *Hölderlin's Dionysiac Poetry*, 5.2.
48. Ibid. EH, in *Nietzsche, Kritische Studienausgabe*, vol. 6, 311. For Nietzsche's critique of Christianity as (1) an abstract, imaginary realm, (2) idiotic, (3) a perversion/exploitation of love, (4) a devious shopkeep er who fails to fulfil l what is promised, (5) and a physical and spiritual sickness—in sum, as (6) "the greatest of all imaginable corruptions" and (7) "the one single eternal blemish on humanity," see AC, in *Nietzsche, Kritische Studienausgabe*, vol. 6, 181–82, 189–91, 215–17, 230–34, 252–53. Murrey, *Hölderlin's Dionysiac Poetry*, 5.2. AC, in *Nietzsche, Kritische Studienausgabe*, vol. 6, 194. BT, in *Nietzsche, Kritische Studienausgabe*, vol. 1, 148.
49. Ibid., 121–22. See also 120, 126 (emphasis added), 123.
50. Galileo Galilei, *The Assayer* (1623), in *Discoveries and Opinions of Galileo*, trans S. Drake (Garden City, NY: Doubleday, 1957), 237–38. Murrey, *Hölderlin's Dionysiac Poetry*, 5.1.
51. BT, in *Nietzsche, Kritische Studienausgabe*, vol. 1, 123. See also 121.
52. Cited in Murrey, *Hölderlin's Dionysiac Poetry*, 7.1. BT, in *Nietzsche, Kritische Studienausgabe*, vol. 1, 86. Murrey, *Hölderlin's Dionysiac Poetry*, 6.1.
53. Murrey, *Hölderlin's Dionysiac Poetry*, 8, 6.1.
54. Ibid., 6.2.
55. Cited in Murrey, *Hölderlin's Dionysiac Poetry*, 7.1, 8. ASC, in *Nietzsche, Kritische Studienausgabe*, vol. 1, 13.
56. BT, in *Nietzsche, Kritische Studienausgabe*, vol. 1, 98.
57. Ibid., 99.
58. Ibid., 116.
59. TL, in *Nietzsche, Kritische Studienausgabe*, vol. 1, 878–79. Although Nietzsche does not use the word "alphabetic," it is clear that he is first concerned with criticizing a Western (and hence alphabetic) experience and concept of language, in particular one that is caught up in the dangers of Western (visual) media and its progress in modern time.
60. Ibid. See also EH, in *Nietzsche, Kritische Studienausgabe*, vol. 6, 311.
61. BT, in *Nietzsche, Kritische Studienausgabe*, vol. 1, 145.
62. BGE, in *Nietzsche, Kritische Studienausgabe*, vol. 5, 195. GS, in *Friedrich Nietzsche, Kritische Studienausgabe*, ed. Giorgio Colli and Mazzino Montinari, vol. 3, *Morgenröte, Idyllen aus Messina, Die fröhliche Wissenschaft* (Berlin: de Gruyter, 1999), 480–81. BT, in *Nietzsche, Kritische Studienausgabe*, vol. 1, 146. See also AC, in *Nietzsche, Kritische Studienausgabe*, vol. 6, 185.
63. BT, in *Nietzsche, Kritische Studienausgabe*, vol. 1, 146.
64. Murrey, *Hölderlin's Dionysiac Poetry*, 6.1. TL, in *Nietzsche, Kritische Studienausgabe*, vol. 6, 104. BT, in *Nietzsche, Kritische Studienausgabe*, vol. 1, 117.
65. Ibid., 130, 116, 143–44.
66. TL, in *Nietzsche, Kritische Studienausgabe*, vol. 1, 880–81.
67. CW, in *Nietzsche, Kritische Studienausgabe*, vol. 6, 27–28.
68. BT, in *Nietzsche, Kritische Studienausgabe*, vol. 1, 131.
69. Ibid., 148, 119, 130, 153.

70. CW, in *Nietzsche, Kritische Studienausgabe*, vol. 6, 27–28. Although I seek to show that Nietzsche's Hellenic thought in its most mature, strongest form, I shall return to his complex, tragic relationship to Wagner in part II.

71. BT, in *Nietzsche, Kritische Studienausgabe*, vol. 1, 146, 153.

72. Ibid., 104. EH, in *Nietzsche, Kritische Studienausgabe*, vol. 6, 313–14.

73. Murrey, *Hölderlin's Dionysiac Poetry*, 2. TI, in *Nietzsche, Kritische Studienausgabe*, vol. 6, 118. See also 118.

74. CW, in *Nietzsche, Kritische Studienausgabe*, vol. 6, 27–28.

75. EH, in *Nietzsche, Kritische Studienausgabe*, vol. 6, 357.

76. Ibid.

Chapter Two

Apollo and Dionysus

"TRAGIC MYTH"

Similar to Hölderlin once again, Nietzsche unconsciously resists the *visualized chronotope* (a monetized style of seeing that alienates individuals from nature and one another) by retrieving an esoteric Dionysian experience. Turning to "the Olympian theocracy of joy" that conquers "the original Titan theocracy of terror"—and this means by turning *downward* to "the roots" of "the Olympian magic mountain"—Nietzsche invokes the myth "and entire philosophy of the forest god."[1] Although references to the Dionysian "lightning-flash" and a *Bacchae*-inspired "earthquake" (through which tyrannical states are "shaken to ruins") evoke Dionysus's mythical birth, it is "the tragic myth" of the "dismembered god"—the time when Dionysus "as a boy had been dismembered by the Titans"[2] —to which Nietzsche is most attracted.

On the one hand, "the original suffering" of "Zagreus" expresses the horror of "individuation."[3] The "primal desire for appearance"—an original longing for the illusion of "a single world-image"—and the "glance into the horrible" recall Dionysus's fatal attraction to his image in a mirror.[4]

On the other hand, interest in the blindness and death to which "the god of darkness" succumbs—we also hear of "Demeter sunken in eternal sorrow"—looks forward to an "eternal rebirth."[5] At the heart of Dionysus's mythical "transformation into air, water, earth and fire" is a "ray of joy cast upon the visage of a ruined world torn into individuals."[6] "The richest creature, brimming over with vitality" and who with his "satyr[s]" and maenads—Nietzsche is especially fond of "Ariadne," the "queen of Dionysian women"—conquers tyrants as "millions sink awestruck into the dust"[7] represents a transition from one style of seeing to another. The isolated "glance into the horrible"—what we may refer to as *tragic seeing*—is transfigured into a

15

radiant picture of enchantment—what we may call *Dionysian seeing*: "A lightning flash. Dionysus becomes visible in emerald beauty."[8] Cosmological confusion is thus limited through the reestablishment of a cosmic (vertical) axis. No longer a reflection of Titanic isolation and horror, the image becomes a source of earthly and heavenly union: "the genius of heart . . . to lie placid as a mirror, that the deep sky may be reflected in it."[9]

As we should expect, parallels with Hölderlin flourish. Nietzsche's picture of "the Dionysian festival procession from India to Greece"—"Dionysus's chariot is showered with flowers and wreaths: under his yoke stride panthers and tigers"—evokes Hölderlin's image of "the god of joy / . . . coming from the Indus all-conquering / . . . with holy / Wine waking the people from sleep" (v 1–4)[10]—Dionysus,

> Who
> Harnessed tigers to
> The chariot and coming down
> From the Indus
> Giving joyful service
> Establishes the vineyard and
> Held back the fury of people. (v 53–59)

Nietzsche's picture of "primal unity" that ascends "out of the smile of this Dionysus" recalls further Hölderlin's "smile from imprisoned / Souls" (v 157–58) that "lights up" (v 158) alongside Dionysian "eyes [that] thaw out from the light" (v 158).[11]

Also like Hölderlin, Nietzsche's fascination with the psychic change from *tragic-* to *Dionysian seeing* is rooted in linguistic transition. I have accented Hölderlin's retrieval of Semele's *Jammer* (v 41), "wailing" and "lamentation."[12] Nietzsche's interest in "the intimate relation of music and myth," specifically his references to Archilochus (who "leads off the dithyramb thunderstruck in [his] mind with wine") and the tragic "earthquake" of music that he "heard"[13] in his youth, suggest the earth-shattering sounds of Semele's mythic death. As if enhancing Hölderlin's *tragic language*, "the Dionysian primal element of music" includes, for Nietzsche, the sounds of "the tortured martyr."[14] Again, one thinks of the tragic demigod just after he gazes upon his reflection in a mirror. The dismemberment of language that emerges from the unbearable (*unhearable*) sound of "the horrific" is further linked to the "[l]ament of Ariadne."[15] Now "the primal pain in music"—"the musical relation of dissonance" associated with the individual whose isolated eyes lead to blindness and death, that is, a loss of "breath [and] deathly silence"—reveals Dionysus's unparalleled power to "impos[e] silence and attentiveness on everything loud and self-conceited."[16]

Hölderlin's transition from Semele's "wailing" (v 41) to Dionysus's "joyful cry" (v 24), furthermore, seems to recur when Nietzsche's "deathly silence" is followed by "Dionysian music."[17] Eyes once lost in the dark come forth to celebrate their origin in a language of earth and community—one that, because it is more sensually open, is no longer tyrannized by seeing alone. The "vision-like new world of appearance" is described as arising "like an ambrosial scent."[18] And because seeing issues forth from the ecstasy of that which cannot be seen in isolation, it is stronger: the "glance is sharper."[19] Consider Ariadne, whose power to hear is enhanced by Dionysus's gentle whisper, and who makes her epiphany as the "gathering of sun in light."[20] The invisible "voice" of the god who "can descend into the netherworld of every soul" gives "the picture," in other words, "the power of music."[21]

"SECRET CELEBRATIONS OF DRAMATIC MYSTERIES"

Although Hölderlin similarly turns to "the staging of myths" in the "terrifying-exciting mysteries," Nietzsche's interest in "the tribe of tragic mysteries"—"in the secret celebrations of dramatic mysteries . . . always in ancient mythical clothing"[22] —is more historical. Firstly, there is the reenactment of "the suffering Dionysus of the mysteries" at "cult gatherings": Gestures to "the agonizing glass case of . . . human individuality" and "the tempter god" seem as if to evoke, once again, the mystic mirror of the "compassionate companion re-enacting [Dionysus's] sufferings."[23] Ghostly visions that haunt the "aimless wanderings" of the initiand who "knew and felt the terrors and horrors of being" culminate in a "convulsive distension of all emotions."[24]

But the goal of "the painfully broken vision of the Dionysian person" is to "transfigure" the "glance into the horrible" into a "golden light" of the "great mysterious one."[25] The mortal who succumbs to "all-powerful time"— *pagkratès chrónos* (v 609)—is "released from the bad [kakôn]" (v 282) and becomes a mystic "free of fear and circling in the dance of the deathless god" (v 235).[26] Nietzsche thus recalls "the moments of liberation" in Hölderlin's *Hyperion*, as when "[i]t seemed as if the old world died and new one began with us": "a new world" arises "from the ruins of toppled old ground."[27] Also like his *Lieblingsdichter* (2.1), Nietzsche senses the sociopolitical potential,

> [i]n this enchantment [when] the Dionysian reveller sees himself as a satyr and, as a satyr, he sees in turn the god i.e. in his metamorphosis he beholds a new vision outside himself.[28]

As the "terrible image of the world fades away charmingly," the "mild tempered ruler" founds the most "powerful unwritten laws" of "the state."[29] The democratic spirit of nature and community transcends the individual ego. Nietzsche calls forth an "image of the sexual omnipotence of nature" that is enhanced by "the narcotic draught [and] . . . potent coming of spring."[30]

This retrieval of the language of ritual is also more historical than that which we find in Hölderlin's translations, poems and essays.[31] The "staging" of Semele's "lament" (v 41) and Dionysus's silent melancholy, as when he approaches his mother's gravestone in Thebes, now gives way to explicit "tragic dissonance."[32] The linguistic feel of "the ugly and disharmonic . . . [in the] content of the tragic myth" is reexperienced by "the solitary person" caught "in the centre of a world of miseries."[33] This "most delicate and severe suffering" originates in the mystic chorus who "through its symbolism of dance, tones and word . . . sees how the god suffers."[34] Individualism and visual isolation—all that is "morally reprehensible"[35] —succumb to the linguistic (primal psychic) dismemberment of the original teeth-gnashing, "tortured martyr." Not only blinded (that is, "sunken in eternal sorrow"), but also "breathless," the mystic initiand suffers the "primal re-echoing" of "deathly silent clamour."[36] Nietzsche speaks of "a hollow sigh [that] arises from the abyss of being."[37]

We have heard the linguistic transition that Hölderlin retrieves: the "wailing" (v 41) of the isolated Semele that contrasts "the joyful cry" (v 24) of Dionysus and his mystic "chorus" (v 21), as when the god makes his epiphany to reveal his "secret initiations" (v 22).[38] Nietzsche's reenactment of "tragic dissonance" similarly concludes in a Dionysian "song of exultation."[39] Nevertheless, this "echo" of the "blessed *yes to life*"—"the saving act of Greek art"[40] —makes the mystical relation between sound and image (that is only implicit in Hölderlin's work) more explicit. When language is experienced as ascending from the invisible (and hence incalculable) darkness of earth below—that is, the dark energy that supports communal life (and alongside the wondrous "gifts"[41] of bread, Demeter, and wine, Dionysus)—and not from the unlimited ego of an individual isolated from nature and others—the sound of the word creates a more powerful, more beautiful picture. Nietzsche invites us to consider the magical "sparks of images [that] ceaselessly spray out of a melody."[42]

This brings us to the power of language that, being rooted in a cosmic (vertical) axis, enables the mystic to "move her limbs for the dithyrambic dance, and give herself without hesitation to an orgiastic feeling of freedom."[43] Nietzsche speaks "a second pouring"—an instant when "music appears to the artist like dream images that through the Apolline dream-effect become visible."[44] This means that "mystical self-purging" opens out "the whole capacity of speech" to call forth a vision of the "lord and master Dionysus."[45] The "gleaming image" of the god, enriched by "the inner illumination of music," enriches, in turn, the "chorus of dancing, singing satyrs."[46] Now the "mystic sensation of unity" witnesses the ascent of the image out of (a previsual) earthly and communal sound—what Nietzsche also hints at when he speaks of "the fire-magic of music."[47] One recalls the choral imagination of Dionysus on the mountain peaks of Parnassus as "chorus-leader of fire-breathing stars" (v 1144–45).[48]

"THE PUBLIC CULT OF TRAGEDY"

But like Hölderlin, Nietzsche's retrieval of the *Dionysiac chronotope* is clearest in his study of the adaption of myth and ritual during *The Birth of Tragedy*. The chthonic openness of "the Greek theatre [that] reminds us of a lonely mountain valley" opens out "sentences intelligent only to a few" to "the public cult of tragedy."[49] The Dionysian and Apolline "artistic powers that arise . . . from nature" are fused to one another "by a metaphysical miracle of Hellenic 'will.'"[50]

On the one hand, "this immense opposition" produces a new individual: the tragic hero whose image is "shot" out of the Dionysian "musical excitation" of the chorus into a "visible middle-world"—what Nietzsche also names "an Apolline region of images."[51] Abandoning "the Dionysian storm and excess," "Apolline artistry"[52] arouses "a parallel dream image" that is for a brief moment disconnected from the "universality"[53] of earth and communal life. Crucial is the enhancement of the power of language and sound to invoke pictures by "Apollo, . . . the god of all visualising forces . . . who, according to his root as the 'Shining one,' is the divinity of light."[54] With this visual enrichment, "the Dionysian chorus . . . discharges itself ever anew into an Apolline image-world."[55]

Given Nietzsche's attraction to "those luminous appearances of Sophoclean heroes, in short the Apolline of the mask,"[56] it is easy to recall characters who appear as if by choral breath. "I see / Antigone coming" (v 804–5),[57] the chorus cries out just before the heroine enters the stage. Being "nothing more . . . than a gleaming picture i.e. appearance through and through," the ghost of the Persian king ascends from an underworld of "darkness and gloom" (v 220–23).[58] "The Apolline frenzy excites the eye above all, so that it gains the power of vision."[59]

But seeing is the source not only of a balmy, healing power. It is also the origin of a dangerous detachment of the individual from earth and community. As I have implied in the previous chapter, "the soothing power of Apollo can even construct the illusion that the Dionysian is really in the service of the Apolline" (2.2).[60] One thinks of the self-destructive visions of Oedipus, Kreon, and Pentheus.

But on the other hand, the "beautiful mixture"[61] of the Dionysian and Apolline reintegrate the *visualized* (and isolated) tragic hero. This becomes clear when Nietzsche examines "the world of appearance in the image of the suffering hero."[62] Here he sees the public tyrant absorbed into secret ritual. "It is the people of tragic mysteries who fight the Persian wars."[63]

To clarify "[t]his difficult to grasp primal phenomena of Dionysian art" whose spectator "beholds the transfigured [Apolline] world of the stage and yet denies it"—who "shudders at the sufferings that shall befall the hero and yet anticipates in them a higher, much more overpowering desire," Nietzsche reminds us "that Greek tragedy in its earliest form had for its sole theme the sufferings of Dionysus and that for a long time the only stage hero was Dionysus himself": "all the celebrated figures of the Greek stage, Prometheus, Oedipus, etc., are mere masks of this origin hero, Dionysus," and this means "the suffering Dionysus of the mysteries . . . torn to pieces by the Titans."[64] We have noted the dismemberment that Pentheus suffers at the end of *Bacchae*.[65]

That "the one truly real Dionysus appears in a variety of forms, in the mask of the struggling hero, and entangled, as it were, in the net of the individual will . . . through the work of the dream interpreter Apollo"[66] suggests that the "primal desire for appearance" and the illusion of "a single world-image" amplify the power of the mystic mirror to intrigue and temporarily distract. "The enchantment" of the Dionysian "tempter-god"—"the precondition of all dramatic art"—when combined with the "Apolline power of transfiguration," projects a stronger, even more lethal, "luminous picture" of "the suffering glass case of . . . human individuality"—one whose "reassuring effect can even create the illusion that the Dionysian is really in the service of the Apolline"—and "this all-illuminated total visibility cast[s] a spell over the eyes and prevent[s] them from penetrating deeper."[67] Nietzsche implies a relation between "this glorious Apolline illusion" and the individual desire to repress the natural flow of time, as witnessed in a succession of musical tones: "the Apolline in tragedy, by means of its illusion, gain[s] a complete victory over the primal Dionysian element of music."[68]

Although implicit, the connection between the mortal who strives for immortality ("the greedy thirst for existence" that we see in the *visualized* "tragic hero") is tied to the spirit of consumer society—"bourgeois mediocrity" (2.2)—that devours "the public cult of tragedy": "the vulture of the great lover of humankind, Prometheus"—himself "a Dionysian mask"—"the terrible fate of the wise Oedipus, the family curse of the Atridae which drove Orestes to matricide," and finally "the sufferable anticipation of the twilight of the gods"[69] are all linked to the cosmological confusion that emerges from the "morally reprehensible" desire *to see* that which is naturally limited (for instance, mortal finitude) as unlimited.

Nietzsche's reference to Midas, who transforms everything by his touch into gold and fails "to capture" Silenus, "the companion of Dionysus, in the forest," touches upon the "morally reprehensible" desire that is unleashed in individuals from "the (disastrous) unlimited homogenising power of money."[70] The limitless essence of money is connected to the (unnatural) understanding of individual time as limitless. This invites us to see the "blunting of the Apolline point" of light through "Dionysian magic"—the crucial moment when the tragic play "leads the world of appearances to its limits, where it denies itself"[71] —as the "blunting" of the *visualized* tragic hero by the earthly spirit (and darkness) of mortality.

Similar to Hölderlin, who makes use of "the homeless, blind Oedipus,"[72] Nietzsche returns to the tragic picture of blindness to which the introverted ("mother-marrying"),[73] money-tyrant succumbs. The meaning of tragedy is caught up in the neutralization of detached, individual seeing (the *visualized chronotope*) by an earthly and communal space-time (the *Dionysiac chronotope*). This occurs, firstly, through the absorption of the tragic hero into Dionysus's "original suffering." That the "enigmatic characteristic (of) the sorrow and fate of the hero" is related to the reenactment of Dionysian ritual—"[t]hat behind all these masks there is a divinity"—is suggested by the bond of the performer and "*Dionysus*, the actual hero of the stage and central point of vision."[74] After this absorption, the return of "[t]he satyr-chorus of the dithyramb" (3.2)—embodied in the "satyr-play": the "ancient Dionysiac nucleus"—facilitates the rebirth of "the Dionysian [which] predominates once again."[75]

Although the birth of tragedy from the monetization of Greece[76] is only implicit in Nietzsche's thought, the neutralizing of the *visualized chronotope* (the visual culture that arises alongside money) by a Dionysian space-time is clearer. "In the total effect of tragedy the Dionysian takes the lead; it ends with a sound that could never arise from the realm of Apolline art."[77] We have noted "the balmy power of Apollo [that] can even construct the illusion that the Dionysian is really in the service of the Apolline." "But in essence," Nietzsche clarifies, "the relation of music to drama is precisely the opposite: music is the actual idea of the world, drama only a reflection of this idea, a single silhouette of the same."[78] "And thus the Apolline illusion reveals itself as what it is, the veiling during tragedy of the actual Dionysian effect."[79]

Similar to Hölderlin, Nietzsche sees the sensual reversal with which the tragic play concludes—when a "new world" ascends "from the ruins of toppled old ground"—as rooted in the return of *Dionysiac language*:

> we have now come to the insight that the scene and its action was originally thought of only as a *vision*, that the only "reality" is the chorus who produces the vision from out of itself and who speaks with the entire symbolism of dance, tone and word. This chorus sees in its vision its lord and master Dionysus and is thus eternally the *serving* chorus: it sees the god suffer and transform himself beautifully, and therefore does not itself *act*. With this, its position in regard to the god, it is the highest Dionysian expression of *nature* and thus speaks, like her, in spiritualised oracular words of wisdom.[80]

One thinks of Hölderlin's evocation of the Dionysian "oracle word."[81] Also like his predecessor, Nietzsche understands the "drama of words" at the heart of tragedy—Hölderlinian "speech against speech"—as gradually revealing "the underground and birth place of the word . . . the becoming of the word from the inside out."[82] This "change-of-harmony" that gently ascends out of "deathly silence" recalls Hölderlin's "Creator-of-names," as when the chorus, in search of Dionysus's "immortals words" (v 1184), cries out to its king to "become manifest" (v 1149–50).[83]

To illustrate this more clearly, let us consider the transfiguration of the (*visualized*) tragic hero. "The most sorrowful figure of the Greek stage, the unfortunate Oedipus," Nietzsche suggests, "through his monstrous suffering radiates finally a magical, blessed strength."[84] As we have seen, Hölderlin's *Oedipus at Kolonus*, with the song of "[t]he returning nightingale" (v 7), "choruses of muses" (v 28) and "the reveler / Dionysus" (v 11–12) himself, not only glimpses, but also *listens to* a Dionysian paradise.[85] "The reconciling tones from another world sound purest," for Nietzsche, "in *Oedipus at Colonus*." This recalls "the pure word"[86] of Hölderlin's commentary on Sophocles. Oedipus's "*suffering organs*," in particular the blinding and death to which his unlimited individualism succumbs,[87] gives way to a cosmic (vertical) axis of language. From "the inner illumination" of earthly and communal sound, eyes magically come forth wherein the "glance is sharper." "Singing and dancing the human expresses himself as a member of a higher communality."[88]

To conclude, "the essence of Greek tragedy and with it the most profound revelation of Hellenic genius" is "a visualisation of Dionysian wisdom through Apolline artistry."[89] Hölderlin also gestures to "this brotherhood of Apollo and Dionysus"—whose effect is like that of "a noble, inflaming, but contemplative wine"—as when he pictures the Dionysian spirit of "thundering waves" (v 2) and "snow-swept / Mountain wilds" (v 3–4) alongside the "eternal benevolence" (v 10–13) of "King Apollo / Known to Delos."[90] Through "these two art drives" and the development of "their powers in strict proportion to one another," the spirit of tragedy—"exciting, purifying and discharging the entire life of a people"—opens out the "homecoming" of the once *visualized* (and isolated) individual back "to the primal source of his being."[91]

NOTES

1. BT, in *Friedrich Nietzsche, Kritische Studienausgabe*, ed. Giorgio Colli and Mazzino Montinari, vol. 1, *Die Geburt der Tragödie, Unzeitgemäße Betrachtungen I–IV, Nachgelassene Schriften 1870–1873* (Berlin: de Gruyter, 1999), 35–36.

2. EH, in *Friedrich Nietzsche, Kritische Studienausgabe*, ed. Giorgio Colli and Mazzino Montinari, vol. 6, *Der Fall Wagner, Götzen-Dämmerung, Der Antichrist, Ecce homo, Dionysos-Dithyramben, Nietzsche contra Wagner* (Berlin: de Gruyter, 1999), 401. NCW, in *Nietzs-*

che, Kritische Studienausgabe, vol. 6, 425. BT, in *Nietzsche, Kritische Studienausgabe*, vol. 1, 153, 72.

    3. BT, in *Nietzsche, Kritische Studienausgabe*, vol. 1, 136–37, 72.

    4. Ibid., 39, 137, respectively. Although Nietzsche is speaking of the amplification of the Apolline through the Dionysian in tragedy, the danger of "self-destruction" that accompanies an experience of (seductively) distracting light, that is, becoming distracted by an attractive image that is unhinged from the darkness of earth below, is something that Nietzsche increasingly recognizes as central to our modern dilemma. NCW, in *Nietzsche, Kritische Studienausgabe*, vol. 6, 425–26. Lucas Murrey, *Hölderlin's Dionysiac Poetry: The Terrifying-Exciting Mysteries* (Heidelberg, New York, Dordrecht, London: Springer, 2015), chapter 2, sections 1–2 (2.1–2.2). Although Nietzsche does not mention (and most likely did not know about) the mirror in Dionysian myth, this etiological episode complements, even enhances his understanding of Dionysus.

    5. EH, in *Nietzsche, Kritische Studienausgabe*, vol. 6, 352. BT, in *Nietzsche, Kritische Studienausgabe*, vol. 1, 72. EH, in *Nietzsche, Kritische Studienausgabe*, vol. 6, 345. The important relation between Dionysus and Zarathustra is treated in the next chapter. See also BT, in *Nietzsche, Kritische Studienausgabe*, vol. 1, 39; and EH, in *Nietzsche, Kritische Studienausgabe*, vol. 6, 311–12.

    6. BT, in *Nietzsche, Kritische Studienausgabe*, vol. 1, 72.

    7. NCW, in *Nietzsche, Kritische Studienausgabe*, vol. 6, 425–26. BT, in *Nietzsche, Kritische Studienausgabe*, vol. 1, 55, 29. See, for instance, Nietzsche's "Lament of Ariadne." EH, in *Nietzsche, Kritische Studienausgabe*, vol. 6, 398–401, 348. Nietzsche even makes reference to his own "almost maenad-like soul." ASC, in *Nietzsche, Kritische Studienausgabe*, vol. 1, 15. Cited in Murrey, *Hölderlin's Dionysiac Poetry*, 3.2–3.3.

    8. EH, in *Nietzsche, Kritische Studienausgabe*, vol. 6, 401.

    9. BGE, in *Friedrich Nietzsche, Kritische Studienausgabe*, ed. G. Colli and M. Montinari, vol. 5, *Jenseits von Gut und Böse, Zur Genealogie der Moral* (Berlin: de Gruyter, 1999), 237.

    10. BT, in *Nietzsche, Kritische Studienausgabe*, vol. 1, 132, 29. Murrey, *Hölderlin's Dionysiac Poetry*, 8.

    11. Ibid., 72. Cited in Murrey, *Hölderlin's Dionysiac Poetry*, 8.

    12. Ibid., 7.2.

    13. BT, in *Nietzsche, Kritische Studienausgabe*, vol. 1, 153, 42–45. Fr. 120, in Daniel Mendelsohn, "Synkeraunô: Dithyrambic Language and Dionysiac Cult," *CJ* 87 (1992): 105–24. The typical theme of the early dithyramb is the (Theban) birth of Dionysus accompanied by a thunderbolt. See Plato Laws 700b, in *Plato, Laws, Books VII–XII*, trans. Robert Bury, vol. 11 (Cambridge: Harvard University Press, 2011); Arthur Pickard-Cambridge, *The Dramatic Festivals of Athens* (Oxford: Oxford University Press, 1968). NCW, in *Nietzsche, Kritische Studienausgabe*, vol. 6, 425.

    14. BT, in *Nietzsche, Kritische Studienausgabe*, vol. 1, 139, 35.

    15. Ibid., 57. EH, in *Nietzsche, Kritische Studienausgabe*, vol. 6, 398–401. Nietzsche may have been thinking of the maenad-like motionlessness (and silence) of Catullus's Ariadne. See Catullus, 64, 60.

    16. BT, in *Nietzsche, Kritische Studienausgabe*, vol. 1, 44, 153. HAH, in *Friedrich Nietzsche, Kritische Studienausgabe*, ed. G. Colli and M. Montinari, vol. 2, *Menschliches, Allzumenschliches I und II* (Berlin: de Gruyter, 1988), 544. BGE, in *Nietzsche, Kritische Studienausgabe*, vol. 5, 237.

    17. Cited in Murrey, *Hölderlin's Dionysiac Poetry*, 10.2. EH, in *Nietzsche, Kritische Studienausgabe*, vol. 6, 313.

    18. BT, in *Nietzsche, Kritische Studienausgabe*, vol. 1, 39.

    19. NCW, in *Nietzsche, Kritische Studienausgabe*, vol. 6, 426.

    20. EH, in *Nietzsche, Kritische Studienausgabe*, vol. 6, 401, 348.

    21. BGE, in *Nietzsche, Kritische Studienausgabe*, vol. 5, 237. Murrey, *Hölderlin's Dionysiac Poetry*, 2.3, 4.3.

    22. Cited in Murrey, *Hölderlin's Dionysiac Poetry*, 7.1–7.2, 10.2. BT, in *Nietzsche, Kritische Studienausgabe*, vol. 1, 132, 73.

23. Ibid., 72, 135, 58. ASC, in *Nietzsche, Kritische Studienausgabe*, vol. 1, 16. BGE, in *Nietzsche, Kritische Studienausgabe*, vol. 5, 237. Murrey, *Hölderlin's Dionysiac Poetry*, 2.1.

24. BT, in *Nietzsche, Kritische Studienausgabe*, vol. 1, 145, 35, 136.

25. Ibid., 58, 151, 132. BGE, in *Nietzsche, Kritische Studienausgabe*, vol. 5, 237.

26. Sophocles, *Oidipous at Kolonus*, in *Sophoclis fabulae*, ed. Hugh Lloyd-Jones (Oxford: Clarendon Press, 1990), 383. Euripides, *Bacchae*, *Euripides fabulae*, ed. Jones Diggle, vol. 3, *Helena, Phoenissae, Orestes, Bacchae, Iphigenia, Avlidensis, Rhesus* (Oxford: Oxford University Press, 1994), 303. Murrey, *Hölderlin's Dionysiac Poetry*, 13.

27. Cited in Murrey, *Hölderlin's Dionysiac Poetry*, 7.1. BT, in *Nietzsche, Kritische Studienausgabe*, vol. 1, 65.

28. Ibid., 61–62.

29. Ibid., 154, 72, 145.

30. Ibid., 58, 28–29.

31. Murrey, *Hölderlin's Dionysiac Poetry*, 10–11.

32. Ibid., 10.2. BT, in *Nietzsche, Kritische Studienausgabe*, vol. 1, 114.

33. Ibid., 152, 28. Nietzsche's immature turn to Schopenhauer, also in regard to the narrowness of Nietzsche's own insight into Greece, is something that shall be discussed in part II.

34. Ibid., 56, 62–63.

35. Ibid., 72.

36. Ibid., 136, 44. EH, in *Nietzsche, Kritische Studienausgabe*, vol. 6, 404.

37. BT, in *Nietzsche, Kritische Studienausgabe*, vol. 1, 136.

38. Murrey, *Hölderlin's Dionysiac Poetry*, 7.2, 10.2.

39. BT, in *Nietzsche, Kritische Studienausgabe*, vol. 1, 72.

40. Ibid., 135, 57. EH, in *Nietzsche, Kritische Studienausgabe*, vol. 6, 345.

41. Ibid., 29.

42. Ibid., 49.

43. Ibid., 134.

44. Ibid., 44. Here Nietzsche is also speaking of tragedy. One of the problems with his youthful, if exceptionally creative, first book, *The Birth of Tragedy*, is its failure to clarify the difference between myth, ritual, and tragedy. This is something to which I return in part II and the conclusion.

45. Ibid., 31, 50, 63.

46. Ibid., 150, 59.

47. Ibid., 30, 131.

48. Murrey, *Hölderlin's Dionysiac Poetry*, 2.3.

49. BT, in *Nietzsche, Kritische Studienausgabe*, vol. 1, 59–60, 135, 73.

50. Ibid., 32, 25–26.

51. Ibid., 104, 149–50.

52. Ibid., 140.

53. Ibid., 137.

54. Ibid., 27.

55. Ibid., 62.

56. Ibid., 65.

57. Sophocles, *Antigone*, in *Sophoclis fabulae*, 215.

58. BT, in *Nietzsche, Kritische Studienausgabe*, vol. 1, 65. Aeschylus, *Persai*, in *Aeschyli septem quae supersunt tragoedias*, ed. Denis Page (Oxford: Clarendon Press, 1972), 10.

59. TI, in *Nietzsche, Kritische Studienausgabe*, vol. 6, 118.

60. BT, in *Nietzsche, Kritische Studienausgabe*, vol. 1, 137.

61. Ibid., 133–34.

62. Ibid., 151.

63. Ibid., 132.

64. Ibid., 152, 140–41, 71–72.

65. Murrey, *Hölderlin's Dionysiac Poetry*, 3.3.

66. BT, in *Nietzsche, Kritische Studienausgabe*, vol. 1, 72.

67. Ibid., 61, 155, 150.

68. Ibid., 137, 139.

69. Ibid., 134, 35–36, 71, 35–36, 68.
70. Ibid., 35. Richard Seaford, *Ancient Greece and Global Warming: The Benefits of a Classical Education, or: Learn from the Past to Live in the Present* (Exeter: Credo Press, 2011). Murrey, *Hölderlin's Dionysiac Poetry*, 3.1.
71. BT, in *Nietzsche, Kritische Studienausgabe*, vol. 1, 141.
72. Murrey, *Hölderlin's Dionysiac Poetry*, 7.1.
73. BT, in *Nietzsche, Kritische Studienausgabe*, vol. 1, 66.
74. Ibid., 151, 71, 63.
75. Ibid., 57, 139. BGE, in *Nietzsche, Kritische Studienausgabe*, vol. 5, 99. Murrey, *Hölderlin's Dionysiac Poetry*, 2.3, 4.3. Euripides, *Cyclops*, with an Introduction and Commentary by Richard Seaford (Oxford: Oxford University Press, 1988), 29.
76. Murrey, *Hölderlin's Dionysiac Poetry*, 3.1.
77. BT, in *Nietzsche, Kritische Studienausgabe*, vol. 1, 139.
78. Ibid., 138.
79. Ibid., 139.
80. Ibid., 62–63.
81. Murrey, *Hölderlin's Dionysiac Poetry*, 11.1.
82. BT, in *Nietzsche, Kritische Studienausgabe*, vol. 1, 110, 138. Murrey, *Hölderlin's Dionysiac Poetry*, 11.1.
83. BT, in *Nietzsche, Kritische Studienausgabe*, vol. 1, 137–38. Murrey, *Hölderlin's Dionysiac Poetry*, 11.1.
84. BT, in *Nietzsche, Kritische Studienausgabe*, vol. 1, 65.
85. Murrey, *Hölderlin's Dionysiac Poetry*, 7.1, 10.1.
86. Ibid., 11.1.
87. Ibid., 9.1.
88. BT, in *Nietzsche, Kritische Studienausgabe*, vol. 1, 30.
89. Ibid., 104, 141.
90. Ibid., 149–50, 133–34. Murrey, *Hölderlin's Dionysiac Poetry*, 9.2.
91. BT, in *Nietzsche, Kritische Studienausgabe*, vol. 1, 155, 134, 128–29.

Chapter Three

Dionysian Philosophy

"THE HELLENIC MODEL"

Although Nietzsche's retrieval of the *Dionysiac chronotope* is strikingly similar to that which we see in Hölderlin, it is his adaption of this ancient experience of earth and community to absorb the *visualized chronotope* in modern time where the deeper similarity between the philosopher and poet truly comes forth.

This is not to say that Nietzsche's understanding of Greece does not also complement Hölderlin's critique of money. The "selfish attitude" of greedy capitalists and scientists who desire "despicable gold," *schnödem Gold*, and "disgraceful profit," *schändliche[r] Gewinn* (v 1097)—and who are "tyrannical towards nature"—is continued in Nietzsche's critique of the "un-Dionysian spirit"[1] of nineteenth-century consumer culture. Now "bourgeois mediocrity" (2.2)—a mass of "ponderous herd animals with uneasy consciences (who commit themselves to promoting egoism" (1.1)—reduces the greatness of life to a vengeful "loan" of "happiness" (1.1).

Nevertheless, it is the critique of *visualized* nature and being—humans and their place in the cosmos reduced to abstract images that can be calculated for profit—wherein philosophy and poetry coalesce. For Hölderlin, as I have shown, the isolation to which money leads, as when "[e]ach individual is nailed alone / . . . in the din of workplace / Hearing only himself and caught up in an insane labour" (v 242–44),[2] is linked to modern visual technology. "The telescope" through which we "coun[t] and / Nam[e] the stars of heaven with names" (v 51–52)[3] is the preeminent example.

For Nietzsche, the monetized spirit of "bourgeois mediocrity" is also caught up in the "treacherous eyes" (2.1) of the *"theoretical man"* who replaces myth with "a *deux ex machine* of its own, namely the god of machines . . . in the service of higher egoism" (2.2). Because this new, abstract individual "is unable to behold a vision, he forces the machinist and decorative artist into his service" (2.2). And like Hölderlin who warns us about a *visualized language* no longer in balance with nature and communal life—as when we "coun[t] and / Nam[e] the stars of heaven with names" (v 51–52)—Nietzsche's critique extends to the rapid uprooting (and homogenization) of language in the nineteenth century (1.2). The degenerate "speaking-style" of "the 'journalist,' the paper slave of the day" (2.2) recalls the spirit of linguistic vengeance in Hazlitt and Burke (1.2).

As we should expect, Nietzsche seeks to adapt the *Dionysiac chronotope* to rescue "authentic art" from "this gloomily depicted wilderness of our exhausted cultures."[4] In a sense, he seeks to purify the unlimited (*visualized*) individualism of the present by absorbing its "poisonous eye of *ressentiment*" into the "Apolline illusion" (2.2). This, in turn, can be transfigured into a Dionysian experience of space, time and language. The problem, however, is that

> our aestheticians know nothing of this return to a primal home, of the brother-hood of the two gods of art in tragedy, nor of the Apolline or Dionysian excitation of the listener.[5]

When Nietzsche asks: "How does the *chorus* and the entire musical-Dionysian underground of tragedy appear on the new Socratic-optimistic world-stage?," he is also asking: In what way can the monetary and visual egoism of "bourgeois mediocrity" in the present be related to the cleansing "foundation of all existence, the Dionysian substratum"?[6] After all, "to form a true estimate of the Dionysian capacity of a people"—and this includes us moderns—they must be brought before "the only sincere, pure and purifying fire-spirit . . . the unerring judge, Dionysus."[7]

Given the primal meaning of Greece, it is no surprise that Nietzsche declares that "to be able to learn from the Greeks is itself a great honour and distinguishing rarity."[8] In particular, it is the significance of "such a miraculous sudden awakening of tragedy . . . for the innermost life-ground of a people [that] can be learned only from the Greeks."[9] Coupled with the socio-political potential that accompanies the birth of tragedy, this leads Nietzsche to claim that, "only as an aesthetic phenomenon is existence and the world eternally justified."[10] "To purify our aesthetic insight," therefore, "we have borrowed from each separate kingdom of art [Kunstreich]."[11] One thinks of Hölderlin's dream of "founding / A kingdom of art," *ein Reich der Kunst* (v 3–4).[12] Tragedy "as the quintessence of all prophylactic powers of healing . . . must confront us, as it did the Greeks" and "art" which "must above all demand purity in its sphere"—especially when humankind is enslaved by the tyranny of "abstract ones"—that is, "when the danger to the will is the greatest"—shall make her epiphany "as a healing sorceress."[13]

This brings us to that which Nietzsche discovers when he, inspired by "the Hellenic model," departs on a journey to find "a single, vigorously developed root [Wurzel]" and "healthy soil [Erdboden],"[14] namely a Dionysian myth of the present. "I am a disciple of the philosopher Dionysus," he proclaims. "I have learned much, all too much about the philosophy of Dionysus,"[15] he continues,

> and, as I said, from mouth to mouth—I, the last disciple and initiate of the god Dionysus: and perhaps I might at least begin to give you, my friends, as far as I am allowed, a taste of this philosophy? In a hushed voice, as is but fitting: for it has to do with much that is secret, new, strange, wonderful and uncanny. Already that Dionysus is a philosopher, and that gods also philosophise, appears to me as something new, and which is not un-ensnaring, that which perhaps arouses suspicion precisely among philosophers.[16]

As we have seen, philosophy emerges from the unlimitedness of money that creates an unconscious imagination that, in turn, sees the universe as ruled by an abstract, singular and unlimited substance.[17] Nietzsche's antipathy to the *monetized* and *visualized* modern "herd animals with uneasy consciences" of "bourgeois mediocrity"—the new mass of self-isolating individuals "who commit themselves to promoting egoism" in our present—is also aimed at the tyranny of self-isolating philosophers.[18]

Let us return to Pentheus, who asks Dionysus if he can spy on his maenads in exchange for an enormous payment of money (v 810–12).[19] Like this tyrant, Parmenides, Plato, Descartes, Kant, and Mill—to name just a few—unconsciously reduce earth and community to self-isolating abstractions that not only fail to question, but even reinforce the monetary (and visual) spirit of the ancient and modern worlds to which each belongs. "Before me this translation of the Dionysian into a philosophical pathos did not exist," Nietzsche declares and proceeds to mourn the lack of real thinking that plagues philosophy since its inception: "tragic wisdom is lacking,—I have searched in vain for signs of it even among the great Greek philosophers from the two centuries before Socrates."[20] Indeed, the birth of thinking that embraces communal life in balance with nature while resisting the destructive force of the (unlimited) visual media of money—"a Dionysian philosophy"[21] —is something "which is not un-ensnaring, that which perhaps arouses suspicion precisely among philosophers."

Looking back, the mature Nietzsche is acutely aware of his "Dionysian nature."[22] Speaking "[i]n a hushed voice, as is but fitting" for the "initiate," he describes even his youthful musings as issuing forth from "a mystic and almost maenad-like soul."[23] "I began by interpreting Wagner's music as the expression of a Dionysian powerfulness of soul" and "by these means discovered the idea of 'tragedy.'"[24] We should note that the hopes and dreams kindled by "[t]he blessed tribe of the Greeks," in particular belief in "the Dionysian life and rebirth of tragedy,"[25] contrary to what many Nietzsche scholars seem to prefer to believe, never die. "After all I have absolutely no reason to renounce my hope for a Dionysian future of music,"[26] Nietzsche writes as late as 1888. "I promise a *tragic* age."[27]

Part of this confidence in the return of the Dionysian comes from Nietzsche's understanding of the unique power of myth to purify the harmful essence of *monetized* and *visualized chronotopes*. On the one hand, the mythical realm to which his Bacchic thought leads glows with rage. Inspired by Dionysus's power to "impos[e] silence and attentiveness on everything loud and self-conceited" (3.1), Nietzsche battles the "evil eye" (2.1) of "the vampire of imperium Romanum" and its "elevated form of piracy."[28] One thinks of the title *Ecce homo*—or another, more direct exultation: "Have I made myself clear?—Dionysus versus the crucified."[29]

As we have noted, the mythic philosopher (who "should prefer to be even a satyr to being a saint")[30] sees the concentrated "bourgeois mediocrity" of classical Greece within the "profoundly nihilistic" essence of Christianity as severing the original tie between Western civilization and Dionysian art, but also the original tie to "the weaker degrees of Apolline art": "neither Apolline nor Dionysian," the "kingdom . . . not of this world" whose "physiological evilness" (2.2) still more aggressively alienates nature and community. Given that there is no difference between the genesis of language in Judeo-Christianity—when "Adam" gave names "to the beasts"—and that which we see in modern time—that is, our "consuming desire for knowledge" (2.2)—Nietzsche understands his new myth that is rooted "in the name of a Greek god" as "purely artistic and anti-Christian."[31] Again, one thinks of Hölderlin's "telescope" (v 51) with which all-too-Judeo-Christian moderns (similar to Adam) "coun[t] and / Nam[e] the stars of heaven with names" (v 51–52). Nietzschean myth struggles with the tragic silence that haunts our time of unlimited money and sinister visual media when "sacred names are missing" (v 101).[32]

But the goal is always the Dionysian rebirth of love. The spirit of Christianity wherein "evil" perversely becomes "good"[33] is absorbed into and transfigured by

> the genius of heart, which teaches the clumsy and too hasty hand to hesitate, and to grasp more delicately; which scents the hidden and forgotten treasure, the drop of goodness and sweet spirituality under thick dark ice, and is a divining-rod for every grain of gold, long buried and imprisoned in mud and sand.[34]

Science that sees nature as a dead machine whose parts can be infinitely plundered for the glory of God gives way to a more universal (and beautiful) picture of earth and humankind as a pulsating, Dionysian whole that, in turn, requires a joyful, *fröhliche Wissenschaft ("la gaia scienza")*. The deterioration of "authentic art" into "superficial entertainment"—into a modern "decadence-music" and language (2.2)—is redeemed by "the Dionysian wisdom of tragedy"[35] that speaks (even sings) in Nietzsche's *Dionysus-Dithyrambs*.

But because the time to which Nietzsche belongs struggles with the modern *visualized chronotope*, the myth of "the Dionysian human"[36] today tends to evoke a peculiarly tragic picture: "one thinks of some great athlete heroically swimming against a violent current in the attempt to reach an invisible country one knows he will never see."[37] Among the many wild and tragic (and popular) Nietzschean myths "The Madman." The despairing and breathless "tortured martyr" in search of the sacred makes his epiphany to a crowd at "the marketplace."[38] This invites us, incidentally, to see this entire scene against the background of "bourgeois mediocrity." The resentful words and laughter that erupt from this modern mass of secular "herd animals" gesture to a *monetized language* that is disconnected from earth and community:

> As many of those who did not believe in god were standing around just then, he provoked much laughter. Has he become lost?, said one. Did he lose his way like a child?, said another. Or is he hiding? Is he afraid of us? Has he gone on a voyage? Emigrated?—thus they screamed and laughed wildly.[39]

Terrifying metaphors gesture to our "self-destructive [self-consuming] culture of the unlimited."[40] "But how did we do this? How could we drink up the sea? Who gave us the sponge to wipe away the horizon?"[41] This is followed by a reference to the "higher egoism" to which those "with uneasy consciences . . . commit themselves." "Must we ourselves," given the unfathomability of this event, "not become gods simply to appear worthy of it?"[42]

We have noted how the industrialization of space and time in the nineteenth century, as illustrated by a train cutting through a rural landscape, extends the "paradox of an unlimited abstract territoriality" that existed already in the imagination of early historic Greece, one that encompasses not only "all geographic space," but also, "beyond that, the whole cosmos" (1.1).[43] Speaking to this unprecedented cosmic uprootedness, the madman asks:

> What were we doing when we unchained this earth from its sun? To where is it moving now? To where are we moving? Away from all suns? Are we not plunging ceaselessly? Backwards, forwards, sideways, in all directions? Is there still an up or down? Are we not lost, as if wandering through an infinite nothing? Do we not feel the breath of empty space?[44]

The frenzied (out-of-his-mind) individual gestures to the accelerated loss of the unique place of human in the cosmos. Following the religious crisis to which early historic Greece succumbs just after the introduction of money and its visual culture,[45] the velocity of this tragic event increases exponentially alongside the emergence of modern (industrial) energy capture, which then gives rise to the modern money and the visual technologies.

> Is it not the case that since Copernicus the self-diminution of the human and his *will* to self-diminution has made unstoppable progress? Alas, faith in his dignity, uniqueness, irreplaceability in the chain of being is gone,—the human has become an *animal*, not metaphorically, but absolutely and unconditionally, he who in his earlier faith was almost god ("child of god," "god-man") . . . Since Copernicus the human appears to have slipped onto an inclined plane,— now he rolls always faster away from the centre—to where? into nothingness? into the "penetrating feeling of his nothingness"?[46]

As we might expect, Nietzsche's myth of cosmic rootlessness includes a critique of the *visualized chronotope*. Because the man of today "is unable to behold a vision"—one thinks of Galileo reading the "grand book" of "the universe, which stands continually open to our gaze," through his "spyglass" (2.2)—the madman gestures to blindness in the present. "Who gave us the sponge to wipe away the horizon?" Absence of visual perspective is reinforced by distorted (and horrifying) images that the maniac embodies (and performs). Appearing with "a lantern in the bright morning hours,"[47] Nietzsche's modern myth begins by expressing the loss of an epiphany of magical light. In this darkness, the meaning of the story lights up:

> The madman leapt into their midst and pierced them with his eyes. . . . Is not night ceaselessly closing in on us? Do we not need to light lanterns in the morning? . . . [he] fell silent and looked again at his listeners; and they, too, were silent and stared at him in astonishment. At last he threw his lantern on the ground, and it broke into pieces and he departed.[48]

But what makes "The Madman" truly a new Dionysian myth is its absorption of modern carelessness into mystic horror that, in turn, prefigures the epiphany of an earthly and communal light. Although the vengeful crowd has still to sense the transformative power of "[l]ightning and thunder,"[49] they are implicitly gathered into a whole, even if only in a negative sense. The impossibility of release—"How can we console ourselves, the murderers of all murderers?"—evokes mystic isolation and despair (3.2).[50] The lack of purifying "water" and "festivals"—one thinks of Hölderlin's "holidays [that] / Do not blaze through the night" (v 46–47)—implies the return of Dionysus's secret rites, including the purifying fountains of water that leap out of the earth (v 704–10).[51] Lastly, "the noise of the gravediggers" and "smell . . .

of divine decomposition"[52] alongside the breathlessness of the screaming messenger (and the terrifying "breath of empty space") indirectly suggest that this blinding of "bourgeois mediocrity" by "deathly silent clamour" (3.2) looks forward to the luminous, synaesthesia of Dionysian redemption.

"INCIPIT TRAGOEDIA"

But of all Nietzsche's myths, *Thus spoke Zarathustra, A book for all and none*, is his most profound adaption of the *Dionysiac chronotope* to challenge the *visualized* (and *monetized*) space-time of the present. The "world-historic" (2.2)[53] significance of Greece now blends most perfectly into modern time. Consider the reflection of the mature, self-proclaimed "mystic" looking back upon his *Birth of Tragedy*.

> The whole representation of the dithyrambic artist is a picture of the already existing author of Zarathustra and it is drawn with an abysmal depth that does not even once come into contact with the real Wagner. (2.2)[54]

In no insignificant way, Nietzsche had always been (and never stopped) dreaming of *Zarathustra*. And that this myth represents both an indirect and direct gesture to the Dionysian is suggested already in its conception. Horrific images of the dis*organ*ization of humanity in modern time—one thinks of the isolated eyes and ears in *The Madman* that have not yet "seen and heard"[55] (that is, not yet been transformed by) "lightning and thunder"—give way to glimpses of a Dionysian paradise.

Firstly, there is the previsual, musical ecstasy out of which the image of the tragic hero ascends. "One may count the entirety of Zarathustra among music;—surely the rebirth of art was doubtlessly *to be heard*."[56] "The phoenix of music flew by," Nietzsche confides, "with lighter and more luminous feathers than he had ever shown."[57] This return to the magical spirit of music, specifically this return to the rebirth of the secret power of sound to call forth images—the winged spirit of music who makes his epiphany "with lighter and more radiate feathers"—takes us back to *The Birth of Tragedy*.

Prescribing the antidote to modern homelessness, Nietzsche encourages those who have become lost in the (endless) wanderings of the present to "merely listen to the delightful, luring call of the Dionysian bird that hovers above him and wants to reveal the way."[58] Elsewhere we hear of a "striving for infinity, the winged-beat of longing."[59] Here we touch upon the secret meaning of the *soul-bird* in mystic initiation.

As we have seen, the fluttering soul (v 214) of Pentheus, who runs "feverishly this way and that" (v 625), reflects "the fluttering agitation" of the "internally felt" soul-bird of the initiand (v 332, 326, 359).[60] This is implicit in *Bacchae* where the "softness" (v 969) of the *visualized* (and *monetized*) fluttering soul of the tyrant (that succumbs to Dionysian dismemberment) is contrasted with the cosmic unity (v 73) of Dionysus's female mystics, described as "a rising flock of (non-fluttering) birds" (v 748).[61] The Apolline picture of *Zarathustra* is thus born out of Nietzsche's power to transcend the *visualized* philosophy of modern time—"Bentham's footsteps" of thought restlessly "moving this way and that" (1.2)—and return to the previsual beauty of a Bacchic underworld.

This brings us to the second way in which the concept of *Zarathustra* is directly Dionysian. "When Zarathustra was thirty years old," Nietzsche tells us, "he left his home and the lake of his home, and went into the mountains. Here he enjoyed his spirit and his loneliness and for ten years he did not grow tired."[62] Individual communion with nature gives way, nevertheless, to a need to explore this relationship.

> At last, however, his heart changed,—and one morning he arose with the morning red, stepped before the sun and spoke to it thus: "You great star! What would happen to your happiness, if you did not have those who you illuminate! For ten years you have come up to my cave; without me, my eagle and my snake, you would have grown tired of your light and this way; but we waited for you each morning, took from you your excess and blessed you for it."[63]

This "excess" of sunlight hints at the Dionysian that, as we have noted, lurks secretly within the Apolline. In fact, it is an earthly superabundance of (real) thinking that compels Zarathustra to abandon his isolation and seek a communal experience. "Alas, I am weary of my wisdom, like bees who have collected too much honey, I need outstretched hands."[64]

Whereas "The Madman" searches in vain for Dionysian fountains of "water" (4.1), Zarathustra is not only witness to an earthly epiphany; he suffers its superabundance. As we have seen, Dionysus, who "gave the pain-removing delight of wine equally to the wealthy man and to the lesser man" (v 421–23), "wants honours in common from all, and to be magnified while distinguishing nobody" (v 208–9).[65] Now Nietzsche's mythical hero also longs to give the miraculous "honey" that "the earth . . . gives."[66] "I would like to bestow and distribute until the wise have once again joyously become their foolishness and the poor once again their wealth."[67]

But to found a relation between one's communion with nature and others, one must embrace his or her individual mortality. "For this reason I must descend into the depths," Zarathustra explains, "as you do in the evening, when you dip behind the sea and bring light to the underworld, you superabundant star!"[68] A picture of gleaming rebirth that ascends out of the darkness below now appears. "I must, like you, *go down*, as humans name it, to them I want to descend."[69] As we have noted, the hubris of the mortal who strives for immortality ("the greedy thirst for existence" that we see in the *visualized* "tragic hero") is tied to a self-destructive, unlimited consumer society—"bourgeois mediocrity" (2.2). And it is the "downfall, not [the] victory" of "the struggling hero" that "prepares"[70] Dionysus's return. "We should recognise," Nietzsche says elsewhere in *The Birth of Tragedy*, "how everything that comes into existence must be prepared for a suffering downfall."[71] This means that only when we resist unlimited (*visualized* and *monetized*) individualism—by shattering of the "agonising glass case of . . . human individuality" (2.2)—can an authentic experience of earth and community return.

> So bless me then you peaceful eye that can behold the greatest happiness without envy! Bless the cup that shall overflow, that the water may flow golden out of it and carry everywhere the reflection of your delight! Look! These cups want to be empty again, and Zarathustra wants to be human again.—Thus began Zarathustra's going down.[72]

This idyllic image of one's relation to nature and others demands that one embrace even the horror of individual death, that is, accept the humble place of the individual within humankind's cosmic (vertical) axis. The penultimate part of Nietzsche's search for a *happy science* culminates with the title "*Incipit tragoedia*," a name that introduces his modern Dionysian myth of Zarathustra: "*Tragedy begins.*"

NOTES

1. Cited in Lucas Murrey, *Hölderlin's Dionysiac Poetry: The Terrifying-Exciting Mysteries* (Heidelberg, New York, Dordrecht, London: Springer, 2015), chapters 8–9 (8–9). BT, in *Friedrich Nietzsche, Kritische Studienausgabe*, ed. Giorgio Colli and Mazzino Montinari, vol. 1, *Die Geburt der Tragödie, Unzeitgemäße Betrachtungen I–IV, Nachgelassene Schriften 1870–1873* (Berlin: de Gruyter, 1999), 115.
2. Murrey, *Hölderlin's Dionysiac Poetry*, 8.
3. Ibid.
4. BT, in *Nietzsche, Kritische Studienausgabe*, vol. 1, 131–32.
5. Ibid., 141–42.
6. Ibid., 95, 155.
7. Ibid., 153, 128.
8. Ibid., 129.
9. Ibid., 132.
10. Ibid., 47.
11. Ibid., 147.
12. Murrey, *Hölderlin's Dionysiac Poetry*, 9.2.
13. BT, in *Nietzsche, Kritische Studienausgabe*, vol. 1, 134, 152, 145, 57.
14. Ibid., 128, 131.
15. EH, in *Friedrich Nietzsche, Kritische Studienausgabe*, ed. Giorgio Colli and Mazzino Montinari, vol. 6, *Der Fall Wagner, Götzen-Dämmerung, Der Antichrist, Ecce homo, Dionysos-Dithyramben, Nietzsche contra Wagner* (Berlin: de Gruyter, 1999), 258. BGE, in *Nietzsche, Kritische Studienausgabe*, Giorgio Colli and Mazzino Montinari, vol. 5, *Jenseits von Gut und Böse, Zur Genealogie der Moral* (Berlin: de Gruyter, 1999), 237.
16. Ibid.

17. Murrey, *Hölderlin's Dionysiac Poetry*, 5.2.
18. Ibid.
19. Ibid., 2.2, 2, 2.3.
20. EH, in *Nietzsche, Kritische Studienausgabe*, vol. 6, 312.
21. Ibid., 313.
22. EH, in *Nietzsche, Kritische Studienausgabe*, vol. 6, 366.
23. ASC, 3, in *Nietzsche, Kritische Studienausgabe*, vol. 1, 15.
24. NCW, in *Nietzsche, Kritische Studienausgabe*, vol. 6, 425. EH, in *Nietzsche, Kritische Studienausgabe*, vol. 6, 312.
25. BT, in *Nietzsche, Kritische Studienausgabe*, vol. 1, 155–56, 132.
26. EH, in *Nietzsche, Kritische Studienausgabe*, vol. 6, 313.
27. Ibid.
28. Murrey, *Hölderlin's Dionysiac Poetry*, 5.2.
29. EH, in *Nietzsche, Kritische Studienausgabe*, vol. 6, 374.
30. EH, in *Nietzsche, Kritische Studienausgabe*, vol. 6, 258.
31. BT, in *Nietzsche, Kritische Studienausgabe*, vol. 1, 120. ASC, in *Nietzsche, Kritische Studienausgabe*, vol. 1, 19.
32. Murrey, *Hölderlin's Dionysiac Poetry*, coda.
33. BGE, in *Nietzsche, Kritische Studienausgabe*, vol. 5, 273–74.
34. Ibid., 237.
35. BT, in *Nietzsche, Kritische Studienausgabe*, vol. 1, 57.
36. Ibid.
37. Eliza Butler, *The Tyranny of Greece over Germany: A Study of the Influence Exercised by Greek Art and Poetry over the Great German Writers of the Eighteenth, Nineteenth and Twentieth Centuries* (Cambridge: Cambridge University Press, 1958), 314.
38. GS, in *Friedrich Nietzsche, Kritische Studienausgabe*, ed. Giorgio Colli and Mazzino Montinari, vol. 3, *Morgenröte, Idyllen aus Messina, Die fröhliche Wissenschaft* (Berlin: de Gruyter, 1999), 480.
39. Ibid.
40. Murrey, *Hölderlin's Dionysiac Poetry*, 6.1.
41. GS, in *Nietzsche, Kritische Studienausgabe*, vol. 3, 481.
42. Ibid.
43. Murrey, *Hölderlin's Dionysiac Poetry*, 3.1.
44. GS, in *Nietzsche, Kritische Studienausgabe*, vol. 3, 481.
45. Murrey, *Hölderlin's Dionysiac Poetry*, 3.2.
46. GM, in *Nietzsche, Kritische Studienausgabe*, vol. 5, 404.
47. GS, in *Nietzsche, Kritische Studienausgabe*, vol. 3, 480.
48. Ibid., 480–81.
49. Ibid., 481.
50. Ibid. Murrey, *Hölderlin's Dionysiac Poetry*, 2.2.
51. GS, in *Nietzsche, Kritische Studienausgabe*, vol. 3, 481. Murrey, *Hölderlin's Dionysiac Poetry*, 8, 7.2.
52. GS, in *Nietzsche, Kritische Studienausgabe*, vol. 3, 481.
53. EH, in *Nietzsche, Kritische Studienausgabe*, vol. 6, 314.
54. Ibid.
55. GS, in *Nietzsche, Kritische Studienausgabe*, vol. 3, 481.
56. EH, in *Nietzsche, Kritische Studienausgabe*, vol. 6, 335.
57. Ibid.
58. BT, in *Nietzsche, Kritische Studienausgabe*, vol. 1, 149. The important problem of Nietzsche's nationalism is something to which we turn in part II.
59. Ibid., 153.
60. Richard Seaford, *Dionysus* (London and New York: Routledge, 2006), 108. Murrey, *Hölderlin's Dionysiac Poetry*, 4.2.
61. Ibid., 4.2, 2.3.
62. GS, in *Nietzsche, Kritische Studienausgabe*, vol. 3, 571.
63. Ibid.

64. Ibid.

65. Murrey, *Hölderlin's Dionysiac Poetry*, 5.2, 2.3.

66. BT, in *Nietzsche, Kritische Studienausgabe*, vol. 1, 30.

67. GS, in *Nietzsche, Kritische Studienausgabe*, vol. 3, 571.

68. Ibid.

69. Ibid.

70. BT, in *Nietzsche, Kritische Studienausgabe*, vol. 1, 134.

71. Ibid., 109. Nietzsche's relation to pre-Socratic thought, including this reference to Anaximander, is treated in the Conclusion.

72. GS, in *Nietzsche, Kritische Studienausgabe*, vol. 3, 571.

Chapter Four

Fifty Mirrors around You

"THEY JINGLE WITH THEIR GOLD"

It is clear that *Zarathustra* elaborates the Dionysian myth of *The Madman* (4.1). Early in the preface, the tragic hero—similar to he who appears at the marketplace—is surprised that there are still those who have failed to notice "that God is dead!"[1] Nevertheless, something has changed. *Zarathustra* is not only a maniac.

As if reflecting (by way of compact metaphor) Nietzsche's critique of monetary greed that descends from medieval Christianity to the nineteenth century—from "an elevated form of piracy" (the crusades) to "bourgeois mediocrity" (2.2)—we come across an earthly, but self-isolating "saint" in the forest who is unaware that he, like all Judeo-Christian priests, is *out of work*.[2] We continue to "the nearest city" where "many people" have "assembled at the marketplace."[3] Similar to the madman, Zarathustra is concerned about the absence of spirituality. But unlike his despairing and frenetic (and fiendish) predecessor, Zarathustra does not hesitate to speak of a future spirit, or of this being's coming significance. "Behold, I teach you the *Übermensch*," he declares to the crowd: "The *Übermensch* is the meaning of earth."[4]

To explain what "the meaning of earth" *means*, Zarathustra invites the scattered individuals at the marketplace to reflect upon their isolation: "what does your body reveal about your soul? Is not your soul poverty and pollution and disgraceful self-satisfaction?"[5] "Truly, the human is a polluted river,"[6] he continues. "One must already be a sea to be able to take on a polluted river without becoming impure."[7] This is the explanation of the godlike being of earth: "he is this sea, in him your vast contempt can perish."[8]

By defining "the *Übermensch*" as an oceanic form of purification, Nietzsche gestures to the nature of the disease to which the crowd has succumbed. Their "hour of vast contempt" is related in particular to rapid industrialization: the reduction of human life to "glow and fuel."[9] Bourgeois "culture" and "education"—*Bildung*—that emerges from this (unlimited) exploitation of nature produces, in turn, "the last human": an individual who is incapable of real love, creation, and wonder.[10] The "happiness" of a mass consumer society—the descendent of "'Greek cheerfulness'"[11] —reduces the meanings of earth (and its ancient resources) to its industrialized, "homogenized sensibility" (1.1). "Everything" that is originally unique and powerful becomes "equal."[12] And as witness to the loss of earth's primal power, Zarathustra foresees the (earthly) exhaustion to which modern humans lead. "But that soil," he says, "will one day be poor and exhausted, and no lofty tree will any longer be able to grow thereon."[13]

Although Zarathustra implores the crowd to heed his message—"the *Übermensch shall be* the meaning of earth! . . . I swear to you, my brothers, *remain true to the earth!*"—"[t]hey do not understand"[14] him. Unable to conceive "the *Übermensch*," "the desire of the masses" cries out, instead, for "the last human."[15] Prophecy of divine being—"the meaning of earth"—is then eclipsed by a (visual) desire for entertainment for which the crowd at the marketplace gathered to see.[16]

In fact, the *monetized chronotope*, as expressed by the resentful "desire of the masses" at the *marketplace*, is an important theme in *Zarathustra*. It returns when the hero arrives before the gates of "the great city."[17] As we have noted, the abrupt rise in population in the nineteenth century is tied to an explosion of urban centers—and this means an explosion of *monetized* space-times (1.1). For Nietzsche, "this city, which steams with the vapour of slaughtered spirit," is ruled by isolated individuals who "jingle with their gold."[18] Although we hear of an urban "prince," he seems to be secretly ruled by "the gold of the shop-keep."[19] The "bourgeois mediocrity" with which Nietzsche is concerned—"the desire of the masses" that Zarathustra confronts at the marketplace—is related to the sickness that is making our earthly place in the cosmos "poor and exhausted." The "polluted river" into which humankind has degenerated is thus a result of money-tyrants who "jingle with their gold."

This brings us to the historical metaphor of humanity with which Nietzsche initiates his central Dionysian myth.

> Meanwhile the rope-dancer began his work: he had stepped out of the little tower and made his way upon the rope, which was stretched between two towers and so hung over the marketplace and people.[20]

By this time Zarathustra has already declared that "the human being is a rope tied between animal and *Übermensch*,—a rope over an abyss."[21] "But then something happened that made every mouth silent and froze every eye."[22] "As [the rope-dancer] was mid-way across,"[23] we hear,

> the little tower opened once again and out leapt a colourful fellow, similar to a buffoon, who went with quick steps after the first one. "Forward, lame-foot," he screamed in a terrible voice, "forward sloth, interloper, pale-face! lest I tickle you with my heel! What are you doing here between towers? You belong in the tower, one should lock you up, a better one than you, for you block the way!" And with every word he came nearer and nearer: but as he was just one step behind him, the terrible event occurred that made every mouth silent and froze every eye: he bellowed a shout as if a devil and jumped over and beyond he who was in his way. But this one, when he saw his rival triumph, lost his head and rope; he threw his balancing stick and shot faster than it down in a whirl of arms and legs into the depth. The marketplace and people like a sea before a storm: everything flew apart, in particular there where the body would crash.[24]

Given the metaphor of the rope as humankind, we can perhaps think of the (present) ropedancer as modern man suffering his "world-historic" (4.1) destiny. For does not this unstable spirit succumb (unconsciously) to a suicidal impulse, as expressed by (in fact, embodied in) his distasteful, aggressive, and lethal "fellow"?

That which is critical for understanding this tragic event is revealed already in the first two words that the "buffoon-like" creature screams: "Forward, lame-foot!" I have shown the tragic fate to which the *monetized* mind of Oedipus—whose name means "lame-foot"—succumbs.[25] And as we have seen, "the terrible destiny of the wise Oedipus" is transfigured, for Nietzsche—as it is for Hölderlin—into "a magical, blessed strength" (3.2). At the core of Zarathustra's first representation of the *monetized chronotope* is the destruction to which money leads and—through the "philosophy of the forest god" (3.1)—the earthly cleansing that such destruction requires. Although the isolated "rope-dancer" suffers a tragic individual death, his mortality is absorbed into (and redeemed by) Dionysian myth. The dismembered, dying body escapes the (inhuman) vengeance of Judeo-Christian and scientific secularization, reaches out to the friendly hero, and, far away from those who "jingle with their gold," returns to the communal spirit of earth.[26]

"LOATHSOME VERBAL-SWILL"

At the core of Nietzsche's critique of the *monetized chronotope* is his critique of *monetized language*. When Zarathustra fails to speak of "the meaning of earth" (5.1), it is "the shouting" at "the marketplace" that "interrupt[s] him."[27] "Too long perhaps I lived in the mountains," he reflects, "too long I *listened* to streams and trees [Bäche und Bäume]."[28] "And now they look at me and laugh: and in their laughter, they hate me still more. There is ice in their laughter."[29]

This conflict between *Dionysiac language*—the word that reveals the divine, purifying powers of earth and ascends from the Dionysian sounds of streams and trees—and *monetized language*—the resentful "shouting and desire of the masses," specifically the "ice" in the "laughter" of those who "jingle with their gold" (5.1)—culminates in tragic silence. When Zarathustra had spoken these words he looked again at the people and was silent. "There they stand," he spoke to his heart, "there they laugh: they do not understand me, I am not the mouth for these ears."[30]

The language of money that reinforces (unlimited) individualism—the words of "glow and fuel" (5.1) that, in "promoting egoism" (1.1), makes "our soil . . . poor and exhausted" (5.1)—is also an important theme. When Zarathustra comes to the gates of "the great city" that is ruled by "the gold of the shop-keep" (5.1), he finds at the center of this *monetized* dystopia a malevolent *monetized language*. Just before he hears of those who "jingle with their gold," he learns that within this nightmarish urban zone "spirit has here become a verbal game. . . . Loathsome verbal-swill does it vomit!"[31] The *monetized* "screaming-throats [of] overheated ambitious ones" emerge, we learn, from the spirit of "vengeance."[32]

As we have seen, Nietzsche connects the "vengeance"[33] that festers and consumes individuals (for instance, in the time that follows their traumatic loss of and alienation from earth) to a "fundamental deterioration of fantasy" (2.1). Instead of listening to the cleansing "meaning of earth," the unlimited "desire of the masses" craves "the poisonous" (2.1) spirit of "superficial entertainment" (2.2). Consider the modern poets who abandon "authentic art" (2.2), in particular how they give up on the terrestrial "depth of tones."[34] "They are not pure enough," Zarathustra warns: "they muddy all their waters so that they appear deep."[35] The cognitive dissonance of "all the jingle-jangling of their harps"—their "[g]host-breath and—whizzing"[36] —recalls the malicious *monetized sounds* of individuals who "jingle with their gold."

This brings us to the deeper meaning of Nietzsche's critique of *monetized language*, one to which he gestures already in the preface. We have suffered the shrill, inhuman words of the "colourful fellow": "'Forward, lame-foot,' he *screamed in a wretched voice*,"[37] and the mouth-silencing "cry" that he subsequently (demonically) "bellowed" (5.1). That this linguistic *ressentiment* is representative of "the desire of the masses" ("gold of the shop-keep") is made clear when the hero departs from the city with the maimed body of the ropedancer. After solemnly reflecting, he took the corpse on his back and set out on his way. And before he went a hundred steps, there stole up to him a person and whispered into his ear—and behold! He who talked was the buffoon from the tower. "Go away from this city, oh Zarathustra," he said; "too many hate you here. The good and the righteous hate you and they name you their enemy and despiser; the believers of the true belief hate you, and they name you the danger of the masses. You were lucky that one laughed at you; and truly, you talk like a buffoon. You were lucky that you trafficked with the dead dog; as you degraded yourself, you saved yourself today. But leave this city—or tomorrow I shall leap over and away from you, a living one over a dead one." And as he had said this, the person disappeared; Zarathustra but went further through the dark allies.[38]

But whereas the *Dionysiac word* that speaks of "the meaning of earth" is met with malicious *monetized silence*, the vengeful spirit of *monetized language* is met (and transformed) by the beauty of *Dionysiac silence*. This we hear in what follows after the (Oedipus-like) ropedancer dies among the "deathly silent clamour" (3.1) of the marketplace. After Zarathustra reassures him that "there is no devil and no hell," the dying individual anxiously responds: "'If you speak the truth,' he then said, 'I lose nothing when I lose life. I am nothing much more than an animal that one taught to dance with blows and small bites.'"[39] Given Nietzsche's critique of modern humans as "ponderous herd animals with uneasy consciences (who commit themselves to promoting egoism)" (1.1), and his critique of the reduction of humankind "to an animal, not metaphorically, but absolutely and unconditionally," the language of the dying ropedancer threatens to remain *monetized*—that is, to slip forever "into the 'penetrating feeling of his nothingness'" (4.1).

In this time of individual desolation and death, the *Dionysiac language* of the hero ascends:

"Not at all," Zarathustra said, "you have made danger your calling, therein is nothing contemptible. Now you perish by your calling: for this I shall bury you with my hands." When Zarathustra had said this, the dying one no longer answered; but he moved his hand, as if he sought the hand of Zarathustra to be thankful.[40]

As we have seen, the Dionysian hero carries the corpse of the ropedancer far away from those who "jingle with their gold" into the forest. Among the Bacchic "streams and trees [Bäche und Bäume]" to which Zarathustra himself "*listened*"—that is, far away from the *monetized*, "[l]oathsome verbal-swill" of the city—the dead body finds its home encircled by the sound of earth's pulsating silence.

"FIFTY MIRRORS AROUND YOU"

Inseparable from Nietzsche's critique of the *monetized chronotope* is his depiction of *visualized* space and time. This is clear in the preface when Zarathustra learns of the visual spectacle that is driving "the desire of the masses" as well as those who "jingle with their gold" (5.1). When he "came to the nearest town along the forest Zarathustra found the people gathered at the marketplace: for it was announced that one would *see* a ropedancer."[41]

Important is the connection that the Dionysian hero makes between "the hour of vast contempt [Verachtung]" and (industrialized) "glow and fuel" (5.1). Terrifying images of modernization—we have seen the "whole region [that] burns like a volcano spitting fire from a thousand tubes of brick" (1.1)—are related, through the spirit of perverse hatred, to Christianity.

> Once the soul looked contemptuously [verächtlich] at the body: and then this contempt [Verachtung] was the greatest:—it wanted it to be wasted, ghastly, famished. Thus the soul thought to escape the body and earth.[42]

This modern "contempt," *Verachtung*, with which Zarathustra struggles is rooted in ancient visual perversions: the "'evil eye,'" *'böser Blick,'* "the poisonous eye of *ressentiment*," *das Giftauge des Ressentiment*, and "treacherous eyes," *verrätersich[e] Augen*" (2.1). Neglecting "the meaning of earth" (5.1), the *visualized* space-time (unconsciously) issuing forth from "the gold of the shop-keep" (5.1) seeks a new picture of the suffering other.

> When Zarathustra had thus spoken, one of the people screamed: "We now heard enough of the ropedancer; now let us also *see* him!" And all the people laughed at Zarathustra. The ropedancer, however, who believed that the word applied to him began his work.[43]

The visual emptiness and horror with which the beauty of earth is met in modern time—"When Zarathustra had spoke these words, he *looked* again at the people and was silent" (5.2)[44]—leads to a critique of what we may call the *visualized* education, *Bildung* (5.1) to which "bourgeois mediocrity" (2.2) gives rise. Later, when he directly confronts "the present-day ones and . . . the land of culture [Bildung],"[45] Zarathustra addresses the hyper-visual (and self-isolating) technologies to which this *monetized* "culture" and "education" has led: "And with fifty mirrors around you," he says aghast, "you flatter and slander your play of colours!"[46] We have noted Nietzsche's attraction to Dionysus's dismemberment: the "primal desire for appearance"—for the illusion of "a single world-image"—and the "glance into the horrible," all of which recall the fatal attraction of the youthful (still maturing) demigod to his image in a mirror (3.1). Already in the preface to *Zarathustra*, Nietzsche seeks to transcend this *visualized chronotope* that knows nothing of our earthly place in the cosmos or Dionysian cosmic light. Consider "the last human" who "blinks" while gazing (indifferently) at love, creation, and wonder (5.1), and who opposes the luminous magic of "a dancing star" ascending from "chaos."[47]

That the *tragic seeing* of the present (that is ruled by money) shall be neutralized by Dionysian light is made clear when Zarathustra gazes upon "the great city" (5.1). As we have seen, "this city, which steams with the vapour of slaughtered spirit," is dominated by individuals who "jingle with their gold" (5.1). The "bourgeois mediocrity" that worries Nietzsche—"the desire of the masses" with which Zarathustra struggles at the marketplace— is at the core of the lethal illness that is making our earthly place "poor and exhausted" (5.1). Inseparable from the disease of *monetization* is a mass "of compressed souls and slender breasts and *pointed eyes*."[48] *Monetized seeing* is contrasted, in turn, when Zarathustra pictures "the pillar of fire in which [the great city]"—along with its anonymous mass of "pointed eyes"—"will be consumed!"[49] This reminds one of the "flame that once Zeus's thunderbolt left" (v 597–98) that catches fire on Semele's tomb while Dionysus's mystic chorus repeats the story of the demigod's birth in *Bacchae*.[50] The house of the *visualized/monetized* tyrant Pentheus is destroyed by a mystic thunderbolt, that is, a Dionysian "pillar of fire."

In many ways, Zarathustra's critique of the *visualized chronotope* is an act of exposure—that is, exposing the (visual) corruption that lurks in the dark to the transformative power of daylight (and daylight understood as a metaphor of public consciousness). Poets and artists who abandon "authentic art" and disregard the earthly "depth of tones" "are not pure enough: they muddy all their waters so that they appear deep" (5.2). Whereas the dissonance of "all the jingle-jangling of their harps"—their ghastly "[g]host-breath and whizzing"—recalls the selfish sounds of those who "jingle with their gold" (5.2), their visual illusions of profundity—the dark surface that is, in fact, only muddy shallow water—significantly recalls the "elevated egoism" of a *visualized* (Wagnerian) "hallucination" (2.2).

As we might expect, the preface of *Zarathustra* already prefigures the transition from *tragic—*to *Dionysian seeing*. The "superficial entertainment" (2.2) that the resentful (*monetized*) crowd has gathered to "see"—the concentrated picture of the isolated (Oedipus-like) ropedancer who reminds us of the single actor who emerges as the (choral) "Dionysian basis of tragedy begins to disintegrate" (2.2)—is followed by the hideous image of "a colourful fellow" and the tragic (visual) event that "froze every eye" (5.1). The (unseeable) spectacle that occurs at "the marketplace"—one wonders about the "pleasures" that Burke and Hazlitt would report (1.1)—the dismembered body of the dying ropedancer, the sinister (and resentful) return of the "colourful fellow," and the sharp, nocturnal image of the corpse-carrying Zarathustra (whose precise visual identity remains obscure) by "gravediggers" who "illuminate him with the torch in the face"[51] are all transformed into the epiphany of an ecstatic (simultaneously external and internal) light whose cosmic significance cannot be denied.

> But at last his eyes opened: enchanted, Zarathustra looked into the forest and the stillness; enchanted, he gazed into himself. Then he arose quickly, like a seafarer who suddenly sees land, and joyously cried out: for he saw a new truth. And thus he then spoke to his heart:
> A light has dawned upon me: I need companions and living ones. [52]

"TO HEAR WITH THE EYES"

To conclude this chapter, we turn to the center of the *visualized chronotope* with which Zarathustra struggles, namely what we have called *visualized language*—a style of speaking and writing that produces an unlimited number of images that, in turn, distract us from the lethal essence of money. As we have noted, the perverse spirit of "contempt," *Verachtung*, is tied to the "glow and fuel" of industrialization and a Judeo-Christian visual hatred of earth—the time when "the soul *looked* contemptuously [verächtlich] at the body"—when "the soul *looked*" with its *'böser Blick,' Giftauge des Ressentiment*, and *verrätersich[e] Augen*" (5.3). When Zarathustra's *Dionysiac language* of "streams and trees" confronts the *monetized language* of those who "jingle with their gold" at "the marketplace" (5.2), it confronts also the *visualized language* "of the masses" assembled to "*see* a ropedancer" (5.3). This is clear at the beginning of the preface. The Dionysian "meaning of earth" of which the hero speaks is (automatically) consumed by the *visualized sounds*—and *language* of the crowd: "When Zarathustra had thus spoken, one of the people screamed: 'We now heard enough of the ropedancer; now let us also *see* him!' And all the people laughed at Zarathustra" (5.3).

Unlike *The Madman*, Zarathustra reflects upon the (linguistic) battle in which he finds himself—that is, the struggle of words between, on the one hand, earth and community, and, on the other hand, money and a money-driven visual culture.

> When Zarathustra had spoken these words, he *looked* again at the people and was silent. "There they stand," he spoke to his heart, "there they laugh: they do not understand me, I am not the mouth for these ears." (5.3, 5.2)

Physical dis*organ*ization—the abyss between the language of Zarathustra's (Dionysian) mouth and the (*monetized, visualized*) ears of the crowd—invites us to understand the tension at the heart of Nietzsche's Dionysian myth in regard to the linguistic dismemberment with which tragedy culminates (3.3). [53] Consider again the tragic individual death to which the "lame-foot" (Oedipus-like) "ropedancer, who but believed that the word applied to him" (5.1, 5.3), succumbs. As he reflects upon the coming rebirth of a cosmic (vertical) axis of language rooted in earth and community and which necessarily ascends out of the dismemberment of *monetized* and *visualized language*, Zarathustra wonders: "Must one first dismember their ears, so that they learn to hear with the eyes?"[54]

At first, the hero entertains the (narrowed) style of language that is recognizable to those whose brains have been poisoned by money and its destructive visual culture. "Must one clatter like kettledrums and preachers of repentance? Or do they believe only he or she who stammers?"[55] As he considers the *Bildung* of "bourgeois mediocrity," in particular "the masses" of modern individuals who surround (and isolate) themselves "with fifty mirrors" (5.3), Zarathustra rallies himself: "Because they prefer not to hear the word 'contempt' in regard to themselves, I will speak to their pride."[56]

The attempt to conquer the *visualized language* of the crowd with the *Dionysiac language* of "lightning" and "madness"[57] nevertheless fails. Blinking, "the mass" of scattered persons willfully associates itself, through its addiction to *visualized language*, with that of "the last human" (5.1). Zarathustra remains isolated within his reflections upon the (Dionysian) dismemberment to which such words tragically lead.

> And all the people rejoiced and smacked their tongues. But Zarathustra was sad and said to his heart:
> "They do not understand me: I am not the mouth for these ears.
> Too long have I lived in the forest, too long I listened to streams and trees: now I speak to them like goatherds.
> Unmoved is my soul and clear like the mountains in the morning. But they believe I am cold and that I mock them in terrible jests.
> And now they look at me and laugh: and in their laughter they hate me still more. There is ice in their laughter.[58]

Here we approach the critique of *visualized language*, which is inseparable from the heart of *Zarathustra*. Given the discussion above, this is to be expected. In "the great city" ruled by the gleaming "gold of the shop-keep" (5.1), "spirit has here become a verbal game. . . . Loathsome verbal swill does it vomit!" (5.2). The mass "of compressed souls and slender breasts and *pointed eyes*" (5.3) who over-populate "this city, which steams with the vapour of slaughtered spirit," is significantly tied to the dark surfaces of poets who "muddy all their water so that they appear deep" (5.2, 5.3).

Nevertheless, what makes Nietzsche's critique of *visualized language* powerful is its extension to the emergence of modern text as not only a part, but also at the core of a media culture whose distractions know no limit. When Zarathustra learns that "spirit has here become a verbal game . . . Loathsome verbal swill does it vomit," he learns at the same time that "they make newspapers out of this verbal-swill."[59] "Do you not see the souls hanging like limp, dirty rags?—And they even make newspapers out of these rags!"[60]

Nietzsche also seems to connect the explosion of newspapers that follows from the invention of the steam rotary process in the nineteenth century (1.2) to the industrialization of (Western) alphabetic writing that facilitates, with unprecedented speed, the absorption of languages (and cultures) into the *monetized chronotope*. Alongside the "glow and fuel" of a visual culture of text (newspapers, journals, etc.) that dominate "the great city" there is "[m]uch appointable virtue with scribe-fingers."[61] The vengeful *monetized* and *visualized* spirit of the "screaming-throats [of] overheated ambitious ones" (5.2) includes, let us not forget, "the pen-demagogues."[62] The industrialization of alphabetic writing thus concentrates "the homogenized sensibility" (1.2) to which modern humans succumb unaware. We have noted Nietzsche's abandonment of his typewriter in the basement of his rural home in Sils-Maria, Switzerland (1.1).

We have also noted Nietzsche's critique of the "'journalist,' the paper slave of the day," who willfully serves the textual "*deux ex machine*" (1.2) of modern time. Given his resistance to such literary *decadence* where individual "words leap out of the sentence in which they belong . . . and obscure the sense of the whole page" (2.2)—one thinks of the language of corporate advertising—and Nietzsche's belief that "[t]he transformation of neural stimuli in sounds" echoes earth and communal locality—to which "[t]he various languages that exist alongside one another" (2.2) testify—it is to be expected that the act of reading (text) in modern time is often inextricably tied to the vengeful spirit of (unlimited) egoism. "I hate reading idlers,"[63] Zarathustra declares. "He who knows the reader does nothing more for the reader. Another century of readers—and spirit itself will stink."[64]

Finally, as we have also seen, Nietzsche identifies the concentration of *monetized* and *visualized languages* as they descend from ancient Greece through medieval Christianity into our mass consumer culture of modern time (2). The explosion of media culture that is exclusively ruled by those who "jingle with their gold" is one of the (unsuspecting) great dangers to our species. "Once spirit was God, then it became human and now it becomes the masses."[65] Facilitating this spiritual denigration is the (mass) printed word. One imagines "reading idlers" surrounded by "fifty mirrors." One thinks of an isolated individual *Facebooking* or *Tweeting* while the corporate money behind this visual media lobbies for political power, and to increase its control of "public opinion."[66] "That everyone is able to learn to read in this mass, homogenized way corrupts not only writing, but also thinking."[67]

This brings us at last to the concealed (and compact) meaning of *Zarathustra*'s preface. When the Dionysian hero carries the Oedipus-like (blind and dismembered) body of the ropedancer far away from the city into the forest, he transcends not only the *monetized* and *visualized chronotopes* of our industrialized, modern world, but also its *monetized* and *visualized languages*. Alongside the "[l]oathsome verbal swill" of those who "jingle with their gold," the presence of the "pointed eyes" of "reading idlers" is now transfigured into "a magical, blessed" (3.3) language of earth and community.

> there he looked inquisitively into the heights—for he heard above him the sharp call of the bird. And behold! An eagle swept through the air in broad circles, and on him a serpent hung, not like prey, but as a friend: for she kept herself coiled about his neck.
> "They are my animals!" Zarathustra said and his heart rejoiced.[68]

NOTES

1. Z, in *Friedrich Nietzsche, Kritische Studienausgabe*, ed. Giorgio Colli and Mazzino Montinari, vol. 4, *Also sprach Zarathustra. Ein Buch für Alle und Keinen* (Berlin: de Gruyter, 1999), 14.

2. Ibid. See, for instance, "Ausser Dienst." Z, in *Nietzsche, Kritische Studienausgabe*, vol. 4, 321–26.

3. Ibid., 14.

4. Ibid. It is important to note that the German word *Übermensch* does not specify gender, thus making the English word "superman" a bad translation. Given Nietzsche's interest in transcending modern (industrialized) humans, both the creativity and danger of this interest in that which shall be above and beyond—*über*—must be taken into consideration.

5. Ibid., 15.

6. Ibid.

7. Ibid.

8. Ibid.

9. Ibid., 16.

10. Ibid., 19.

11. Ibid. BT, in *Friedrich Nietzsche, Kritische Studienausgabe*, ed. Giorgio Colli and Mazzino Montinari, vol. 1, *Die Geburt der Tragödie, Unzeitgemäße Betrachtungen I–IV, Nachgelassene Schriften 1870–1873* (Berlin: de Gruyter, 1999), 115.

12. Z, in *Nietzsche, Kritische Studienausgabe*, vol. 4, 20.

13. Ibid., 19.

14. Ibid., 15, 18, 20.

15. Ibid., 20.

16. Ibid., 16.

17. Ibid., 222.

18. Ibid., 222–23.

19. Ibid.

20. Ibid., 21.

21. Ibid., 16.

22. Ibid., 21.

23. Ibid.

24. Ibid.

25. Lucas Murrey, *Hölderlin's Dionysiac Poetry: The Terrifying-Exciting Mysteries* (Heidelberg, New York, Dordrecht, London: Springer, 2015), chapters 2–3 (2–3).

26. Z, in *Nietzsche, Kritische Studienausgabe*, vol. 4, 22, 25.

27. Ibid., 20.

28. Ibid. Emphasis added. As I suggest in my Hölderlin monograph, there is a potentially significant echo of the flowery and watery spirit of the ancient Greek god *Bacch*us in the modern German word(s) for stream/streams: *Bach, Bäche*.

29. Ibid., 21.

30. Ibid., 18.

31. Ibid., 223.

32. Ibid., 224.

33. GM, in *Nietzsche, Kritische Studienausgabe*, ed. Giorgio Colli and Mazzino Montinari, vol. 5, *Jenseits von Gut und Böse, Zur Genealogie der Moral* (Berlin: de Gruyter, 1999), 270.

34. Z, in *Nietzsche, Kritische Studienausgabe*, vol. 4, 165.

35. Ibid.

36. Ibid.

37. Emphasis added.

38. Ibid., 23.

39. Ibid., 22.

40. Ibid.

41. Ibid., 14. Emphasis added.

42. Ibid., 15.

43. Ibid., 16. Emphasis added.

44. Emphasis added.

45. Ibid., 153.

46. Ibid.

47. Ibid., 19.

48. Ibid., 224. Emphasis added.

49. Ibid., 225.

50. Murrey, *Hölderlin's Dionysiac Poetry*, 2.3.

51. Z, in *Nietzsche, Kritische Studienausgabe*, vol. 4, 24.

52. Ibid., 25.

53. Murrey, *Hölderlin's Dionysiac Poetry*, 2–4.

54. Z, in *Nietzsche, Kritische Studienausgabe*, vol. 4, 18.

55. Ibid.

56. Ibid., 19.

57. Ibid., 16.

58. Ibid., 20–21.

59. Ibid., 223. One thinks of the *New York Times*—and every other agenda-setting newspaper.

60. Ibid.

61. Ibid.

62. Ibid., 224.

63. Ibid., 48.

64. Ibid.

65. Ibid.

66. Ibid., 223.

67. Ibid., 48.

68. Ibid., 27.

Chapter Five

The Meaning of Earth

"A BIG EYE"

In an important sense, *Zarathustra* can be understood as an exploration of the origin of the vengeful spirit of *monetized* and *visualized chronotopes*. This becomes clear when we consider again the dis*organ*ized state that the Dionysian hero temporarily suffers. After recognizing that "they do not understand me," Zarathustra dejectedly reflects, "I am not the mouth for these ears" (5.4).

Following the projection of Dionysus's myth and cult into tragedy (3.3), the act of individual dismemberment is horrific, but transfiguring. "Must one first dismember their ears, so that they learn to hear with the eyes?" (5.4). This gesture to gruesome, but transformative dis*organ*ization prefigures not only the dismemberment and release of the body of the "lame-foot" (Oedipus-like) ropedancer (5.1), but also the horrific scene later described in *Of redemption*.

> When Zarathustra one day went over the great bridge, cripples and beggars surrounded him and a hunchback spoke to him thus:
> "Behold, Zarathustra! Even the people learn from you and win faith in your teaching: but, so that they believe you fully, one thing is still needed— you must first convince also us cripples! Here you have a fine selection and truly, an occasion with more than one opportunity! You can heal the blind and make the lame run; and from him who has too much behind, you could also take a little away—that, I think, would be the right way to make cripples believe in Zarathustra!"[1]

As we might expect, the Dionysian prophet cautions against (self-serving) snap decisions and directs the group of invalids to the perversions that have consumed (non-crippled) individuals of the present.

> But Zarathustra then responded to he who spoke: "If one takes the hump away from the hunchback, then he takes his spirit—thus teach the people. And if one gives eyes to the blind, he sees so many bad things on earth: he thus curses he who healed him. He but who makes the lame run does him the greatest injury: for as soon as he runs does his vices run away with him—thus teach the people about cripples. And why should Zarathustra not learn from the people, if the people learn from Zarathustra?"[2]

Having associated himself with the "blind" spirit of ("lame-foot") Oedipus, Zarathustra turns to the sickness that plagues modern life—one that has degraded the wholeness of the human being into that of a cripple.

> "But that is the least of my concerns since I have been among humans, that I see: this one is missing an eye and this one an ear and the third a leg, and others who have lost their tongues or noses or heads."[3]

Now we enter the inner orbit of Zarathustra's critique of present-day humankind, one that is significantly similar to that of the *visualized chronotope* found in Hölderlin's poetry.

> "I see and saw worse and many so despicable that I would like neither to speak nor remain silent of them: namely, humans who lack everything except that they have one thing too much—humans who are nothing other than a big eye or a big mouth or a big belly or something else big—inverted cripples I name such ones."[4]

We have noted Nietzsche's interest in the "primal desire for appearance"—for the illusion of "a single world-image"—as well as his interest in the "glance into the horrible"—and how such interest recalls Dionysus's fatal attraction to his image in a mirror (3.1). We have also noted Nietzsche's critique of the *visualized chronotope* in his central Dionysian myth: the *monetized* spirit of *Bildung* whose "pointed eyes" aggressively isolate themselves "with fifty mirrors" (5.3). Taken together, this scene of wandering, homeless lame-ones and beggars that gives way to a perverse (oppositional) picture of modern humans (who have "one thing too much . . . who are nothing other than a big eye") evokes Hölderlin's adaption of Oedipus to resist the *visualized* space-time of science and capitalism in modern time.

For Hölderlin, before Oedipus is transfigured by "a magical, blessed strength" (3.3)—to which he gestures in his translation of *Oedipus at Kolonus*—the fallen, wandering, and homeless individual models the modern human who, absorbed in philosophical hyper-abstractions, degenerates into "a beggar when he reflects."[5] And before Oedipus succumbs to such horrifying (self-)dismemberment, the mentally ill tyrant uses his eyes like modern scientists and greedy capitalists to sustain his (limitless) individualism. This means that just as humans of today instrumentalize visual technologies like "[t]he telescope" (v 51), through which they "*sca[n]* and coun[t]" (v 50)[6] and finally "exploit the spirit" (v 37) of nature "to make / A little money" (v 39-40), Oedipus declares that he shall "*scan* every word" (v 295).[7] As if repeating Hölderlin's critique of *monetized* and *visualized* tyrants—for instance, when he tells us that "king Oedipus has one eye too many," *ein Auge zuviel*[8] —Nietzsche's *Zarathustra* sees modern humans as tyrants who have "one thing too much," *eins zuviel*, as those "who are nothing other than a big eye," *ein großes Auge*.

Given the rapidly increasing division of labor within universities (already during the nineteenth century)—the compartmentalizing of thought that accompanies industrialization (*monetization* and *visualization*), what Nietzsche names "the problem of science" (2.2)—Hölderlin's critique of the isolation of "[e]ach individual . . . to his own affairs, in the noise of his compartment" (v 242–46)[9] that implies physical dis*organ*ization (and dismemberment) is enhanced.

> "And when I came out of my loneliness and went over this bridge for the first time: I did not believe my eyes and looked again and again and finally said: 'That is an ear! An ear as big as a human!' I looked more closely: and really, under the ear something still moved, something that was pitiful and poor and wasted. And truly, the monstrous ear sat upon a little thin stalk—but the stalk was a human! One who put a glass before the eye could even still see a little envious face; also that of a bloated little soul that hung on the stalk. But the people said to me that the big ear was not only a human, but a great human, a genius. But I never believed the people when they spoke of great humans— and I held to my belief that it is an inverted cripple who has too little of everything and one thing too much."[10]

This brings us to the wretched (Hölderlinian) image of humanity in modern time that haunts the heart of Nietzsche's *Zarathustra*. The cause of this visual horror—the *visualized chronotope*—is then absorbed into the myth of a new tragic image of isolation, dismemberment, and death.

When Zarathustra had so spoken to the hunchback and to those who whom he was their mouthpiece, he turned with profound discontent to his disciples and said:

> "Truly, my friends, I wander among humans as among the fragments and limbs of humans!
> This is that which is most wretched to my eye, that I find humans broken and scattered as upon a battle- and butcher-ground.

And when my eye flees from now to then: it always finds the same:
fragments and limbs and gruesome accidents—but no humans!" [11]

Nietzsche invokes Hyperion's critique of modern Germans who, having become "more barbaric through industry and science and even through religion," are "like fragments of a tossed out vessel." [12] The grisly landscape of the present with its "the fragments and limbs of humans" deepens the relation of Nietzsche's critique of modern life to the tragic hero who suffers blindness, (self-)dismemberment, and death. "So I came to the Germans," Hyperion declares, "like the homeless, blind Oedipus at the gates of Athens, where the grove of the goddesses receive him: and the beautiful souls greet him." [13] .

Associating the nightmarish image of the present with the language of Hölderlin, Nietzsche seeks to absorb (and thus transfigure) the *visualized* space and time into a *Dionysiac chronotope*. Witness, for instance, the parallel of visual horror between, on the one hand, Zarathustra: "This is that which is most wretched to my eye, that I find humans broken and scattered as upon a battle- and butcher-ground," and, on the other hand, Hyperion: "is this not like a battlefield where dismembered hands and arms and all body-parts lie cast about while their life-blood drains into the sand?" [14] This mirror image of visual horror concentrates the relationship between the *visual vengeance* of humans who are ruled by money in modern time (5) and the mystic transfiguration that Hölderlin retrieves from Greece. Hölderlinian despair that threatens to consume the heart of Nietzsche's *Zarathustra* constructs a bridge between the *monetized* visual culture of the present (its "pointed eyes" surrounded by "fifty mirrors") and Dionysus's ancient mystic mirror. "It is a hard word, but I say it nonetheless, for it is the truth," Hyperion declares, "I can think of no people more torn apart than the Germans. You see craftsmen, but no humans, thinkers, but no humans, priests, but no humans." [15] Implicitly gesturing to Dionysian release, Zarathustra continues Hyperion's visual despair: "And when my eye flees from now to then: it always finds the same: fragments and limbs and gruesome accidents—but no humans!"

But this gesture to the absorption (and potential redemption) of the *visualized chronotope* into a primal experience of earth and community invites us to wonder: How are we to understand the deeper philosophical (and psychological) origins of the present dis*organ*ization of humanity? From where does our (ancient, but in modern time exponentially increasing) estrangement from nature and ourselves emerge? That such questions lead to the more profound exploration of identity is clear.

A prophet, one who wills, a creator, a future itself and a bridge to the future—and alas, even still the equal to a cripple on this bridge: all this is Zarathustra.
And you also often ask yourselves: "who is Zarathustra to us? What is his meaning to us?"
And like me myself you gave your questions as the answer.

Is he a promiser? Or a fulfiller? A conqueror? Or a inheritor? An autumn? Or one who ploughs? A doctor? Or a healer?
Is he a poet? Or a truth-sayer? A Liberator? Or one who captures? A good one? Or a bad one?[16]

Inseparable from this deeper investigation of identity is Nietzsche's search to redeem the gruesome (*monetized* and *visualized*) dismemberment to which humankind has succumbed.

I wander among humans like fragments of the future: that future upon which I gaze. And that is all my poetising and aspiration, that I compose and bring together into one that which is fragmentary and riddle and gruesome chance.
And how I could endure to be human, if the human was not also a poet and solver of riddles and redeemer of chance![17]

"TEETH-GNASHING AND MOST LONELY MELANCHOLY"

Seeking the ancient source of the scattered limbs and overgrown organs that plague the present, Nietzsche turns to an authentic experience of release, which is defined as the acceptance of the irreversibility of time. "To redeem the past and to look anew upon every 'it was' as a 'So I wanted it!'—to me only that is redemption!"[18]

Once again, we find ourselves entering the orbit of Hölderlinian language. "Will—the name of the liberator and bringer-of-joy: thus I teach you, my friends! And now learn this also: the will is still a captive."[19] I have noted Hyperion's "moments of liberation, when the divine bursts open the prison, . . . when it is for us as if the unchained spirit . . . returns to the halls of the sun."[20] Zarathustra declares, "[w]illing liberates" and then wonders, "but what is *that* which also imprisons the liberator in chains?"[21] The spirit of Dionysus, who is imprisoned and who then magically liberates himself and his mystic initiates in *Bacchae*,[22] is resurrected through Hölderlin's voice. Naming the "will" the "liberator and bringer-of-joy," *Freudenbringer*, recalls Hölderlin's "god-of-joy," *Freudengott* (v 1), an adaption of the liberating spirit of Dionysus the *Freudengott* (v 1169) at the end of Sophocles's *Antigone*.[23]

In search of "*that* which also imprisons the liberator in chains," Nietzsche continues: "'It was': thus is the name of the will's teeth-gnashing and most lonely melancholy. To be powerless against *that* which has occurred—it is an evil spectator of all that is past."[24] On the one hand, the "evil spectator" into which the will degenerates recalls the Judeo-Christian "*slave revolt in morality*" (2.1) as well as the modern "gold of the shop-keep" who rules "the great city" (5.1).

On the other hand, "the will's teeth-gnashing and most lonely melancholy" evokes the *monetized* tyrant of Greece. As we have seen, Nietzsche's description of "Bentham's footsteps" as "moving this way and that" recall Pentheus running "feverishly this way and that" (v 625; 1.2). Like the "evil" spirit of the "teeth-gnashing" will, the tyrant who imprisons Dionysus "breathes out his soul" (v 620) and is heard "gnashing his teeth in his lips" (v 625).[25] When Zarathustra declares, "[t]hat time does not run backward, that is its animosity; 'That which was'—thus is the name of the stone that he cannot roll,"[26] we are invited to associate modern (*monetized*) "animosity" with Judeo-Christianity and early historic Greece.

This becomes clearer as Zarathustra explains the hateful, mob-like and greedy nature of the will. "And so it rolls out stones of animosity and ill-humour and exercises revenge on anyone that does not, equal to it, feel animosity and ill-humour."[27] "Thus the will, the liberator, became a torturer," he continues, "and upon all that can suffer, it takes revenge for not going back."[28]

Whereas the rhetoric of "the antipathy of the will against time" and "[t]he spirit of revenge" once again evoke the ancient ethical inversion underlying modern "common sense"—the life-destroying "madness" that the will "preached" looks to the "insanity"[29] that (monetized) humans of today aggressively project onto the (non-monetized) past—the language of the Dionysian hero, nevertheless, culminates in a reference to "the original Titan theocracy of terror" (3.1). "'And this is itself justice, this law of time that must devour its children': thus preached madness."[30]

By defining the "law of time" as that which is fated to "devour its children" Nietzsche evokes the devouring spirit of mortality projected onto the tragic stage. One recalls a few verses from *Oedipus at Kolonus* where the chorus declares that,

> alone to the Gods
> do old age and dying never come to pass.
> But all other things are swallowed by all-powerful time [chrónos].[31] (v 607–09)

Nietzsche is not unaware of the *aetiological chronotope*[32] from which the Greek cosmos issues forth.

> Like Uranos who does not let his children come to light, but instead, as soon as they are born, conceals them in the womb of earth, *Kronos* devours his own right after birth.[33]

In particular, Nietzsche is interested in "the tragic myth"[34] of Dionysus who "as a boy had been dismembered [and devoured] by the Titans" (3.1).[35]

When Zarathustra declares that "time . . . must devour its children," he implies that "the spirit of revenge" (to which "the will" succumbs) is caught up in the individual finitude with which the tragic hero struggles. The all-consuming individualism of *Kronos* (who devours the spirit of earth and community) that echoes in the confrontation of the tragic hero with "all-powerful *chrónos*" (v 609)[36] expresses the resentful perversion into which "the will" can degenerate. "Alas, unmoveable is the stone 'It was': all punishments must also be eternal!"[37]

This turn to Greece significantly sustains the linguistic orbit of Nietzsche's *Lieblingsdichter* (1.1) whose exploration of tragic heroes and mortality is also inextricably tied to the *aetiological chronotope*. In *Nature and Art or Saturn and Jupiter* Hölderlin evokes the law-giving power of "Kronion!" (v 25), and Zeus's father Kronos.[38] This gives the philosophical (and psychological) analysis of the origin of the vengeance new depth.

The "evil" spirit into which "the will" transforms is associated with the *monetized chronotope* and *language* of Judeo-Christianity and the present—from the vengeance of "the *slave revolt in morality*" (2.1) to the sound of those who "jingle with their gold" (5.1) in "the great city." Critical is the new negative community of (mass) "envy" and "jealousy"[39] that emerges from the desire of "the will" to "exercis[e] revenge on anyone that does not, *equal* to it, feel animosity and ill-humour."[40] *Monetized* individuals who recklessly celebrate "the gold of the shop-keep"—that, through the homogenization (the *unlimited* making equal) of the original powers of earth and community with industrial technology, becomes concentrated in the nineteenth century—, are named "preachers of equality, of the tyrannical-insanity of powerlessness."[41] "'Vengeance we want to exercise and insult on all those who are not equal to us'—thus celebrate the tarantula-hearts."[42]

Zarathustra makes it clear that the "evil" spirit of the will that manifests itself at the modern "marketplace" (5.1) has deep roots. "Antagonised arrogance, guarded envy, perhaps the arrogance and envy of your fathers: from you breaks forth the flame of the madness of revenge."[43] The Dionysian hero is especially clear about *the language of revenge* from which the "[l]oathsome verbal-swill" (5.2) of *monetized language* emerges. "In all their lamentations sounds vengeance,"[44] he says.

> And "will to equality"—that itself shall henceforth become the name for virtue; and against everything that has power we want to raise a cry!
> You preachers of equality, of the tyrannical-insanity of powerlessness shout thus for "equality": your secret tyrannical-desires thus disguise themselves in virtuous words![45]

Important is the *visualized chronotope* that Nietzsche associates with the origin of revenge. "'It was': thus is the name of the will's teeth-gnashing and most lonely melancholy. To be powerless against *that* which has occurred—it is an *evil spectator* of all that is past."[46] The words "evil spectator," *böser Zuschauer*, evoke not only the "pointed eyes" (of "reading idlers") in modern time that surround themselves with "fifty mirrors" (5.3–5.4), but also the Judeo-Christian "evil eye," "*böser Blick*," "for all things" (2.1). This connection between the philosophical (and psychological) origin of revenge and the ancient *visualized chronotope* returns when Zarathustra declares in *Of the tarantula*: "Revenge sits in your soul: wherever you bite grows a black scab; with revenge your poison sets the soul spinning!"[47] Just as modern "contempt," *Verachtung*, through its tie to the Judeo-Christian "soul [that] looked contemptuously," *verächtlich*, "at the body," emerges from ancient "treacherous eyes," *verrätersich[e] Augen*" (2.1), the "poison," *Gift*, of the tarantula through which "revenge" emerges now is associated with the Judeo-Christian "poisonous eye of *ressentiment*," *das Giftauge des Ressentiment* (2.1).

This brings us to the more profound gesture that gives Nietzsche's understanding of the origin of revenge its unparalleled modern power. Having exposed the relationship between, on the one hand, the vengeance to which "the will" succumbs when it confronts the irreversibility of time and, on the other hand, the *monetized* and *visualized chronotopes* in modern and ancient Judeo-Christian times, the Dionysian hero rolls back the (almost) unmovable stones of *money* and *seeing* to early historic Greece.

As we have noted, "the will's teeth-gnashing and most lonely melancholy" evokes the Greek tyrant Pentheus who, having imprisoned the spirit of earth and community, is heard "gnashing his teeth in his lips" (v 625). This complements the other references in *Zarathustra* to the tragic hero, in particular to Oedipus. Consider again the "lame-foot" ropedancer who suffers tragic dismemberment and individual death, and the "blind . . . and lame ones" (6.1) whom Zarathustra meets in *Of redemption*. Consider also "[t]he hunchback" who, like a mystic initiand, "had covered his face"[48] while Zarathustra spoke of "the will's teeth-gnashing and most lonely melancholy."

Nietzsche's search for the (timeless) origin of vengeance—both modern and ancient Judeo-Christian—shifts to the tyrant of early historic Greece. But here he turns not simply to a confrontation with individual finitude, but also to the perverse spirit into which "the will" degrades itself when, through reckless individualism—"the greedy thirst for existence" (3.2)—that is, "being," is no longer is in balance with nature and itself, and therefore "must be eternal deed and guilt."[49]

For Hölderlin, Oedipus's declaration that he shall "*scan* every word" (v 295) recalls modern humans who instrumentalize visual media like "[t]he telescope" (v 51), through which they "*sca[n]* and coun[t]*" (V 50) and finally "exploit the spirit" (v 37) of nature "to make / A little money" (v 39–40; 6.1). But at stake is not only the *monetized*, "wrathful . . . spirit of Oedipus, all-knowing," but also the *visualized vengeance* of the tyrant's "machine process," that is, "king Oedipus [who] has one eye too many," *ein Auge zuviel* (6.1).[50]

For Nietzsche, Oedipus is also an original lens through which we can see the origin of the *monetized*, "mechanistic world-dumbing" (1.1), as well as an expression of *visual resentment*. The desire of the tyrant "[t]o *make* all beings thinkable"—to imprison the world within his isolated and tyrannical "will to power"[51] —is related to Oedipus having "one thing too much" *eins zuviel,* namely "a big eye," *ein großes Auge* (6.1).

In fact, it is precisely the *monetized* and *visualized* "will to power" of the tyrant from which "breaks forth the flame of the madness of revenge." When Zarathustra sadly reflects, "I am not the mouth for these ears" (5.4), and then later looks upon the bloody landscape of the present—that is, a modern nightmare of "fragments and limbs of humans," in particular of "inverted cripples" with, for instance, "a big eye" (6.1)—he gazes upon the individual (self-)dismemberment to which the original, "*suffering organs*"[52] of Oedipus succumb. "Against your [*monetized* and *visualized*] will all-seeing time [chrónos] has found you out" (v 1213).[53] The origin of "revenge" into which "the will" degenerates is thus the absorption of the individual who refuses to accept his or her humble, limited mortal place in the cosmos.

"TWINKLING STARS AND GLOW-WORMS"

By associating the origin of "the spirit of vengeance" (that descends from Judeo-Christianity to modern time) with the tragic hero, Nietzsche moves closer to his final goal. More specifically, the association of the will's revenge with tyrants in tragedy looks forward, if implicitly, to the absorption (and hence transfiguration) of *monetized* and *visualized chronotopes* into the *Dionysiac chronotope.*

This is not to say that "the spirit of vengeance" does not remain a lethal threat to the Dionysian hero. Zarathustra understands not only that the new world into which he has descended is ruled by revenge, but also that he must guard himself from the impurity of its spirit. "I find your contempt contemptible," he says to his "grunting-pig" before the gates of "the great city."[54]

From love alone shall my contempt and warning bird take flight: but not from the swamp!—
[...]
But this lesson I give you, fool, in farewell: where one can no longer love, there should one—*pass by!*—[55]

This brings us to the urgent question concerning "the will." If it has degenerated since ancient times into a concentrated expression of (*monetized* and *visualized*) *ressentiment,* then in what way can Zarathustra redeem its degenerate spirit? How can that which has made itself dirty once again become clean?

Similar to Hölderlin, by associating the vengeance of the modern world with its ancient origins in Greece, Nietzsche constructs a bridge between *the historical* and *the Dionysian eternal*—that is, between time and timelessness—through which the possibility of cosmic cleansing is opened out. To illustrate this, we briefly turn to the end of *Of redemption*.

Zarathustra begins to speak of a time when "the will," now named "a creator," "finally releases itself."[56] Gesturing to the acceptance of Dionysian destruction and rebirth (3.1–3.2), he gestures further to the moment when "the will" has "unlearned the spirit of revenge and all teeth-gnashing"—and become "its own liberator and joy-bringer."[57] But then the speech abruptly breaks off.

> And who has taught it reconciliation with time, and something that is higher than all reconciliation? Something higher than all reconciliation must the will want, which is the will to power—: but how does this happen to it? And who taught it also to go backward?
>   —But here in his talk Zarathustra suddenly paused and he looked like one extremely terrified. With a terrified eye he looked at his disciples; his eye pierced their thoughts and afterthoughts like arrows.[58]

We have noted the danger of "the will to power" in hands of tyrants, for instance, in Oedipus's desire "[t]o *make* all beings thinkable" (6.2). In *Of self-overcoming—Von der Selbst-Überwindung*—a title that evokes Nietzsche's earlier "mystical self-purgation," *mystischen Selbstentäusserung* (3.2), the Dionysian spirit of this event becomes clearer. "It is not the river that is your danger and the end of your good and evil, you wise ones," Zarathustra confides, "but this will itself, the will to power—the inexhaustible procreative life-will."[59] "And this secret life itself said to me," the master proceeds,

> "Behold," it said, "I am that *which must always overcome itself.*
> [. . .]
> Whatever I create and however I love it,—soon must I be against it and my love: thus wants my will."[60]

Returning to the dilemma of modern time, Zarathustra concludes his talk: "And he who must be a creator in good and evil: truly, he must first be a destroyer and smasher or values."[61] This brings us, in a sense, back to "these preachers of equality" whose "souls," given their anti-Dionysian spirit, are missing the earthly magic of "honey."[62] From them "breaks forth the flame of the madness of revenge" (6.2). Like a Dionysian mystic who performs "[m]ostly at night [when] darkness lends solemnity" (v 486), Zarathustra, "trusting the way and the light of stars: for he was an experienced night-walker,"[63] retreats into the darkness, free of modern visual pollution, to purify the impure flame of "pointed eyes" (5.3).

> Night it is: now every gushing fountain speaks louder. And my soul is also a gushing fountain.
> Night it is: just now all the songs of lovers awaken. And my soul is also the song of a lover.

An un-silenced, an un-silence-able is in me; that wants to be sound. A desire for love is in me that speaks itself the language of love.[64]

One recalls Hölderlin's "language of lovers" (v 26)—or the nocturnal, Dionysian "fountain" (v 9) and "streaming word" (v 54) of *Bread and Wine* (precisely that which Zarathustra receives while wandering in the forest at night).[65]

Light I am: alas, that I were night! But this is my loneliness, that I am encircled by light.
Alas, that I were darkness and night! How I would suck upon the breasts of light!
And you yourselves I wanted to bless, you little twinkling stars and glow-worms above!—and blessed be your gifts of light.
But I live in my own light; I drink back in the flames that break forth from me.[66]

Like the chorus who imagines Dionysus at the end of *Antigone* making his epiphany to cleanse the city of the vengeful (*monetized* and *visualized*) tyrant—Dionysus who as "chorus-leader of fire-breathing stars" (v 1144–45)[67] combines celestial and earthly light—Nietzsche imagines Zarathustra purifying "the flame of the madness of revenge" with the lightless-ness of night. From this dynamic darkness a cosmic (vertical) axis of light magically ascends (in the earthly "flames that break forth" from the voice of the singing mystic).

The arc of Zarathustra absorbs the historical *monetized* and *visualized chronotopes* into the eternal *Dionysiac chronotope* which, through its harnessing of the dread of blindness and death, preserves the possibility of visual rebirth.

In the preface, the hero introduces himself as the prophet of Dionysus's transformative lightning-flash, which, as "the meaning of earth," is transformed into "the superior-human" (5.1). "Behold, I am a preacher of lightning and a heavy drop from the cloud: but this lightning is called *super-human*."[68] Already here the epiphany of light out of darkness evokes the *Dionysian seeing* with which mystic initiation culminates.[69] "I want to teach humans the meaning of their being: which is the super-human, the lightning-out-of-dark-clouds human."[70] Again, one recalls Hölderlin's *Nature and Art or Saturn and Jupiter*, this time the "lightning-flash" (v 17) that appears "as if from dark clouds" (v 17).[71]

But as Nietzsche makes his way to the end of his Dionysian myth, he has not only confronted, but also "*pass[ed] by*" those spaces and times "where one can no longer love." When we arrive at *The other dance-song*, we are no longer struggling with modern or Judeo-Christian—nor even Hellenic-tyrannical—*monetized* and *visualized chronotopes*. Instead, we seem to glimpse a Dionysian paradise.

Into your eyes I recently gazed, oh life: I saw gold flash in your night-eyes,—my heart stood still before this ecstasy:

—a golden boat I saw blinking upon forceful waters, a sinking, drinking, once again winking golden swinging-boat!

At my foot, the dance-raging one, you threw a glance, a laughing questioning melting swinging-glance. [72]

This is not to say that the *Dionysian seeing* that conquers the *visualized chronotope* has freed itself of the dread of individual death. "Away from you I leapt and from your serpents: there you stood already, half-turned, the eye full of longing." [73] The playful (visual) tension that erupts between the Dionysian hero and "life" soon betrays the deeper, tragic event to which Zarathustra belongs.

With crooked glances—you teach me crooked paths; on crooked paths my foot learns—pitfalls!

. . .

—Who did not hate you, you great binding one, in-winding one, temptress, seeker, finder! Who did not love you, you innocent, impatient, wind-swift, child-eyed sinner!

. . .

You gnash on me lovingly with white teeth, your evil eyes leap out against me from your little mane of locks! [74]

Neutralizing the "evil eye," *böser Blick* (2.1), of *monetized* tyrants through its absorption into the (Dionysian) "evil eyes," *böse Augen*, of "life" does not free the mortal of mortality, but instead gives this individual the possibility of death.

Thereupon life looked thoughtfully about and around herself and softly said: "Oh Zarathustra, you are not faithful enough to me!

You no longer love me as much as you say; I know that you are thinking about it, that you will leave me soon." [75]

"THE MEANING OF EARTH"

"In the total effect of tragedy the Dionysian takes the lead; it ends with a sound that could never arise from the realm of Apolline art" (3.3). As if recalling his youthful insight into the nature of the tragic play, toward the end Nietzsche has "life" say to Zarathustra:

"There is an old, heavy heavy booming-clock: it booms at night up to your cave:—

—when you hear this clock strike the hours at midnight, then you think between one and twelve thereon—

—you are thinking about it, oh Zarathustra, I know it, that you will leave me soon!"—

"Yes," I answered hesitatingly, "but you know it also—"And I said something to her into the ear between her confused yellow foolish tresses of hair.

"You *know* that, oh Zarathustra? No one knows that."

And we looked at one another and glanced at the green meadow upon the cool evening descended, and we wept with one another.—But then life was dearer to me than all my wisdom. [76]

We then hear the *Drunken Song* with which Nietzsche's myth culminates—wherein dying and the desire that (if not tempered) threatens to lead to *monetized* and *visualized* revenge coincide. Awakening "[f]rom deep dream," a voice cries out in tragic-joyous ecstasy: "But all desire wants eternity—, / —wants deep, deep eternity!" and breaks off when the clock strikes "[t]welve"[77] into pitch darkness (and death).

As we have seen, Nietzsche's hero transcends *monetized* and *visualized* spaces, times and languages (of the present, of Judeo-Christianity, and even of early historic Greece). "Beyond good and evil,"[78] Zarathustra's struggle with mortality is elevated to a cosmic confrontation with time. *Dionysian seeing*—"I saw gold flash in your night-eyes" (6.3)—although interrupted by the hero's revelation of his willingness to die—"'Oh Zarathustra, you are not faithful enough to me!'" (6.3)—remains tempered by gentle (earthly and communal) speech: "'Yes,' I answered hesitatingly, 'but you know it also.'" One recalls Nietzsche's celebration of Dionysian "sentences intelligent only to a few" (3.3). "You *know* that, oh Zarathustra? No one knows that."

Nietzsche's myth is not only a transfiguration of the (*monetized* and *visualized*) vengeance, but also a celebration of the Dionysian ecstasy of seeing and speaking (and writing) that ascends from this primal purification. "Of all that is written I love only *that* which *one* writes with his blood. Write with blood: and you shall experience that blood is spirit."[79] Whereas the hero names modern text and visual media like "newspapers"—because they know nothing of earth and community—"verbal-swill" (5.4), he nevertheless rejoices in text that echoes the "transformation of neural stimuli in sounds" (2.2). This of course has its limits. Even the seductive, challenging picture of "unfamiliar blood"[80] remains bound to the sacred (non-textual) darkness of the ear. "He who writes in blood does not want to be read, but learned by heart."[81]

Passing by the "pointed eyes" of "reading idlers" who surround themselves with "fifty mirrors" (5.3, 5.4), *Zarathustra* crescendos with a frenzy of *Dionysiac language*. "Raise your hearts, my brothers, high higher!" he commands: "And also for me do not forget your legs! Raise also your legs, you good dancers, and better still: stand on your heads!"[82] That the (linguistic) spirit of such chthonic ecstasy remains not only at the heart of Nietzsche's modern myth, but also transcends the *monetized* and *visual languages* is suggested in the reappearance of this passage at the end of his "[s]elf-criticism" from 1886—significantly composed while the mature philosopher continued to reflect upon *The Birth of Tragedy*.[83]

> "This crown of the laughing one, this rose-wreathed crown: to you, my brothers, I throw this crown! Laughter I say is holy: you higher humans, *learn* for me—to laugh!"[84]

But these times of ecstasy and glimpses of Dionysiac paradises are also clues about mortality—and this means Nietzsche's deepest philosophical (and psychological) thoughts on the relation of the human being to image and sound. This is suggested when we return to Zarathustra whispering, "something into the ear [of life] between her confused yellow foolish tresses of hair." The perverse scale and dismemberment of organs in modern time— overgrown ears, mouths, and eyes that, because of the *monetized* and *visualized* "spirit of revenge," no longer correspond to nature nor one another— yield to an organic reconciliation (and ecstasy) of sorts. This natural unity is inspired by Hellenic myth. When Dionysus reveals himself in Nietzsche's *Dionysus-Dithyrambs*, he declares to Ariadne: "You have little ears, you have my ears," and concludes with the mystic saying, "I am your labyrinth."[85]

But this (procreative) coupling gestures further to a more profound meaning. Insofar as Dionysus's aural identification with Ariadne parallels the intimate, but ecstatic sounds that Zarathustra and "life" whisper into each other's ears, the naming of Ariadne Dionysus's "labyrinth" implies that "life" is that which forever wanders within a maze of earth and community. This means, in turn, that Zarathustra echoes that which weds itself to "life" to express its own eternal striving, namely "the will to power"—to whom "life" is "a river [that] through many turns flows back into its source!"[86]

This is not the artificial power of men and women of money with "treacherous eyes" (1A). Instead this is real cosmic power, of which the prehistoric Greeks with their celebration of kings sprung from the earth, *autóchthonas* (2.2), were well aware. Consider the Anthesteria when the wife of the local king, *árchon basileús*, was sexually united with Dionysus—a secret rite that may have reenacted the time when the earth spirit entered "the chamber set apart"[87] for him and his bride Ariadne. One thinks also of Dionysus, who makes his epiphany to purify the *monetized* and *visualized* city under the name *wánax* (v 1150) at the end of *Antigone*.[88]

Although the image is there to reassure, when it becomes disconnected from earth and community, it threatens to consume our struggle with mortality. To cure this illness "the meaning of earth" (5.1) provides a limit through which life can flourish. Consider the time of Zarathustra's last praise of the Apolline spirit of light. The Dionysian hero returns to his cave and gestures to a reconciliation of sunlight with the darkness of earthly tones below (that coalesce within the cave-like organ of hearing). Having spoken the word of individual finitude "into the ears" of the "higher humans"[89] —who also significantly named the "grapevine"[90] —Zarathustra awaits a picture that, liberated from the illusion of immortality to which *monetized eyes* cling, shall ascend from sound.

They sleep still in my cave, their dream still reflecting on my midnight-song.
The ear that listens to me,—that listening ear is lacking in limbs.[91]

NOTES

1. Z, in *Friedrich Nietzsche, Kritische Studienausgabe*, ed. Giorgio Colli and Mazzino Montinari, vol. 4, *Also sprach Zarathustra. Ein Buch für Alle und Keinen* (Berlin: de Gruyter, 1999), 177.
2. Ibid.
3. Ibid., 177–78.
4. Ibid., 178.
5. Lucas Murrey, *Hölderlin's Dionysiac Poetry: The Terrifying-Exciting Mysteries* (Heidelberg, New York, Dordrecht, London: Springer, 2015), chapters 7.1, 10.1 (7.1, 10.1).
6. Emphasis added.
7. Cited in Murrey, *Hölderlin's Dionysiac Poetry*, 8, 11.1.
8. Ibid., 9.2.
9. Ibid., 8.
10. Z, in *Nietzsche, Kritische Studienausgabe*, vol. 4, 178.
11. Ibid., 178–79.
12. Murrey, *Hölderlin's Dionysiac Poetry*, 7.1.
13. Ibid.
14. Ibid.
15. Ibid.
16. Z, in *Nietzsche, Kritische Studienausgabe*, vol. 4, 178.
17. Ibid.
18. Ibid.,179.
19. Ibid.
20. Murrey, *Hölderlin's Dionysiac Poetry*, 7.1.
21. Z, in *Nietzsche, Kritische Studienausgabe*, vol. 4, 179.
22. Murrey, *Hölderlin's Dionysiac Poetry*, 2.3, 4.3.
23. Ibid., 8, 9.1.
24. Z, in *Nietzsche, Kritische Studienausgabe*, vol. 4, 179–80.
25. Murrey, *Hölderlin's Dionysiac Poetry*, 4.1–4.2.
26. Z, in *Nietzsche, Kritische Studienausgabe*, vol. 4, 180.
27. Ibid.
28. Ibid.
29. Ibid., 180, 20.
30. Ibid., 180.
31. Sophocles, *Oidipous at Kolonus*, in *Sophoclis fabulae*, ed. Hugh Lloyd-Jones (Oxford: Clarendon Press, 1990), 382–83.
32. For my discussion of Seaford's concept in regard to Hölderlin, see Murrey, *Hölderlin's Dionysiac Poetry*, 2.
33. Ibid., 3.1. Emphasis added.
34. BT, in *Friedrich Nietzsche, Kritische Studienausgabe*, ed. Giorgio Colli and Mazzino Montinari, vol. 1, *Die Geburt der Tragödie, Unzeitgemäße Betrachtungen I–IV, Nachgelassene Schriften 1870–1873* (Berlin: de Gruyter, 1999), 153.
35. Murrey, *Hölderlin's Dionysiac Poetry*, 2.1, 2.2.
36. Emphasis added.
37. Z, in *Nietzsche, Kritische Studienausgabe*, vol. 4, 181.
38. Murrey, *Hölderlin's Dionysiac Poetry*, 8, 10.3.
39. Z, in *Nietzsche, Kritische Studienausgabe*, vol. 4, 129.
40. Emphasis added.
41. Ibid.
42. Ibid., 128.
43. Ibid., 129.

44. Ibid.

45. Ibid.

46. Emphasis added.

47. Ibid., 128.

48. Ibid., 182.

49. Ibid., 181. Here we should note that, for Nietzsche, "guilt," *Schuld* (also in regard to a Judeo-Christian religious sense of "the believer," *Gläubiger*), is directly linked to the historical transformation of the human being by a new world that is ruled by money. See GM, in *Nietzsche, Kritische Studienausgabe*, Giorgio Colli and Mazzino Montinari, vol. 5, *Jenseits von Gut und Böse, Zur Genealogie der Moral* (Berlin: de Gruyter, 1999), 298.

50. Murrey, *Hölderlin's Dionysiac Poetry*, 9.1, 13.2, 7.1.

51. Z, in *Nietzsche, Kritische Studienausgabe*, vol. 4, 146.

52. Murrey, *Hölderlin's Dionysiac Poetry*, 9.1.

53. Sophocles, *Oidipous Tyrannos*, in Sophocles, *Antigone*, in *Sophoclis Fabulae*, Lloyd-Jones, 167.

54. Z, in *Nietzsche, Kritische Studienausgabe*, vol. 4, 224–25.

55. Ibid., 225.

56. Ibid., 181.

57. Ibid.

58. Ibid.

59. Ibid., 147.

60. Ibid., 148.

61. Ibid., 149.

62. Ibid., 130, 129. See also "Das Honig-Opfer," 295–99.

63. Euripides, *Bacchae*, *Euripides fabulae*, ed. Jones Diggle, vol. 3, *Helena, Phoenissae, Orestes, Bacchae, Iphigenia, Avlidensis, Rhesus* (Oxford: Oxford University Press, 1994), 312. Z, in *Nietzsche, Kritische Studienausgabe*, vol. 4, 20.

64. Ibid., 136.

65. Friedrich Hölderlin, *Sämtliche Werke und Briefe*, Bd. 1, *Gedichte*, ed. Jochim Schmidt (Frankfurt: Deutscher Klassiker Verlag, 1992), 286. Murrey, *Hölderlin's Dionysiac Poetry*, 10.3. Z, in *Nietzsche, Kritische Studienausgabe*, vol. 4, 24.

66. Ibid., 136.

67. Murrey, *Hölderlin's Dionysiac Poetry*, 2.3.

68. Z, in *Nietzsche, Kritische Studienausgabe*, Colli and Montinari, vol. 4, *Also sprach Zarathustra. Ein Buch für Alle und Keinen* 18.

69. Murrey, *Hölderlin's Dionysiac Poetry*, 2.3.

70. Z, in *Nietzsche, Kritische Studienausgabe*, vol. 4, 23.

71. Murrey, *Hölderlin's Dionysiac Poetry*, 10.3.

72. Z, in *Nietzsche, Kritische Studienausgabe*, vol. 4, 282.

73. Ibid.

74. Ibid., 282–83.

75. Ibid., 284–85.

76. Ibid., 285.

77. Ibid., 286.

78. Ibid., 284.

79. Ibid., 48.

80. Ibid.

81. Ibid.

82. Ibid., 366.

83. ASC, in *Nietzsche, Kritische Studienausgabe*, vol. 1, 22.

84. Z, in *Nietzsche, Kritische Studienausgabe*, vol. 4, 368.

85. EH, in *Friedrich Nietzsche, Kritische Studienausgabe*, ed. Giorgio Colli and Mazzino Montinari, vol. 6, *Der Fall Wagner, Götzen-Dämmerung, Der Antichrist, Ecce homo, Dionysos-Dithyramben, Nietzsche contra Wagner* (Berlin: de Gruyter, 1999), 401.

86. Z, in *Nietzsche, Kritische Studienausgabe*, vol. 4, 211.

87. *Ath.Pol.* 3.5. in Aristotle, *The Athenian Constitution, The Eudemian Ethics, On Virtues and Vices,* trans. Horace Rackham (Cambridge: Harvard University Press, 1935), 16. See also Demosthenes, *Against Neaeras,* 74, in *Demosthenes, Orationes,* ed. Michael Rennie, vol. 3 (Cambridge: Harvard University Press, 1991), 317 (1369). Xenophon, *Symposium* 9.2–7, in Xenophon, *Memorabilia Oeconomicus,* trans. Edgar Marchant, *Symposium, Apology,* trans. Otis Todd (Cambridge: Harvard University Press, 2002), 632–34.

88. Murrey, *Hölderlin's Dionysiac Poetry,* 10.1.

89. *Z.* in *Nietzsche, Kritische Studienausgabe,* vol. 4, 397.

90. Ibid., 401.

91. Ibid., 397.

II

Proto-National Socialism

Chapter Six

Despair of the German Spirit

Although it is clear that Nietzsche's "Dionysian philosophy" (4.1) emerges in a way that is independent from Hölderlin's Dionysiac poetry, the *Lieblingsdichter* (2.1) of his youth, nevertheless, facilitates his Hellenic exploration of earth, community, and language—one that, not incidentally, even such able thinkers and poets of the nineteenth century like Marx and Baudelaire could never imagine.

This does not mean that fundamental differences between Nietzsche and Hölderlin do not exist. Whereas Hölderlin stumbles across the sociopolitical power of "mystic initiations"—Dionysus's *Mysterien* and the *Geheimnis* (v 22)[1] of Bacchic rites—when he is about thirty years old during the time of the French Revolution and Napoléon, Nietzsche's exposure to the potential of ancient ritual and "the people of tragic mysteries," *der tragischen Mysterien* (3.2), given that this occurs already in his early twenties (maybe even late teens)—and during the middle of nineteenth century industrialization—is, in a sense, both earlier and later.

But the fact that *this* poet and *this* philosopher are able to see into Dionysus's darkly lit early historical depth leads to that which remains their most productive similarity. By retrieving the *Dionysiac chronotope* and *language*, Nietzsche, like Hölderlin, identifies the visual vengeance that from early historic to modern time underlies the greed of unregulated capitalism. The "most profound revelation of Hellenic genius" (3.3) is adapted to initiate a "*tragoedia*" (4.2) of today where the "higher egoism" (2.2) concealed within the "pointed eyes" (5.3) of modern money-tyrants who "jingle with their gold" (5.1) is absorbed back into the communal "meaning of earth" (6.4). As with my study of Hölderlin, I have sought to show that Nietzsche's "Dionysian philosophy" (4), given its potential openness to all places, peoples, and languages, recalls the spirit of the "democratic god par excellence."[2] One

thinks of his celebration of "the public cult of tragedy" as "exciting, purifying and discharging the entire life of a people" (3.3).

But the similarity that we see between Nietzsche and Hölderlin is not only
positive. In fact, the problems that haunt Hölderlin's retrieval of a Dionysian
space, time, and words, when they reappear in Nietzsche's adaption of
Greece, intensify and become (shockingly) sinister. In the second part of this
study, we turn to two modern spatio-temporal forms and styles of language—
the *racist* and *Judeo-Christian chronotopes*—both of which consume the
democratic potential of the earthly and communal spirit in Nietzsche's "Dionysian philosophy."

"A PERMANENT, LOVING BOND BETWEEN GERMAN AND
GREEK CULTURE?"

Rescuing Nietzsche from National Socialism after 1945 has produced a reassuring, but outlandishly false image of his apparent antinationalism (1.3).
This becomes clear when one takes even a cursory look at Nietzsche's criticisms of his fatherland and mother tongue. Reasonably pointed statements
that expose the selfishness that can accompany modern German culture and
thought soon degenerate into a self-hatred that, in turn, blends into the madness that Nietzsche finally suffers. We have noted his critique of Kant the
(hyper-abstract) "idiot"[3] and Wagner the romantic charlatan (2.2). But such
criticisms of "the end of German philosophy" (2.2) and "this whole petty
German wretchedness"[4] —as justified as they may be—are suspiciously
without end. Like Hölderlin's rejection of the "child-like culture" of barbaric
(non-Dionysian) German industrialists, scientists, and priests—which is reasonable, if abstract—Nietzsche's inspired embrace of that which is "'un-
German'"—for instance, when he rejects that which "smells offensively like
Hegel" or that which is "infected with the cadaverous-bitter perfume peculiar
to Schopenhauer"[5] —often remains unclear and redoubles into a (psychic)
self-mutilation of sorts.

At best Nietzsche's need to transcend the unfortunate narrowness of his
own modern space-time and language gives rise to creative expressions that
we might expect from one with such linguistic talent. Consider his turn to
France, in particular to the French language, to express the primal discontent
against which his "Dionysian philosophy" (4.1) rages. Being unlike any word
in the German language, the French *ressentiment* (2.1) uniquely evokes the
profound hostility that an individual projects onto that which he or she perceives to be the source of an original injustice.

At worst, Nietzsche's aggressive attempts to abandon his cultural and
linguistic inheritance—and thus expose [w]*hat* [he and] *the Germans lack*—
reveals a deeper event of cognitive dissonance. "The Germans have de-

stroyed for Europe the last great cultural harvest."⁶ From here he proceeds to gesture, if indirectly, to the absence of a German religious leader who is capable of Dionysiac "magic and spectacle."⁷ Referring to the "German monk, Luther" who "came to Rome," he laments how "[t]his monk, with all the vengeful-addict instincts of an unsuccessful priest in him, raised a rebellion *against* the Renaissance."⁸ To interpret Nietzsche's discontents with his own (German) culture and language as simply a sign of his unquestionable antinationalism—although comforting after 1945—neglects the profound crisis of nationalism and religious identity to which his work belongs.

We have noted the destructive spirit of *Romanticism* that plagues Hölderlin's poetry. When "German humanism took over the Greek world from Winckelmann as an artistic revelation just as much as it took it over as a scientific object,"⁹ it tragically *germanified* Greek culture, that is, willfully submitted ancient Greece to the tyranny of modern Germany. Given Nietzsche's (self-reflexive) admonishments about his forerunning "wakers-of-the-dead" (2.2), one would expect to see in his work a new style of German thinking that transcends such Germano-centric, self-serving resurrections. This leads to the question: Did Nietzsche understand the lethal depths of his own romances and wakings-of-the-dead?

As I have noted, Hölderlin's retrieval of the *Dionysiac chronotope* is never free of nationalism. One thinks of his poems *The Dying Vaterland, Death for the Vaterland,* and *Song of the Germans,* as well as his (nationalist) phantasm of an ancient "*Volk* of rare excellence hidden" living secretly "in the depths of Asia"—one that is significantly tied to the search for "[o]ne race."¹⁰ Unsettling is Hölderlin's restriction of the universal spirit of humankind that Greece opens out to modern Germany. Elegies and odes such as *The Archipelago, Homecoming,* and *Heidelberg* make it clear that the perceived "springtime of Greece" (v 272) is a metaphor not only of the ascendency of the ancient Greeks, but also that which shall give way to the fated "autumn" (v 173)¹¹ of their German successors. After all, as Hölderlin declares in *To the Germans,* "the mountains of German / Land are the mountains of the muses" (v 35–36).¹² Democracy inherent in the Dionysian transition from tragic isolation and suffering to earthly and communal joy is absorbed into modern nationalism. "Only one thing matters for the day, the *Vaterland* and into the sacrifice's / Festive flame everyone throws his own" (v 29–30).¹³

Like Hölderlin, Nietzsche narrows the identity of those who may access the magic of Greece to the German people. "Also during medieval Germany," it just so happens, "the same Dionysian power drove ever increasing groups of singing and dancing people from place to place."¹⁴ Furthermore, it also just so happens that "Kant and Schopenhauer made it possible for the spirit *of German philosophy* to destroy the complacent desire for the existence of scientific Socraticism" and thereby reintroduce "*Dionysian wis-*

dom"[15] to modern time. Unaware of the depth of Hölderlin's relation to Greece, Nietzsche expectedly ascribes the way in which "the German spirit has been able to learn most resolutely from the Greeks" to "the most noble intellectual struggles of Goethe, Schiller and Winckelmann."[16] Here Nietzsche prepares the tyranny of Germany over Greece that is implicit in the belief that "German humanism took over the Greek world from Winckelmann as an artistic revelation just as much as it took it over as a scientific object."

Also like his *Lieblingsdichter*, Nietzsche understands the exclusive retrieval of Greece in Germany as an unfinished project—and this means (potentially) unlimited in its influence on other races in the future. Hölderlin's restriction of the spirit of Dionysus to German demigods—one thinks of the Dionysian *Rhine* and *Germania* who found "cities" (v 89) and "holidays" (v 109)—consumes not only the present, but also the near and even distant future.[17] His invocation of Dionysian/German "poets!" (v 57) around 1800 to make their epiphany in the coming months gives way to a future *Memento* of 1803–1804.[18] Now the heroism of Dionysian/German "poets" (v 59) may take years, decades, and perhaps a century to reveal itself.[19]

But with Nietzsche the tragic time before the epiphany of a Germano-Greco genius absorbs nineteenth-century industrialization: "it must also be noted," he continues in his reflection on Winckelmann, Schiller, and Goethe,

> that since their time and with regard to the subsequent effects of their struggles, the endeavour to achieve a path of intellectualism equal to the Greeks has become weaker and weaker in an incomprehensible way.[20]

Once again, the fact that Nietzsche is unaware of the Dionysian depths of Hölderlin's poetry plays into his romanticizing of the failure of his forerunning German poets and philosophers.

> Should we, in order to not have to completely despair of the German spirit, not be able to draw the conclusion that in some essential points even these heroes [Winckelmann, Schiller, and Goethe] could not succeed to penetrate the core of Hellenic being and found a permanent, loving bond between German and Greek culture?[21]

"So that perhaps an unconscious sense of this shortcoming also in regard to serious natures raises disheartening doubt," Nietzsche proceeds, "whether they, after such predecessors, could advance further on this intellectual path and be able to reach the goal at all."[22]

"CONFUSED OUR GAZE SEARCHES"

Nietzsche's understanding of the reef upon which the German retrieval of Greece shipwrecks is more historical than that which we find in Hölderlin. In particular, there is now a historical critique of the general, superficial mood of those who dominate the politics of modern universities and colleges while misidentifying (or simply being wholly ignorant of) Greece's profound meanings for humankind. "Therefore we see since this time," he notes, "the value of the Greeks for education degenerate in the most alarming way; the expression of compassionate superiority is heard." Nietzsche goes on,

> in the most varied intellectual and non-intellectual camps; elsewhere a wholly ineffectual, if educated idle chatter flirts with "Greek harmony," "Greek beauty," and "Greek cheerfulness."[23]

But what seems like a universal problem of learning is caught up in the (romantic) restriction of the magic of ancient Greece to modern Germany.

> And in these very circles, whose dignity could be to create the salvation [Heil] of German education from the indefatigable Greek riverbed, in the circles of teachers at places of higher education one has learned best to settle with the Greeks in a timely and comfortable way such that a skeptical valuation of the Hellenic ideal and complete perversion of the true intention of classical studies is abandoned.[24]

"Whoever has not exhausted himself in these circles through his devotion to becoming a reliable corrector of ancient texts or linguistic microscope of natural history"—one recalls Nietzsche's criticism of the modern "big eye," *ein großes Auge* (6.1)—

> is perhaps trying to assimilate Greek antiquity, alongside other antiquities "historically," and this means with the method and supercilious airs of our present intellectual historiography.[25]

This brings us to one of the essential dangers of Nietzsche's Greco-Germano romance, namely how his belief that the retrieval of Greece belongs exclusively to Germany is often masked with the appearance of a new planetary historical weakness. "There has never been another period of art," Nietzsche says as if speaking of all cultures everywhere, "in which so-called education and authentic art have been so estranged and opposed as that which we can see with our eyes in the present."[26]

> We understand why such a weak education hates true art; for through it, it fears its own downfall. But should not an entire style of culture, namely the

Socratic-Alexandrian, have exhausted itself after culminating in such a dainti-
ly-weak point as that of the present intellectualism?"[27]

As one reads on, however, it becomes unavoidably clear that the failure of
the present to retrieve Dionysian Greece, if a global problem, is nevertheless
one that can be resolved *only* through German culture, in particular through
new German heroes. "If such champions like Schiller and Goethe were not
able to succeed in breaking down the enchanting gates that lead into the
Hellenic magic mountain," Nietzsche declares,

> if with their courageous striving they could not advance further than that of
> that longing gaze which Goethe's Iphigenia sends home from barbaric Tauris
> across the sea, for what could the epigones of such heroes hope, if not for them
> suddenly, in a wholly different direction from that of all the toiling of previous
> culture, that is, from an untouched side, the gates opened up themselves—from
> the mystic sound of the re-awakening of tragedy's music.[28]

This attempt to confine the potential sociopolitics of Greece to Germany
ends in a reckless despair and euphoria. "Let no one try to diminish our belief
in a never-before-experienced rebirth of Hellenic antiquity," Nietzsche proclaims, "for in it alone do we find our hope for the renewal and purification
of the German spirit through the fire-magic of music."[29]
    At this point he introduces a German visual culture that anticipates the
rebirth of Dionysian Greece in modern Germany.

> A desolate, lonely individual could not choose a better symbol than the knight
> with death and devil, as Dürer drew him for us, the armoured knight with the
> iron, hard gaze who, undeterred by his gruesome companions, and, although
> hopeless, alone with his horse and dog, knows to take his terrible path.[30]

Now we are in a position to see how Nietzsche's retrieval of the *Dionysiac chronotope* is tragically absorbed into a *nationalized* space-time—the
nationalized chronotope.[31] Firstly, there is the isolated German hero who
mirrors the isolated mystic initiand. "One such Dürer knight was our Schopenhauer: he lacked all hope, but he wanted the truth. He has no equal."[32]
Secondly—and similar to Hölderlin—Nietzsche *adapts the adaption* of the
epiphany of Dionysus as a magical light in tragedy—for instance, when the
god appears to and raises up his mystic initiates from their desolate isolation
and darkness in *Bacchae*[33] —to express the Hellenic spirit's revelation in
Germany.

> Confused our gaze searches for that which has disappeared: for what they see
> is as if from out of a sunkenness raised by a golden light, so full and verdant,
> so luxuriantly alive, so full of incalculable longing.[34]

Thirdly (and lastly), the combination of the German hero and the power of ritual as revealed in the tragic play fuse together to facilitate—somehow?—Germany's planetary redemption of modern time. After hysterically citing the second version of Goethe's *Faust*, the youthful philologist frothingly proclaims to his countrymen,

> Yes, my friends, believe with me in the Dionysian life and in the rebirth of tragedy. The time of the Socratic human is past: wreath yourselves with ivy, take the thyrsus in your hand and do not be surprised when tigers and panthers fawning about your knees lay themselves down. Now only dare to be tragic humans: for you shall be redeemed. You shall lead the Dionysian festival procession from India to Greece! Arm yourselves for hard strife, but believe in the wonder of your god![35]

NOTES

1. Lucas Murrey, *Hölderlin's Dionysiac Poetry: The Terrifying-Exciting Mysteries* (Heidelberg, New York, Dordrecht, London: Springer, 2015), chapters 7.2 (7.2).
2. Ibid., 2.3.
3. Ibid., 6.2.
4. TI, in *Friedrich Nietzsche, Kritische Studienausgabe*, ed. Giorgio Colli and Mazzino Montinari, vol. 6, *Der Fall Wagner, Götzen-Dämmerung, Der Antichrist, Ecce homo, Dionysos-Dithyramben, Nietzsche contra Wagner* (Berlin: de Gruyter, 1999), 104. EH, in *Nietzsche, Kritische Studienausgabe*, vol. 6, 314.
5. Cited in Murrey, *Hölderlin's Dionysiac Poetry*, coda, 14. EH, in *Nietzsche, Kritische Studienausgabe*, vol. 6, 314.
6. AC, in *Nietzsche, Kritische Studienausgabe*, vol. 6, 250.
7. Ibid., 251.
8. Ibid., 251–52.
9. Murrey, *Hölderlin's Dionysiac Poetry*, 6.2.
10. Ibid., 12.1, 12.4.
11. Ibid., 12.1.
12. Ibid.
13. Ibid.
14. BT, in *Friedrich Nietzsche, Kritische Studienausgabe*, ed. Giorgio Colli and Mazzino Montinari, vol. 1, *Die Geburt der Tragödie, Unzeitgemäße Betrachtungen I–IV, Nachgelassene Schriften 1870–1873* (Berlin: de Gruyter, 1999), 29.
15. Ibid., 128.
16. Ibid., 129.
17. Murrey, *Hölderlin's Dionysiac Poetry*, 12.2, 12.4.
18. Ibid., 12.4.
19. Ibid.
20. BT, in *Nietzsche, Kritische Studienausgabe*, vol. 1, 129.
21. Ibid.
22. Ibid.
23. Ibid., 129–30.
24. Ibid., 130.
25. Ibid.
26. Ibid.
27. Ibid., 130–31.
28. Ibid., 131.
29. Ibid.

30. Ibid.

31. For my first use of the term *nationalized chronotope*, see Murrey, *Hölderlin's Dionysiac Poetry*, 12.1.

32. BT, in *Nietzsche, Kritische Studienausgabe*, vol. 1, 131.

33. Murrey, *Hölderlin's Dionysiac Poetry*, 1.3, 7.1–7.2, 8, 9.1–9.2.

34. BT, in *Nietzsche, Kritische Studienausgabe*, vol. 1, 131–32.

35. Ibid., 132.

Chapter Seven

Patriotic Excitation and Aesthetic Opulence

"IN THE TERROR AND SUBLIMITIES OF THE RECENTLY OUT-BROKEN WAR"

As we should expect, at the center of Nietzsche's nationalizing of the *Dionysiac chronotope* is his abandonment of the language of earth and community for that of a *nationalized language*. On the one hand, this reminds us of Hölderlin.

As I have shown, the (universal) Dionysian spirit of "[t]he language of lovers" (v 26) and "the language of the land" (v 27) is absorbed into "the sound of the *Volk*!" (v 28)[1] where "people" refers more and more exclusively to German *Volk*. Now the democratic potential of "the pure word," *das reine Wort*, of Greece becomes restricted to a linguistic experience that is peculiar to German natural phenomena. One recalls "the pure voice," *die reine Stimme* (v 95), of the German river *Der Rhein*.[2] Modern German "poets" (v 57) of the present—who are also referred to as "the wine-god's holy priests" (v 123), retrieve the language of Dionysus that is opened out in tragedy "to sing of the angels of the holy *Vaterland*."[3]

This adaption of *Dionysiac language* to express "the height and pure joyfulness of the songs of the *Vaterland*"—also celebrated as the "German song" (v 226)—culminates in Hölderlin's return to the language of "a *Volk* of rare excellence hidden" secretly "in the depths of Asia."[4] In *Memento* the epiphany of Dionysian "breath" (v 37)—and this includes the "times/Of secrets," *Zeiten/Des Geheimnisse* (v 43), that are prophesied to reappear "in Germany" (v 44)—dissolves into a distant (and unlimited) projection of *The Voice of the Volk*.[5] No longer set to appear in the coming months, the German "wine-god's holy priests" are transfigured into the German "poets" (v

59) of a distant, unlimited future.[6] This means, finally, that at an unspecified time that could be years, decades, even centuries, having returned to their "forefathers" (v 12) who arose "[f]rom the forests of the Indus" (v 10), German poets shall found the language of the "German race," *Deutsch[es] Geschlecht* (Fragment 72).[7]

As we have also seen, Nietzsche's narrowing of the universal significance of Greece to Germany is, in essence, a musical-linguistic degeneration.

> Let no one try to diminish our belief in a never-before-experienced rebirth of Hellenic antiquity, for in it alone do we find our hope for the renewal and purification of the German spirit *through the fire-magic of music*.[8]

This musical-linguistic core of the global future is—somehow?—exclusively Greek and German. This returns in many, even outlandish forms. "Also during medieval Germany, the same Dionysian power drove ever increasing groups of singing and dancing people from place to place." (7.1)

It is significant that most of the citations above come from the early Nietzsche. And indeed, to understand this musical-linguistic derangement of Nietzsche's nationalism, one has to confront a youthful soul mesmerized by the nationalist spirit of an older, fatherly musician. This is not to say that the relationship between these two is never heartwarming. One recalls Nietzsche's "Preface to Richard Wagner" with which he strikes the first note of *The Birth of Tragedy Out of the Spirit of Music*. The no-longer-fatherless, ecstatic son calls forth the magical time when his "highly esteemed friend"—who himself "to the close of the *Eumenides* . . . remained in a state of ecstasy" (2.1)—"will receive this text: when you, perhaps after a wintry outing in the snow, seeing the liberated Prometheus on the cover, read my name."[9]

Instead, this is to say that the inner core of Nietzsche's relationship to Wagner is, nevertheless, stained by German nationalism. The otherwise beautiful tradition of German music and enchanting sounds of Greece's "terrifying-exciting mysteries"[10] is, if Nietzsche is to be trusted, forced to fight a modern battle against the non-German. "You shall then remember," he confides,

> that I, at the same time when your beautiful *Festschrift* for Beethoven arose, that is, in the terror and sublimities of the recently out-broken war, gathered myself for these thoughts.[11]

What first presents itself as harmless quickly is degraded into the exclusion of the music and language of the other.

> If one transformed Beethoven's *Ode to Joy* into a painting and did not hold back his imagination when millions sink into the dust horrified: then could one approach the Dionysian.[12]

What is arguably Nietzsche's most profound insight into tragedy—the mystery of images that spark and leap out of sounds (3.3)—now comes dangerously close to Wagner's *nationalizing* of Beethoven. "We experience it again and again," he declares,

> how a symphony of Beethoven compels the individual listeners to speak visually, though the configuration of the different world of images produced by a musical piece may never be so fantastically colourful, and even contradictory. [13]

"MONSTROUS INTRUSIVE POWERS FROM THE OUTSIDE"

What makes the otherwise innocent statements above threatening is that they culminate in a sinister concentration of language as both sound (music) and image (text) wherein the spirits of Greece and Germany are exclusively intertwined: "to where does the mystery of this oneness of German music and philosophy lead us," Nietzsche asks, "if not to a new form of being whose content we can teach ourselves only by sensing Hellenic analogies?" [14] "At the same time there lives in us the feeling," he proceeds, "as if the birth of a tragic age means for the German spirit only a homecoming to itself, a blessed self-rediscovery." [15]

At this point we are introduced to something ominous, something whose unfortunate intensity transcends that which we see in Hölderlin's nationalism. For Nietzsche, the Hellenic "oneness of German music and philosophy" shall reemerge only when the "monstrous intrusive powers from the outside" that have reduced Germans "to slavery" [16] are annihilated. Written just after the Franco-Prussian War, this can mean the German conquest of the French: the hateful "leading-strings of a Roman civilization." [17]

The music and language of Germany, uniquely fused as they are with the music and language of Greece, gradually acquire a cosmic significance with respect to their historic destinies to purify the present of all inauthentic peoples and languages. "But let the liar and hypocrite beware of German music," Nietzsche warns,

> for among all our cultures, it is the only pure and purifying fire-spirit from which and toward which, as in the teaching of the great Herakleitos of Ephesus, all things move in a double orbit. [18] (4.1)

"Tragedy absorbs the highest musical orgasm into itself," as Wagner's *Tristan and Isolda* suggests, "such that it, as with the Greeks and as with us, brings music to its perfection." [19] The nationalist, Wagnerian spirit not only rebels against the disenchantment of "bourgeois mediocrity" (2.2), but also seeks to destroy the "monstrous intrusive powers from the outside" that have reduced the German people and language "to slavery." This is particularly clear when Nietzsche infuses his "Dürer knight" with Wagnerian magic.

> For our comfort there were signs that the German spirit, undestroyed in beauti-
> ful health, depth and Dionysian strength, in an inaccessible abyss nevertheless
> rests and dreams, like a knight sunken in slumber: out of this abyss Dionysian
> song ascends to us, to let us know that this German knight still now in his
> ancient Dionysian myth dreams in blessed, serious visions. [20]

The seemingly innocent spirit of birdsong that evokes a Bacchic paradise (4.2)—"Let no one believe that the German spirit has forever lost its mythic home, if it still so clearly understands the voices of birds that tell of this home"[21]—degenerates into the (unlimited) nationalism and racism that Wagner writes into his operas. "One day it will find itself awake in all the morning freshness of a tremendous sleep," Nietzsche declares, "then he will kill dragons, destroy vicious dwarves and awaken Brünhilde—and not even Wotan's spear will be able to stop his way!"[22]

On the one hand, the music and language of nationalism seem to belong only to the young Nietzsche. The ecstatic cry of Dionysus, who liberates the spirit of earth and community from destructive, *visualized* money-tyrants (such as Pentheus) regresses into the tyrannical cry of the nationalism of Nietzsche's *Vaterland*.

To illustrate this, let us briefly return to Hölderlin's translation of "the joyous shout," *das Jauchzen* (v 24), of Dionysus's mystic chorus in *Bacchae* that he adapts to express the godlike "joyous shout," *Jauchzen* (v 61), of *The Rhine*.[23] As if a new mythic language describing a godlike German happi- ness, Dionysus's "joyous shout," *das Jauchzen*, is also, for the youthful Nietzsche, adapted to express the sound of Wagnerian ecstasy, as when Nietzsche celebrates "the joyously shouting Kurwenal," *das jauchzende Kur- wenal*.[24]

Of course the mature Nietzsche comes to reject his German master. What the youthful philologist saw as "the primal suffering of modern culture"—a symptom of the degeneration of "authentic art" into "superficial entertain- ment"—is, in the end, associated with the "musician-problem of Wagner" (2.2). This intelligent progression is indebted to Nietzsche's insight into trag- edy in regard to the strength of the (Apolline) image to ascend out of commu- nal and earthly (and hence invisible) Dionysian sound (3.3). Aware that such a deceptively simple (and modest) understanding of the human being and his or her primal relation to nature is lacking in Wagner's egocentric music, Nietzsche associates the inauthentic "gestures" of the nationalist composer that immobilize "especially the muscle sensations" (2.2) with an obsessive visual impulse (we might say the *Wagnerian chronotope*) that fails to honor the audible underworld of the eyes. "Wagner begins with the hallucination: not of sounds, but instead of gestures" (2.2).[25]

We have further noted that Nietzsche is acutely aware of how "Wagner's music" was merely a medium through which he as a young man could discover "the expression of a Dionysian powerfulness of soul" and "by these means discovered the idea of 'tragedy'" (4.1). Thus the distance that the older Nietzsche sees between his central Dionysian myth and Wagnerian "decadence-music" that consumes "the flutes of Dionysus." (2.2):

> The whole representation of the dithyrambic artist is a picture of the already existing author of Zarathustra and it is drawn with an abysmal depth that does not even once come into contact with the real Wagner. (4.2)

But the musical and linguistic tension that haunts Nietzsche's relation to Wagner's nationalism and racism leads to a fundamental question. This becomes clear when we consider Nietzsche's adaptions of Dionysus's "joyous cry," *das Jauchzen*, which is gradually liberated from the *kitsch* of Wagnerian mythology ("the joyously shouting Kurwenal," *das jauchzende Kurwenal*) and replanted in the landscape of his own (explicitly Dionysian) philosophical mythology.

> But at last his eyes opened: enchanted, Zarathustra looked into the forest and the stillness; enchanted, he gazed into himself. Then he arose quickly, like a seafarer who suddenly sees land, and joyously cried out [jauchzte]. (5.4)

The transformation from a Wagnerian to a Zarathustrian *jauchzen* invites us to wonder: Is Nietzsche's abandonment of Wagner also an abandonment of Wagner's nationalism and racism? Or is the anti-Wagnerian philosopher who nevertheless refuses to abandon the illusion that Germans are secretly a superior race descending from (non-Judeo-Christian) ancient races—such as those from India, Greece, and Iran—swimming out to racist-infested waters in whose depths the nonracist, democratic spirit of his *Dionysiac chronotope* is doomed to drown?

"DESTRUCTION OF GREEK CULTURE THROUGH THE JEWISH WORLD"

Although Nietzsche comes to reject the *visualized* and *monetized chronotopes* that rule Wagner's (inauthentic) art, there remains a *proto-National Socialist chronotope* and *language* that, because they sharpen during the transition from Nietzsche's earlier to his later work, tragically consumes his "Dionysian philosophy" (4.1).

In the early Nietzsche, the creation of a sinister space-time and language consists firstly of the creation of a secret community of revolutionary and superior German artists. This is implicit in the rhetorical tone through which he invokes the presence of his isolated, but heroic countrymen. Now "the most noble intellectual struggles" of "such heroes" as Winckelmann, Schiller, and Goethe (and the "Dürer knight" Schopenhauer) give way to the "desolate, lonely individual" of modern Germany who, in turn, is joyfully absorbed into "*our* belief in a never-before-experienced rebirth of Hellenic antiquity."[26] The secret space-time and language of Dionysus's mystery cult—with its "sentences intelligent only to a few" (3.3)—is then neutralized by Nietzsche's (youthful) need for a secret German community:

> Yes, *my friends*, believe *with me* in the Dionysian life and in the rebirth of tragedy. The time of the Socratic human is past: wreath *yourselves* with ivy, take the thyrsus *in your hand* and do not be surprised when tigers and panthers fawning about *your knees* lay themselves down. Now only dare to be tragic humans: for *you shall be redeemed. You shall lead* the Dionysian festival procession from India to Greece! *Arm yourselves for hard strife, but believe in the wonder of your god!*[27]

In no small part *The Birth of Tragedy* is a perverse adaption of the movement in mystic initiation (from individual isolation and suffering to communal and earthly joy) to call forth an elite community of bellicose German artists. "I know that I must lead [führen] the participating friend up to an elevated place of lonely observation where he will have few companions," Nietzsche confides, "and call out to him encouragingly that we have to hold fast to our luminous leaders [Führen] the Greeks."[28] Although alone, "the attentive friend" shall return with his fellow countrymen to their "more nobly endowed natures"—and this means a homecoming to "the nobler natures among artists" that open out "the noble core of our peoples' character [Volkscharakter]."[29]

Secondly, the construction of a racist German space-time and language in the early Nietzsche is related to the perverse application of a cleansing act in Greek tragedy to describe how this secret German community shall disinfect the corruption of modern art. As we have seen, the goal of Nietzsche's retrieval of the tragic play is "[t]o purify our aesthetic insight" (4.1). And as we have also seen, his understanding of "the degenerate form of tragedy,"[30] which yields the still more degenerate "Alexandrian arts of adulation" (2.2), rears its devious face in our "ineffectual, if educated" understanding of antiquity today.

The concept of "degenerate art" (2.2) often represents a creative (and even sometimes truthful) understanding of history. Nevertheless, Nietzsche's rhetoric often slips into a racist language that is peculiar to the emergence of certain strains of nineteenth-century science (such as biology) and betrays his deeper cognitive dissonance. When he and his secret community of battling German artists strive toward "a beautiful inner, healthful primal power,"[31] they seek to identify and eradicate any and all non-German degenerate life-forms. One recalls Nietzsche's question concerning "the degenerate form of tragedy" that is recovered during the *Renaissance*: "From which juices do these parasites of operatic creatures nourish themselves, if not from the true art?"[32]

The third component of the early Nietzsche's destructive Germanic space-time and language is the identity of those who have been selected for cleansing. The purification of the "monstrous intrusive powers from the out-side" that have reduced modern Germans "to slavery" can mean, for exam-ple, the conquest of the French: "the leading-strings of a Roman civilisation." Consider the full citation that accompanies the artistic homecoming to "the noble core of our peoples' character [Volkscharakter]."

> One would also have to despair painfully about our German being if it had inextricably entangled itself in, or become identical with, its culture, as we can observe to our horror in regard to civilised France; and that which was for a long time the great advantage of France and the cause of its vast superiority, namely that unity of being between people and culture, might compel us, in view of this sight, to celebrate ourselves that this so questionable culture has until now had nothing to do with the noble core of our peoples' character [Volkscharakter].[33]

Less well known than the early Nietzsche's racism toward the French is that of his open racism toward the Jews. Even before *The Birth of Tragedy*, writing during the winter of 1869–1870, the Wagnerian-inspired youth iden-tifies the Jews as the murders of Dionysian Greece. "Destruction of Greek culture through the Jewish world,"[34] Nietzsche proclaims in one of his sever-al notes. As we have seen, the older Dionysian philosopher is critical of the Jews who, following the loss of their earthly place in the sixth century B.C.E., degenerate into "that priestly nation of *ressentiment par excellence*" (2.1).

But here we leave the orbit of a creative (and somewhat reasonable) critique of Jewish priests who, "*no longer* united with Israel" (2.1), invent a vengeful cosmological vision. Under the (massive) influence of Wagner's "patriotic excitation and aesthetic opulence,"[35] the early Nietzsche succumbs to what we may call nineteenth-century biological racism. Individuals who start out in a particular people lack the freedom to develop in a way that is communal and earthly. Just because one is born Jewish does not mean that "to live uprooted from native soil" (2.2) in modern time is less painful for him or her than it is for any other (German or, for instance, Palestinian) person. Nietzsche leaves no room for the exceptional Jew who sets out on a

Dionysian journey for "a single, vigorously developed root [and] healthy soil" (4.1) in a way that embraces the non-Jewish other.

"AND IF THE GERMAN SHOULD LOOK ABOUT HESITATINGLY FOR A *FÜHRER*"

This gives us some insight into the limits of the early Nietzsche's otherwise brilliant discovery of Dionysus. Although his retrieval of Hellenic earth and community is without question of rare excellence (even for an ingenious young adult), the impressionable youth remains imprisoned in what he perceives to be "the German problem": the "vortex and turning-point in the very centre of German hopes."[36] This is the voice of one who is writing to he who is identified as complicit "sublime fore-fighter [Vorkämpfer] on this path."[37] "From out of the Dionysian ground of the German spirit a power has arisen which has nothing common with the primal conditions of Socratic culture," the young Nietzsche declares,

> and from which it can be neither explained nor excused, but shall be from this culture much more felt as the horrifically inexplicable, the overwhelmingly hostile—German music, which we understand pre-eminently in its powerful solar orbit from Bach to Beethoven, from Beethoven to Wagner.[38]

Important is Nietzsche's adaption of the political potential of a movement (in ritual) upward from the earth into the light of the sky and heaven above.[39] Although Hölderlin's use of "the joyous shout," *das Jauchzen* (v 24), of Dionysus's mystic chorus in *Bacchae* for the rising "joyous shout," *Jauchzen* (v 61), of *Der Rhein* is similar in its absorption of a cosmic (vertical) axis into German nationalism,[40] Nietzsche's concentration of Bacchic and Germanic breathe is far more fatal.

> From this abyss the German Reformation came forth: in whose choral-hymn the future melody of German music first resounded. So deep, courageous and full of soul, so exuberantly good and delicately did this chorale of Luther intone, as the first Dionysian luring-call that breaks forth from densely grown thickets during the approach of spring. Answering him in emulative echo this consecrated, overly courageous procession of Dionysian revellers for whom we have German music to thank—and for whom we shall thank for *the rebirth of German myth*![41]

Still more significant, Nietzsche's youthful (Wagnerian) nationalism and racism reveals that at the center of the delusion upon which both rest is an abyss of German leadership in the present. "Perhaps some will think that this spirit must begin its battle [Kampf] with the elimination of everything Romantic,"[42] Nietzsche confides, in which they may be able to recognize an external preparation and encouragement in the victorious fortitude and bloody glory of the last war, but one must search for the inner necessity in the ambition to be continually worthy of the sublime fore-fighters [Vorkämpfer] on this way, Luther as well as our great artists and poets.[43]

The glimpse of a Dionysiac paradise is next exploited to empower Nietzsche's search for a German leader. "But never let him believe that he could fight [kämpfen] similar battles [Kämpfe] without the gods of his house, or his mythical home," he feverishly proclaims, "without 'bringing back' all things German!"[44]

And if the German should look about hesitantly for a *Führer* who might bring him back again to his long lost home and whose ways and paths he scarcely knows anymore—so let him only listen to the charming luring call of the Dionysian bird that hovers above and wants to point out the way to him.[45]

NOTES

1. Lucas Murrey, *Hölderlin's Dionysiac Poetry: The Terrifying-Exciting Mysteries* (Heidelberg, New York, Dordrecht, London: Springer, 2015), chapter 12.1 (12.1).

2. Friedrich Hölderlin, *Sämtliche Werke und Briefe*, hg. Jochen Schimdt, Bd. 1, *Gedichte* (Frankfurt am Main: Deutscher Klassiker Verlag, 1992), 330. Murrey, *Hölderlin's Dionysiac Poetry*, 12.2.

3. Ibid., 12.3.

4. Ibid., 12.4.

5. Ibid.

6. Ibid.

7. Ibid.

8. Emphasis added.

9. BT, in *Friedrich Nietzsche, Kritische Studienausgabe*, ed. Giorgio Colli and Mazzino Montinari, vol. 1, *Die Geburt der Tragödie, Unzeitgemäße Betrachtungen I–IV, Nachgelassene Schriften 1870–1873* (Berlin: de Gruyter, 1999), 23.

10. Murrey, *Hölderlin's Dionysiac Poetry*, 1.

11. BT, in *Nietzsche, Kritische Studienausgabe*, vol. 1, 23.

12. Ibid., 29.

13. Ibid., 50–51.

14. Ibid., 128.

15. Ibid.

16. Ibid.

17. Ibid., 128–29.

18. Ibid., 127–28.

19. Ibid., 131.

20. Ibid., 153.

21. Ibid., 153–54.

22. Ibid., 154. Given Nietzsche's understanding of Christianity and Judaism as both loathsome and interwoven (11), it is hardly proof that he is not anti-Semitic when he claims (perhaps falsely) in *Ecce homo* that the Wagnerian "dwarves" to whom he refers are "Christian priests." EH, in *Friedrich Nietzsche, Kritische Studienausgabe*, ed. Giorgio Colli and Mazzino Montinari, vol. 6, *Der Fall Wagner, Götzen-Dämmerung, Der Antichrist, Ecce homo, Dionysos-Dithyramben, Nietzsche contra Wagner* (Berlin: de Gruyter, 1999), 310.

23. Murrey, *Hölderlin's Dionysiac Poetry*, 10.2, 10.3.

24. BT, in *Nietzsche, Kritische Studienausgabe*, vol. 1, 136.

25. CW, in *Nietzsche, Kritische Studienausgabe*, vol. 6, 28.

26. Emphasis added.

27. Emphasis added.

28. BT, in *Nietzsche, Kritische Studienausgabe*, vol. 1, 147.

29. Ibid., 140, 116, 143, 146.

30. Ibid., 76.

31. Ibid., 146–47.

32. Ibid., 126.

33. Ibid., 146.

34. NF1, in *Friedrich Nietzsche, Kritische Studienausgabe*, ed. G. Colli and M. Montinari, vol. 7, *Nachgelassene Fragmente, 1869–1874* (Berlin: de Gruyter, 1988), 83. "Vernichtung der griechischen Kultur durch die jüdische Welt." See also 3 (73) and 3 (76).

35. BT, in *Nietzsche, Kritische Studienausgabe*, vol. 1, 24.

36. Ibid.

37. Ibid.

38. BT, in *Nietzsche, Kritische Studienausgabe*, vol. 1, 127.

39. For a discussion of this vertical movement with which mystic initiation culminates, see Murrey, *Hölderlin's Dionysiac Poetry*, 2.3.

40. Murrey, *Hölderlin's Dionysiac Poetry*, 12.2.

41. BT, in *Nietzsche, Kritische Studienausgabe*, vol. 1, 147.

42. Ibid., 149.

43. Ibid.

44. Ibid.

45. Ibid.

Chapter Eight

Blond German Beasts

"FALSE, FLICKERING LIGHT"

After *The Birth of Tragedy* Nietzsche's secret community of isolated, but elite German artists transform into something even more sinister. Lonely heroes who make their Dionysian epiphany to save humankind from the alienation of modern life reappear as "beasts of prey," *Raubtiere*,[1] who guard themselves from life-denying, inauthentic forms of morality—for instance, the perverse moral code that Nietzsche associates with the Jews (2.1). Through the final conquest of their (mythic and hence timeless) battle against Semitic morality, these "lords of earth," *Herrn der Erde*,[2] presume their destined places as the true leaders of Europe and the entire world.

What makes the concentration of nationalism and racism in Nietzsche's later work particularly tragic is its link to what could be, if one subtracted his nationalist and racist psychoses, an insightful critique of the origins of civilization. Consider the following diatribe against the evil source of the present: "the meaning of all culture,"[3] Nietzsche declares,

> is to breed the beast "human" into a tamed and civilized animal, a house pet; so one must doubtlessly view all of those reactionary and *ressentiment*-instincts [*Ressentiment-Instinkte*] with whose help the excellent races, including their ideals, have been degraded and overpowered, as the actual tools of culture.[4]

Whereas the concept "excellent races," *die vornehmen Geschlechter*, that is, people who are—somehow?—better than others, is outlandish (and despicable), the idea that the emergence of modern culture is caught up in "actual tools" that have "degraded and overpowered" humankind is not without interest (2.1–2.2).

Consider further Nietzsche's description of the (so-called) *less excellent races* whose obsession with money heralds the Christian world.

> They are miserable, there is no doubt, all these rumour-mongers and corner-counterfeiters, even though they crouch down warmly beside each other—but they tell me that their misery is God's choice and sign, one beats the dog he loves most; perhaps this misery is also a preparation, a test, a schooling, perhaps still better—something that one day will be redeemed and paid off with huge interest in gold, no! in happiness. They call this "blessedness."[5]

Nietzsche's "Dionysian philosophy" (4.1) struggles with the resentful spirit of money as well as that of an alienating visual culture (2, 5–6). The criticism of monetized, life-destroying tyrants and their conflation of "interest in gold" with "sacredness" follows another, if indirect, critique of the new form of seeing through which a *monetized morality* emerges.

> —Is there someone who wants to look a little down and into the secret [Geheimniss] of how one *fabricates ideals* on earth? Who has the courage for this? . . . Come on! Here is the open glimpse into this dark workshop. Just wait a moment, my nosy and presumptuous sir: your eye must first accustom itself to this false, flickering light.[6]

At the center of this vengeful lust for money and (artificial) seeing is a vengeful sound- and linguistic experience—one that recalls the *monetized* and *visualized languages* of *Zarathustra* (5.2, 5.4).

> I see nothing, and so I hear more. It is a carefully crafted quiet mongering and devious whispering from all corners and crevices. It seems to me that one lies; a sucrose mildness sticks to every sound. Weakness is falsified into *something of merit*, there is no doubt.[7]

Nietzsche thus adds a dose of deceit to the terror and isolation of the (early industrialized) compartment that we see in Hölderlin's *The Archipelago*: the forerunning "dark workshop" where,

> [e]ach individual is nailed alone
> To his own affairs, in the din of his workplace
> Hearing only himself and caught up in an insane labour,
> With a violent hand, restless, but always and forever
> Bringing about nothing, like the Furies, from the toil of his hands. (v 242–46)[8]

"And powerlessness which does not retaliate,"[9] Nietzsche continues,

> is being falsified into "goodness"; anxious degradation into "humility"; submission before those one hates into "obedience" (namely to One of whom they say commanded this submission,—they name him God). The inoffensiveness of the weak one, cowardice itself, in which he is rich, his standing-at-the-door,

his unavoidable need to wait acquires good names such as "patience." what is also called virtue *itself*: the inability to avenge [das Sich-nicht-rächen-Können] is named not wanting vengeance [Sich-nicht-rächen-Wollen]. perhaps even forgiveness ("for *they* know not what they do—we alone know what *they* do!"). One also talks of the "love of one's enemies"—and sweats while talking of this.[10]

"HAPPY MONSTERS"

But how are we to understand Nietzsche's story of the origin of social organization? In what way does this ideal community of heroes issue forth from the primal (linguistic) separation of, on the one hand, *good* persons who ascend out of a spark of natural energy and genius from, on the other hand, *bad* individuals who, estranged from nature, instrumentally employ the resentful spirit of money and selfish eyes to destroy all that which is naturally heroic in humankind?

> With the excellent ones who create the fundamental concept of "good" straight away and spontaneously. that is. conceived from out of itself and from this arises the first imagination of "bad" it is just the opposite! This "bad" of excellent origin and that "evil" from the cauldron of unsatisfied hatred [ungesättigten Hasses]—the first an imitation. an additional gesture: the second. in contrast. the original. the beginning. the actual deed in the conception of a slave-morality—how differently do both words "bad" and "evil" stand against the apparently same concept "good"! But it is *not* the same concept "good": quite the contrary. one should indeed ask *who* is actually "evil" in regard to the morality of *ressentiment*. Strictly answered: the very "good" of the other morality. that of the excellent. powerful. dominating ones [der Vornehme. der Mächtige. der Herrschende]. only coloured. re-interpreted and seen again through the poisonous eye of *ressentiment*.[11] (2.2)

Regardless of how one romanticizes the elite community that we come across in Nietzsche's later work, one (profoundly uneasy) thing remains. In contrast to Hölderlin's gestures to a preeminent and secret "race" (7.1)—and this includes his later, episodic invocation of the "German race," *Deutsch[es] Geschlecht* (Fragment 72; 8.1)—Nietzsche's projection of "excellent races," *vornehmene Rassen, vonehme Geschlechter* (9.1), is precisely that: a racist phantasm.

Because the infestation of racism is more present in Nietzsche's work than we may tend to think, it is unfortunately impossible to illuminate the keystone of his Dionysian thought without stumbling across at least one of its (glaringly) inhuman outbursts. We have treaded lightly over some of Nietzsche's less explicit racist moments—for instance, when he declares in his reflections on *Völker und Väterlander*: "These Englishmen are no race of philosophers," *philosophische Rasse* (1.2).

But racism is at the core of this destined cosmological death-struggle. Thus Nietzsche uses the word "race" to name the timeless identities not only of those who are superior, but also of those who are forever damned. "A race [Rasse] of such humans of *ressentiment* will necessarily be *more clever* than that of an excellent race," he reveals, "it will also honour cleverness in a completely difference way."[12]

Those who participate in Nietzsche's cosmic death-struggle are not only Germanic in origin. While describing the primal reunion with nature (which transcends civilization and for which all elevated beings sometimes lust), we are given a menu of preeminent tribes who exemplify this racial affliction:

> from time to time this hidden ground needed release, the animal must be let out once again, must return once more back to the wilderness—Roman, Arabic, Germanic, Japanese nobility, Homeric heroes, Scandinavian Vikings—in regard to this need they are all the same.[13]

But even the inter-cultural spirit of this predatory-state that overcomes that of an inauthentic cultural one has a sinister tendency to fade into Nietzsche's infamous phantasm of *the blond, Germanic beast.*

> The deep, icy mistrust that the German [der Deutsche] evokes as soon as he has power, also again in the present—is still the aftermath of that inextinguishable horror that held Europe for centuries from the wrath of blond, Germanic beasts [der blonden germanischen Bestie].[14]

Although he goes on to say that there is little to no relationship between these ancient Germanic heroes and the modern Germans of the present, given the recent explosion of racism that the English Empire, among others, ignites in the nineteenth century, Nietzsche's willingness to celebrate a pale, white colored, cruel ruler from northern Europe—"a blond race"[15]—is unusually unsettling.

But most tragic about Nietzsche's racism is that it neutralizes the spirit of the "democratic god par excellence" (7) that his otherwise brilliant insights work so hard to retrieve. As we have seen, Hölderlin's "happy madness," *frohlockender Wahnsinn* (v 47), which the poet derives from Dionysian "enjoyment," *frohlocken*, also shades into nationalism, as when Hölderlin praises "the height and pure joyfulness of patriotic songs," *das höhe und reine Frohlocken vaterländischer Gesänge.*[16] The absorption of Dionysus's earthly and communal ecstasy into Nietzsche's projection of "happy monsters," *frohlockende Ungeheuer*, is, nevertheless, an appalling new low.

> Here we want at least to not deny one thing: he who acquaints himself with those "good ones" only as enemies acquaints himself also with nothing other than evil enemies, and these same humans who so strictly through custom,

reverence, rite, thankfulness, though still more through mutual protection, through jealousy *inter pares* are held within limits, who otherwise prove themselves in their behaviour among each other to be so inventive in regard, self-control, delicacy, loyalty, pride and friendship—they are with respect to what is outside, there where the foreign, the foreign ones begin, not much better than beasts-of-prey who have been cut loose. There they enjoy freedom from all social demand, they harmlessly behold the tension in the wilderness which emerges from a long imprisonment and enclosure in the peace of community, they enter back into the innocence of the predator-conscience, as happy monsters [frohlockende Ungeheuer] who perhaps after a despicable sequence of murder, burning-down, rape, and torture walk away with a high-spiritedness and balance of soul as if only a student-prank has been executed, convinced that the poets once again have something about which to sing and praise.[17] (9.1)

The monstrous, unnatural spirit of this passage invites the question: In what way is the natural potential of Nietzsche's "Dionysian philosophy" tortured, raped and murdered by his own immature (student) mentality?

"NOT ONLY ONWARD, BUT ALSO UPWARD SHOULD YOU PLANT"

Nietzsche's productive insights into the danger of visual culture and money that emerge in and descend into industrialization from the early historic period in Greece (2.2) are tragically plundered, for instance, by his need to see all Jews as belonging to an unproductive race for humankind.

Consider again the monetized, "bourgeois mediocrity" (2.2) that is inextricably tied to vengeful, "pointed eyes" (5.3) and thus also "the poisonous eye of *ressentiment*," *das Giftauge des Ressentiment* (2.1) that kills the tragic play. As we have noted, "Greek art and especially [vornehmlich] Greek tragedy resisted above all the destruction [Vernichtung] of myth" (2.2).

But even the early Nietzsche makes it clear that the undertones of his *visualized chronotope* can give way to a racist phantasm of Semites secretly conspiring to murder "Greek art and especially [vornehmlich] Greek tragedy." We have noted his following declaration: "Destruction [Vernichtung] of Greek culture through the Jewish world" (8.3).

The "excellent race," *vornehme Rasse* (9.1), of Greece through whom the genius of tragedy ascends is thus "destroyed," *vernichtet*, by the "*more clever*" *monetized* and *visualized* "slave-morality" (9.2) of the Jews. We should note the textual proximity of Nietzsche's reference to "the poisonous eye of *ressentiment*" to, just a few pages later, his infamous "blond, Germanic beast," and other such "happy monsters" (9.2). "Everything that has been done on earth against 'the excellent ones,' the violent ones, the masters, the

powerful ones, ['die Vornehmen,' 'die Gewaltigen,' 'die Herren,' 'die Mach-
thaber'], is not worth mentioning," he declares,

> in comparison with that which *the Jews* have done against them: the Jews, that
> priestly people who knew how to effect satisfaction on their enemies and
> conquerors with finally a radical devaluation of their values, that is an act of
> *spiritual vengeance* [*geistigen Rache*]. (2.1)[18]

The most obvious (and perhaps most tragic) absorption of Nietzsche's
"Dionysian philosophy" (4.1) into a self-destructive nationalism and racism
is that which the *Übermensch* suffers. As we have seen, *der Übermensch* "is
the meaning of earth" (5.1). The terrestrial significance of this being is elaborated as the catalyst of an oceanic cleansing in the present. Modern humans
are "a dirty river" (5.1). And this godlike, earthly essence "is this sea" in
which their "vast contempt [Verachtung] can perish" (5.1). The purification
to which the *Übermensch* points, insofar as it battles against those who with
"treacherous eyes," *verrätersich*[e] *Augen* (5.4, 6.2), "jingle with their gold"
(5.1), can be seen as a battle against *monetized* and *visualized chronotopes* in
the nineteenth century.

Such a battle suggests that behind Nietzsche's *Übermensch* is his retrieval
and adaptation of the chthonic spirit of Dionysus. Just as the prophet Teiresias foretells of the liberation that Dionysus's epiphany in lightning shall
open out to battle the (*monetized* and *visualized*) tyrant Pentheus in *Bacchae*
(v 274–80, 282, 286, 209–10),[19] Zarathustra prophesies to the (similarly
monetized and *visualized*) crowd before him: "'Behold, I teach you the
Übermensch: he is this lightning [Blitz], he is your madness [Wahnsinn]!'"
(5.1). This coincidence significantly repeats. "'Behold, I am a preacher of
lightning [Blitz] and a heavy drop from the cloud: but this lightning [Blitz] is
named *Übermensch*'" (6.3). As we have seen, Nietzsche's central Dionysian
myth crescendos with a community *Of higher humans, Von höheren Menschen*, who begin to dance ecstatically through space and time.

> "Raise your hearts, my brothers, high higher! And also, for me, do not forget
> your legs! Raise also your legs, you good dancers, and better still: stand on
> your heads!" (6.4)

The cosmic meaning that Nietzsche reintroduces to humankind through
the epiphany of the *Übermensch* concludes—perhaps like *Bacchae* con-
cluded in Greece[20]—with the elevated spirit of *Dionysiac language*. "I want
to teach humans the significance of their being [Sein]: which is the
Übermensch, the lightning [Blitz]-out-of-dark-clouds human" (6.3). The
mystery of this teaching is revealed, finally, in the

crown of the laughing one, this rose-wreathed crown: to you, my brothers, I throw this crown! Laughter I say is holy: you higher humans, *learn* for me—to laugh! (6.4)

As we have also seen, *Zarathustra* teaches "the will to power," *der Wille zur Macht* (6.3). Here too I have sought to show that there is something redeeming—even Dionysian—about this new cosmic force. That this "will" is crucial for the revelation of the earthly and communal spirit of the *Übermensch* is clear. "Your will says: the *Übermensch* is the meaning of earth!" (5.1). In particular, I have argued that Nietzsche battles the nineteenth-century origins of our "homogenised sensibility of our hyper-monetised, atomised, and self-destructive culture of the unlimited" (1.1) by calling into question the relatively recent tendency in modern time to reduce nature and human life to unlimited masses of discrete, exchangeable (and visible) phenomena—what we might call a scientific style of the precondition of mass concentrated capitalism. Thus Zarathustra rebels against "these preachers of equality" whose "souls," given their anti-Dionysian spirit, lack the earthly magic of "honey" (6.3).

At the core of this "tyrannical-insanity of powerlessness" (6.2) is the perverse desire "[t]o *make* all beings thinkable" (6.2). One recalls the modern *monetized* and *visualized* spirit of Hölderlin's Oedipus.[21] This brings us to a thoughtful reflection on mortality. Because *the will to power* and *the will to life* are not identical, Nietzsche understands the desire to live as the medium through which the desire for force ceaselessly expresses itself (6.3). Those who embrace *der Wille zur Macht* thus embrace not only life, but also that through which the spirit of life is reborn, namely the cosmological significance of destruction and finally death (6.3).

In light of Nietzsche's explicit racism, however, it is not difficult to see Zarathustra as the prophet of a master race. Although the *Übermensch* is Dionysian, that is, like Dionysus he secretly and mystically embodies "the meaning of earth," the name *Übermensch* and the phrase *Sinn der Erde* evoke the master races to which Nietzsche often gestures. One thinks of "the masters of earth," *Herrn der Erde* (9.1).

This drags us back into the glaringly non-democratic (and non-Dionysian) orbit of Nietzschean racism. Zarathustra's critique of "these preachers of equality" is often seen as a cry against social democracy and the ethics of universal human rights. What is potentially a creative adaption of the earthly and communal spirit of Dionysus to challenge money and its reckless media culture in modern time degenerates into that which excuses (and even legitimates) precisely that against which tragedy battles, namely reckless individualism that encompasses racism and murder.

"Only where life is, is there also the will: but not the will to life, but instead, so I teach you—will to power!

To those who are living there is much that is prized more highly than life itself; indeed from out of this prizing itself speaks—the will to power!
And who must be a creator in good and evil: truly, he must also first be a destroyer [Vernichter] and shatterer of values." (6.3)

This invites to us to wonder: What is it, precisely, that Nietzsche is farming in *Zarathustra*? Are we to look forward joyfully to a more communal and earthly experience of human life? Or are we to feel the icy shudder that accompanies the thought that a master (mostly white and German) race shall emerge whose self-serving cleansing of the present knows no (ethical) limit? It is not difficult to imagine the *Übermensch* as just another "beast-of-prey" (9.2) and "the last human" (5.1) as just another eternal Jew (9.2) who is still standing in the way of that which Nietzsche secretly truly wants: "for I am already touching upon something *serious* to me, on the 'European problem,' as I understand it, on the breeding [Züchtung] of a new ruling caste for Europe" (1.1). One recalls Zarathustra's declaration, already in *Book One*: "Not only onward should you plant [pflanzen], but also upward!"[22]

NOTES

1. GM, in *Friedrich Nietzsche, Kritische Studienausgabe*, ed. G. Colli and M. Montinari, vol. 5, *Jenseits von Gut und Böse, Zur Genealogie der Moral* (Berlin: de Gruyter, 1999), 274–77.
2. Ibid., 282.
3. Ibid., 277.
4. Ibid.
5. Ibid., 282.
6. Ibid., 281.
7. Ibid.
8. Lucas Murrey, *Hölderlin's Dionysiac Poetry: The Terrifying-Exciting Mysteries* (Heidelberg, New York, Dordrecht, London: Springer, 2015), chapter 8 (8).
9. GM, in *Nietzsche, Kritische Studienausgabe*, vol. 5, 281.
10. Ibid., 281–82.
11. Ibid., 274.
12. Ibid., 272–73.
13. Ibid., 275.
14. Ibid., 275–76.
15. Ibid., 263.
16. Murrey, *Hölderlin's Dionysiac Poetry*, 9, 10.3, 11.1, 12.4, 14.4.
17. GM, in *Nietzsche, Kritische Studienausgabe*, vol. 5, 274–75.
18. Ibid., 267.
19. Murrey, *Hölderlin's Dionysiac Poetry*, 2.3, 6.2, 9.1.
20. For the significance of Dionysus's lost speech at the end of Euripides'ss tragedy that (most likely) announced the foundation of his cult in Thebes, which I discuss in regard to Hölderlin, see Murrey, *Hölderlin's Dionysiac Poetry*, 2.3.
21. Murrey, *Hölderlin's Dionysiac Poetry*, 9.1, 11.1.
22. Z, in *Friedrich Nietzsche, Kritische Studienausgabe*, ed. Giorgio Colli and Mazzino Montinari, vol. 4, *Also sprach Zarathustra. Ein Buch für Alle und Keinen* (Berlin: de Gruyter, 1999), 90.

Chapter Nine

Purification of the Race

"THE WISDOM OF HIM WHO IS NOT ONLY THE GOD OF THE JEWS"

To comprehend the nationalism and racism into which Nietzsche's "Dionysian philosophy" (4.1) degenerates, we must place his *proto-National Socialist chronotope* within the historical context from which it emerges. And to do this we must turn not only to the retrieval of ancient Greece in modern Germany, but also to a retrieval of ancient India.

As we have seen, Nietzsche follows Hölderlin's invocation of the ancient picture of Dionysus returning to Greece after conquering the Indians (3.1).[1] "Yes, my friends," he exclaims, "You shall lead the Dionysian festival procession from India to Greece!" (7.2, 8.3). This evokes Hölderlin's gesture to India as an Eastern civilization of sorts to Greece—and this means as the source of an original "race" (7.1). Hyperion speaks of a secret *"Volk* of rare excellence" who descend from out of "the depths of Asia" (7.1).

But this romantic turn eastward should not surprise us. Already in 1786 the Anglo-Welsh philologist William Jones, in a way that has little to do with Indology, makes the influential discovery that Latin, Greek, and Sanskrit must "have sprung from some common source."[2] Hölderlin's sentimental (and mentally unstable) love of Greece—one thinks of the beginning of *The Only One*:

> What is it, that
> Binds me to the ancient, sacred coasts
> That I love still more
> Than my *Vaterland?* (v 1–3)[3]

—even recalls the melancholy confession of the English statesman Warren Hastings: "in truth I love India a little more than my own country."[4] The

97

future voyage with which Hölderlin's poetic *Memento* culminates is a journey to the "forefathers" who arose "[i]n the forests of the Indus" and from
whom the glorious German spirit of tomorrow shall—somehow?—ascend.[5]

As we have seen in the introduction, the "desolate time," *dürftig[e] Zeit* (v
122),[6] that Hölderlin associates with a visual culture that underlies the *unlimitedness* of modern greed and money expands exponentially in the nineteenth
century. This rapid and protracted increase in the estrangement of humans
from nature and themselves (alongside unprecedented population growth)
deepens, in turn, the need for a romantic dream of purgation and release. The
fantasy of a homecoming to an ancient, original world of linguistic and
cultural unity thus accelerates its velocity. This is also easy enough to understand. Given the growing presence of science, the bourgeoisie, and secularization, the search for a sociopolitical form to organize the formless mass of
unlimited (urban) sadness is simultaneously a search for a godlike leader
who can re-enchant an increasingly disenchanted cosmos.

Jones's discovery in 1786 of "the common source"—in German *eine
gemeinsame Quelle*[7] —from which Latin, Greek, and Sanskrit must "have
sprung" prepares the way for research in Germany on Indian epics, hymns,
and myths—what is also named "Indian philosophy." Friedrich Schlegel's
1808 *On the language and wisdom of the Indians*[8] is followed by the work of
Franz Bopp and the rise of popular new concepts such as a "linguistic family," *Sprachfamilie*, that, in turn, kindle the idea of an original language,
Ursprache, and an original people, *Urvolk*. Specifically, it is the concept of
an ancient race of "Aryans" that is introduced into German science by I. F.
Klenker through his translation of (the French orientalist) Abraham Anquetil-
Duperron's *Zend-Avesta. Ouvrage de Zoroatre* from 1771:[9] the sacred texts
of Zoroastrianism, the so-called Iranian counterpart to the Indo-Aryan Vedas—that gains in popularity. Klenker's introduction of the new concept of
"Aryans" into German culture creates a bridge, for instance, between the
work of Bopp (and such concepts as *Sprachfamilie*, *Ursprache*, and *Urvolk*)
and the work of Christian Lassen (whose concept of an "Indo-Germanic
people," *indogermanische Völker*, is popular in Germany already in the
1830s)—and opens the door between linguistics, biology, and anatomy.[10]

Important for Nietzsche are the (racially oriented) concepts of Max
Müller. For Müller, the study of "Indo-Germanic people" is an exploration of
the origin of humankind in a way that transcends the narrow confines of
Judaism. This is clear in his description of the goal of his work, *History of
Ancient Sanskrit Literature* from 1859, which is "to discover in the first gems
of the language, religion and mythology of our forefathers, the wisdom of
Him who is not the God of the Jews only."[11] Having "perfected society and
morals," Müller goes on, the "Aryan nations . . . have been the prominent
actors in the great drama of history."[12]

Such praise of these secret "rulers of history" (that is, "their mission to link all the parts of the world together by the chains of civilization, commerce, and religion") enhances interest in physiological studies (such as those undertaken by Carl Vogt) suggesting that this original race "is tall, dolichocephalic (has a longer, thinner skull), light-skinned, blue-eyed and blond."[13] The spiritual and physiological characteristics of this original race then combines with Social Darwinism. Survival of the races now depends on what Herbert Spencer famously names the "survival of the fittest" in his 1864 study *Principles of Biology*.

Tragically, this search for the secret, real physical and spiritual origin of humankind harmonizes with the anti-Semitism that erupts in Germany during the mid to late nineteenth century. No longer understood as a confession, but as an (unchanging) biological identity—something, incidentally, that many Jews accepted (and would still accept today)—Judaism becomes an inauthentic, Eastern religion that is to be conquered by the (timelessly) authentic *other* Eastern religions of India and Persia which, descending through Greece, directly (both in spirit and biologically) manifest themselves in modern Germans.

The persistent belief that India is "the Asia of Greece"[14] is taken seriously already toward the end of the nineteenth and beginning of the twentieth centuries. Witness "the meaning" that Max Weber ascribes to "India" in regard to "ancient Greece," as well as Wilhelm Schwaner's work *The German Bible. From the Sacred Texts of Germanic Peoples* (1904–1905, second edition 1910), which views the *Vedas* as the true (non-Jewish) "Old Testament"[15] of the Germans.

For Schwaner, the ancient Indians with their language, religion, mythology, and wisdom are, in truth, "our forefathers"—and by "our forefathers" Schwaner means modern Germans are the northern branch of this superior race, namely the "Aryans."[16] Such an outlandish, grotesque mythology, supported by the emerging sciences of religion and linguistics in the nineteenth century, polarizes not only Semitic vs. Hellenic (Japhetic), but also Semitic vs. Aryan and Swabian languages.[17] This new wave of modern (lingo-) anti-Semitism is further plagued by an anxiety of death initiated (in the diseased brains of racists) by the Jews, as is implicit in the many editions of Wilhelm Marr's *Victory of Jewry over Germandom*[18] (published throughout the 1870s—first edition in 1873; fifth edition, 1879).

"THE ARYAN CONQUERING RACE"

For Nietzsche, who is reading Müller (and aware of Spencer's adaption of Darwinism),[19] the anti-Semitism of Germany in the mid to late nineteenth century offers him a chance to invent a new racist program. Although he tends to distance himself from a few of the many "solutions" to "the Jewish problem"—as proposed, for instance, by his brother-in-law Bernhard Förster (who, unable to free Europe of the Jews, eventually founds the colony *New Germany* in Paraguay in 1888—here we should note the significance of the fact that Nietzsche is well aware of contemporary conversations about the founding of a Jewish state in Palestine, Uganda, and Madagascar)—he nevertheless prefers the anti-Semitic concept of (total) assimilation.

This brings Nietzsche close to the anti-Semitism of Wagner, whose anonymous essay "Judaism in Music" Wagner republishes under his own name in 1869—that is, just a few years before *The Birth of Tragedy out of the Spirit of Music*.

But to understand Nietzsche's anti-Semitism, one must first understand the threat to Germans (and humankind) that he feels the Jews represent. Writing in the early 1880s, Nietzsche reflects:

> In our schools Jewish history is presented as sacred: Abraham is more important to us than any person from Greek or German history. And from him that which we feel from David's psalms is so different from than that which excites us when we read Pindar or Petrarch that it seems to be a foreign home. [20]

"This train of products from an Asian, very distant and very peculiar race," Nietzsche proceeds, because Christianity turns not to "people," but instead to individual "humans," has never felt guilty about dividing "the humans of an Indo-Germanic race" with "the religious-break of Semitic people." [21]

Given his fantasy of a special (spiritual, linguistic, and biological) relationship between ancient Greece and modern Germany, Nietzsche's claims that the Jews murdered the Dionysian spirit of Greece expectedly appear alongside the first signs of his racist program. Statements from 1869 such as "Destruction [Vernichtung] of Greek culture through the Jewish world" (8.3) and "Victory [Sieg] of the Jewish world over the weakened will of Greek culture" occur just before he writes (sometime between September of 1870 and January of 1871) of the racial cleansing in which Germans must engage if they want to free themselves of the "[s]candalous theories" of "Judea!": "The vast work of the German being, the shaking off of that foreign, unnational yoke; and it will succeed." [22] This means that we can draw a (rather continuous) line between the anti-Semitism of the early and late Nietzsche. "That Germany richly has *enough* Jews," he declares in the mid-1880s,

> that the German stomach and German blood have trouble (and shall for a long time have trouble), to be finished with this quantum of "Jew"—in the way that the Italians, the French and the English, because of stronger digestion, are finished with them—: that is the clear statement and language of a general instinct to which one must listen, according to which one must act. "Do not let

in any more Jews! And in particular shut the doors to those in the east (also in Austria)!"[23]

Nietzsche's lifelong anti-Semitism is a product of his general theory of races. This is shown in what he describes, a few years earlier, in regard to "[t]he purification of the race," *Die Reinigung der Rasse.*

> There are probably no pure races, but instead those that have become pure, and these only very rarely. The regular races are mixed and in them one always finds, alongside the disharmony of physical forms (for example when the eyes and mouth do not correspond to one another), the disharmony also of habits and concepts of values. (One heard Livingstone say: "God created white and black humans, but the devil created the crossed-races.") Mixed races are always the same as mixed cultures, mixed moralities: they are mostly more evil, cruel and restless. Purity is finally the result of countless adjustments, absorptions and eliminations, and the progress toward purity shows itself insofar as that present power in a race is *narrowed* more and more to a few selected functions, while before it had to concern itself with too many and often contradictory things: such a restriction will at the same time appear as if it was an *impoverishment* and needs be judged with care and delicately. But in the end, if the process of purification has succeeded, all the forces that formerly were wasted in the struggle of the disharmonious qualities are at the command of the entire organism: thus purified races are always *stronger* and *more beautiful.*—The Greeks give us the measure of a purified race and culture: and hopefully a pure European race and culture will succeed.[24]

Nietzsche's racial theory culminates in a death-battle between those whom he names *Aryans* and *Pre-Aryans.* The side to which the Jews (among others) timelessly belong is obvious. "These bearers of repressed and bottled-up instincts,"[25] he declares,

> these descendants of all European and non-European slavery, specifically the whole pre-Aryan population—they represent the decline of humanity! These "tools of culture" are a disgrace to humans, and in fact a suspicion, a counter-argument against "culture" in general! One may be justified in always fearing the blond beast of the excellent races and being on one's guard: but who would not a hundred times prefer to be afraid if one, at the same time, is able to admire, rather than to be free of fear, but to remain within the disgusting glance of the distorted, the dwarfed, the stunted, the poisoned [Vergifteten]? And is this not our doom?[26]

Alarming also is the extent to which Nietzsche's racism festers within his diatribe against modern sociopolitics. All nuance and subtlety of his (otherwise profound) retrieval of Dionysus disappears.

> Who can guarantee that modern democracy, still more modern anarchy, and indeed that tendency to the "Commune," the most primitive form of society,

which is now common to all Socialists in Europe, does not in its main essence signify a monstrous *reversion*—and that the conqueror- and master-race, the Aryan race, is not also becoming physiologically inferior?[27]

We have noted the "parasites" and the "juices" from which they "nourish themselves" (8.3) in *The Birth of Tragedy*. Now the non-Aryan, "worm 'human,'" *das Gewürm "Mensch,"* steps "into the foreground and swarms."[28] The problem, according to Nietzschean racism, is,

> that the "tame human," beyond-help, mediocre and unpleasant, has learned to feel himself as the goal and peak, as the meaning of history, as "higher humans";—yes that he has a certain right to feel like this because of his distance to the superabundance of the failed, sickly, tired and exhausted, from whom Europe today has begun to reek, as long as he is at least relatively successful, at least still capable of living, at least saying "yes" to life.[29]

The presence of this "pre-Aryan population" is a threat not only for "Germany," but also for "all of Europe" where "the conquered race once again obtained the upper hand, in complexion, shortness of the skull, perhaps even in intellectual and social instincts."[30]

Deep within the gloomy, un-beautiful caverns of Nietzsche's anti-Semitic, pro-Indo-Germanic racist program lurks a *proto-National Socialist language*. This means not only a style of speaking and writing that promotes a racist German language, but also the appropriation of language itself as a universal phenomenon that—somehow?—legitimates such German racism.

> In Latin *malus* (which I place alongside *melas*) could have signified the vulgar man as the dark coloured one, above all the black-haired one ("*hic niger est—*"), as the pre-Aryan inhabitants of Italian earth whose complexion formed the clearest distinction from the dominating blondes, namely the Aryan conquering race.[31]

But language is active not only in its genesis of reality; it aggressively destroys the language (and reality) of the non-German other. The "traces of lost languages" that endure in the present echo the time when their original linguistic forces succumbed to the superiority of "the Indo-Germanic languages"—that is, the historical instant when their speakers were "attacked and conquered" by "the wandering Indo-Germanic tribes," *indogermanische Wanderstämme*, and "the language of the conqueror was just as victorious and passed on to those conquered."[32]

For Nietzsche, the only heart of humankind that is to be recognized is the one that resides within the epiphany of an Indo-Germanic language whose philosophical and poetic genius founded the preeminence of "the Aryan conquering race."

The inventors of the Indo-Germanic language had probably belonged to the highest class and used the present, less valuable languages. A high philosophical and poetic education spoke from out of them and formed a corresponding language: this is a self-conscious art-product: it takes musical, poetic genius. For it was a poetic- and wise-language that was later distributed through the next classes and wandered outwards with the warrior tribes [Kriegstämmen]. This was the most precious legacy of home to which one strongly held.[33]

Insofar as language is subservient to the cruel, if creative rulers from whom it springs, the word is a passive tool through which this band of hyperactive, psychotic leaders (arbitrarily) decide what is "good" and what is named "bad."

Indeed, they call themselves in perhaps the most frequent instances simply after their superiority in power (e.g. "the powerful," "the lords," "the commanders"), or after the most obvious sign of their superiority, as for example "the rich," "the possessors" (that is the meaning of arya: and the Iranian and Slavic languages correspond).[34]

"ZARATHUSTRA ... IN THE ARYAN PROVINCE"

Given his insight into Dionysian Greece (3) and adaption of this earthly and communal spirit to challenge modern money and its distracting visual culture (4–6), it is painful to witness Nietzsche degrade his *Dionysiac chronotope* and *language* with the vulgar and finally weak spirit of racism. His critique of the *monetized chronotope*—the "bourgeois mediocrity" (2.2) that cleverly (if perhaps also unconsciously) evokes the precious metal of both Greece in the fifth century B.C.E. and Europe in the nineteenth century—degenerates into the (banal) anti-Semitic belief that being Jewish can only mean seeking "interest in gold" (9.1).

The perception of the dangerous style of seeing that accompanies money—Nietzsche's criticism of "the poisonous eye of *ressentiment*," *das Giftauge des Ressentiment* (2.1)—is absorbed into his fantasy of a non-Indo-Germanic, mostly Semitic, "poisoned" people: the *Vergiftete* ones, an inferior race exhibiting "the disharmony of physical forms (for example, when the eyes and mouth do not correspond to one another)" (10.2). Nietzsche's use of Dionysus thus shipwrecks on the modern reef about which it sets sail. For what could be more *monetized* and recklessly visual than modern racism that culminates, finally, in (mechanized) mass murder?[35] One thinks of the Nazi Holocaust and Israeli destruction of Palestine.

Nietzsche's *proto-National Socialist chronotope* even absorbs the Dionysian spirit of Zarathustra (4–6) who at times can recall Teiresias in *Bacchae* (9.3). In fact, while celebrating Hölderlin as his *Lieblingsdichter* in the 1860s, the excited youth also celebrates "[t]he religion of Zoroaster."[36] Later

Nietzsche praises the time when his Persian hero "went into the Aryan province and composed the *Avesta* in the ten years of his loneliness in the mountains."[37] "[T]he act of a monstrous purification [ungeheure Reinigung] and consecration of humankind"[38] that Nietzsche associates with *Zarathustra* thus evokes not only the ancient power of Dionysus to cleanse a community of *monetized* and *visualized chronotopes* (3.3), but also alas Nietzsche's phantasmagorical "purification of the race," *Reinigung der Rasse* (10.2)— that is, the modern power of the "monsters," *Ungeheuer* (9.2) of "the Aryan conquering race" (10.2) to liberate Germany (and the entire world) from the (mostly Semitic) "monstrous [ungeheure] intrusive powers from the outside" (8.2). "The new problem," after all, is "whether or not *a part of humanity* is to be bred into a higher race at the costs of others."[39] And as we have seen, Zarathustra declares to his disciples: "Not only onward should you plant [pflanzen], but also upward!" (9.3).

But that the Dionysian hero of Nietzsche's central myth degenerates into a prophet of racism is perhaps something that should not surprise us. Upon closer inspection, the potential for such racial purgation is always present. "The myth of Prometheus is an original procession of the entire Aryan tribes,"[40] Nietzsche writes already in *The Birth of Tragedy*,

> and a document of their talent for the profoundly tragic, yes it may well be possible that this myth has the same characteristic meaning within the essence of the Aryan as that of the myth of original sin has for the Semites, and that between both of these myths a relationship like that of brother and sister exists.[41]

Before we underestimate the violence that erupts within the tyrannical family (for instance, between brothers and sisters), let us not forget the aggression that Nietzsche, like many people, associates with the Jews. His comment about the violence of Jews toward non-Jews through the biblical story that Germany is forced to hold sacred—"[i]n our schools Jewish history is presented as holy" (10.2)—gives way to the conspicuous death-struggle that Nietzsche sees Jewish people initiating in modern time. "In regard to the spectacles that the next century will invite us to see,"[42] he writes in the early 1880s,

> is the decision about the fate of the European Jews. That they have cast their die, have crossed the Rubicon, is wholly clear: the only thing that remains for them is either to become the masters of Europe or to lose Europe, as they once a long time ago lost Egypt where they were confronted with a similar either-or fate.[43]

Like many of his countrymen, Nietzsche is not going to give up without a fight, and the (potential) genocide of Indo-Germanic, Aryan races to which

Socraticism, Christianity, and Judaism lead can be redeemed only through the adaption of tragedy. Those who suffer the death of authentic art for which traditional philosophers, Christians, and Jews are responsible must, "like Oedipus first succeed to the meadow of the Eumenides."[44] I have noted the styles of *Dionysian seeing* and *language*, for instance, in the joyous torch-lit procession with which Aeschylus's tragic play culminates (v 1021–46).[45] I have also noted the "state of ecstasy" in which Wagner remained "to the close of the *Eumenides*" (2.2). Finally, like Hölderlin, Nietzsche directly refers to these earthly goddesses of revenge in regard to *Oedipus at Kolonus*.[46]

But unlike Hölderlin, Nietzsche transforms the Greek transformation of ritual for the stage to reinforce a racist program. Thus the goal of the "*tragic time*" (6.2) that he foretells

> takes the higher-breeding [Höherzüchtung] of humanity in the hands, including the relentless destruction [Vernichtung] of everything degenerate and parasitical [Entartenden und Parasitischen].[47]

Only such a modern (and massive) "purification of the race"—and this means only after "humanity has acquired consciousness of the hardest, but most necessary wars, *but without suffering*"—"will the excess of life on earth be made possible, and from which the Dionysian condition must grow again."[48]

To conclude this chapter, I would like to make clear that Nietzsche's greatest tragedy is his dismemberment of *Dionysiac language* with a *proto-National Socialist language*. The communally constructive (and hence universal) "underground and birth place of the word" (3.3) that tragedy reveals is consumed by his unfortunate, even childish need to raise the German language above all other languages.

> For he who has sinned against the German language has desecrated the mystery of all our Germanness: throughout all the mixing and change of nationalities and customs only the German language, as if through a metaphysical magic, has saved itself and with it the German spirit. It alone also conceals the spirit for the future, if it does not itself fall prey to the sacrilegious hands of the present. "But Di meliora" Away pachyderms, away with you! This is the German language, in which humans express themselves, yes, in which the great poets and great thinkers have sung and written. "Hands down!"[49]

What makes this outlandish belief that the German language is superior to other languages particularly problematic is the way that Nietzsche conceals this perversion in his derangement of the secret language of ritual. As I have shown, the sociopolitics of mystery-cult is preserved by Dionysian initiates who regard its language as sacred and shroud its magical powers in secrecy.[50] When Nietzsche openly declares that his texts are intended "only for a few select ears," however, he means "only for a few select ears" of a "higher" race, that is, "the excellent ones," *die Vornehmen*.[51] In contrast to the priests of Dionysus—and in contrast to Hölderlin's wandering Dionysian, German "poets" (v 57; v 59; 7.1), Nietzsche's wandering poets and philosophers are the leaders of elevated "warrior-races," *Kriegstämmen* (10.2). Through their retrieval of "the root," *Wurzel*, of words and their construction of self-aggrandizing (and thus arbitrary) concepts like "the truthful,"[52] these poetic and philosophical warriors legitimate not only the superiority of the Indo-Germanic/Aryan races, but, still more important, the secret dominance of the (oppressed) German race in modern time. One thinks of Stefan George and Martin Heidegger.

NOTES

1. Lucas Murrey, *Hölderlin's Dionysiac Poetry: The Terrifying-Exciting Mysteries* (Heidelberg, New York, Dordrecht, London: Springer, 2015), chapter 9.2 (9.2).

2. William Jones, "The Third Anniversary Discourse, on the Hindus," delivered to the *Asiatic Society* on 2 February 1786. Cited in William Jones, *Selected Poetical and Prose Works*, ed. Michael Franklin (Cardiff: University of Wales Press, 1995), 361.The *Sanskrit* language, whatever be its antiquity, is of a wonderful structure; more perfect than the *Greek*, more copious than the *Latin*, and more exquisitely refined than either, yet bearing to both of them a stronger affinity, both in the roots of verbs and the forms of grammar, than could possibly have been produced by accident; so strong indeed, that no philologer could examine them all three, without believing them to have sprung from some common source, which, perhaps, no longer exists; there is a similar reason, though not quite so forcible, for supposing that both the *Gothic* and the *Celtic*, though blended with a very different idiom, had the same origin with the *Sanskrit*; and the old *Persian* might be added to the same family.

3. Cited in Murrey, *Hölderlin's Dionysiac Poetry*, 9.2.

4. See Hastings's "Letter to Nathaniel Smith" (from the *Bhagvat-Geeta*). Cited in Peter Marshall, *The British Discovery of Hinduism in the Eighteenth Century* (Cambridge: Cambridge University Press, 1970), 184–91.

5. Murrey, *Hölderlin's Dionysiac Poetry*, 9.4, 12.4.

6. Ibid., 8.

7. See Hubert Cancik, *Nietzsches Antike, Vorlesung*, 2. Auflage (Stuttgart: J. P. Metzler, 2000), 125.

8. Friedrich Schlegel, *Über die Sprache und Weisheit der Indier, Ein Beitrag zur Begründung der Alterthumskunde* (Heidelberg: Mohr und Zimmer, 1808).

9. Incidentally, Anquetil-Duperron's subsequent work from 1801 to 1802, *Oupnek*, which presents fifty Upanishads (that had been translated from Sanskrit into Persian in 1656, and which he then translates from Persian into Latin), is the book through which Arthur Schopenhauer first encounters Indian philosophy.

10. For the "scientific" linguistic roots that underlay the myth of "Aryans" in Germany, see Ruth Römer, *Sprachwissenschaft und Rassenideologie in Deutschland* (München: Fink, 1989), 49.

11. Max Müller, *History of Ancient Sanskrit Literature* (London: AMS, 1978), 3, 13.

12. Ibid., 14.

13. Ibid., 15. See Cancik, *Nietzsches Antike, Vorlesung*, 2. Auflage 125.

14. See Schmidt, *Anthropologie*, vol. 2 (1865), 410. Cited in Cancik, *Nietzsches Antike, Vorlesung*, 2. Auflage 193, ft. 25.

15. Max Weber, *Gesammelte Aufsätze zur Religionsoziologie*, II (Tübingen: J. C. B. Mohr, 1972), 363. Wilhelm Schwaner, *Germanenbibel. Aus heiligen Schriften germanischer Völker*, 2 Bd. (Schlachtensee: Volkserzieherverlag, 1904–1905).

16. Ibid.

17. See Schmidt, *Anthropologie*, vol. 2 (1865), 410. Cited in Cancik, *Nietzsches Antike, Vorlesung*, 2. Auflage 193, ft. 25.

18. Wilhelm Marr, *Der Sieg des Judenthums ueber das Germanenthum* (Charleston: Nabu Press, 1879/2010).

19. In particular, Nietzsche is reading Müller's "Beiträge zur vergleichenden Religionswissenschaft" and his "Beiträge zur vergleichenden Mythologie und Ethnologie," which include the theme of Semitic monotheism. KB, in *Friedrich Nietzsche, Kritische Studienausgabe*, ed. Giorgio Colli and Mazzino Montinari, vol. 14, *Kommentar zu den Bänden 1–13* (Berlin: de Gruyter, 1988), 534–35. Potentially significant for this intellectual constellation is Nietzsche's friendship with Paul Deussen, the most interesting German Indologist and for whom the Upanishads and the philosophy of Kant and Schopenhauer were comparable.

20. NF3, in *Friedrich Nietzsche, Kritische Studienausgabe*, ed. Giorgio Colli and Mazzino Montinari, vol. 9, *Nachgelassene Fragmente, 1880–1882* (Berlin: de Gruyter, 1988), 21–22. "In unserem Schulen wird die jüdische Geschichte als die heilige vorgetragen: Abraham ist uns mehr als irgend eine Person der griechischen oder deutschen Geschichte: und von dem, was wir bei Davids Psalmen empfingen, ist das, was das Lesen Pindars oder Petrarca's in uns erregt, so verschieden wie die Heimat von der Fremde."

21. Ibid. Dieser Zug Erzeugnissen einer asiatischen, sehr fernen und sehr absonderlichen Rasse ist vielleicht inmitten der Verworrenheit unserer modernen Cultur eine der wenigen sicheren Erscheinungen, welche noch über dem Gegensatz von Bildung und Unbildung erhaben stehen: die stärkste sittliche Nachwirkung des Christenthums, welches sich nicht an Völker sondern an Menschen wendete und deshalb gar kein Arg dabei hatte, den Menschen der indogermanischen Rasse das Religionsbuch eines semitischen Volkes in die Hand zu geben.

22. NF1, in *Nietzsche, Kritische Studienausgabe*, ed. Giorgio Colli and Mazzino Montinari, vol. 7, *Nachgelassene Fragmente, 1869–1874* (Berlin: de Gruyter, 1988), 80. "Sieg der jüdischen Welt über den gewächten Willen der griechischen Kultur"; and 3 (76) 81. "Skandaleuse Theorie! Judaea!" Ibid., 100. "Ungeheure Arbeit des deutschen Wesens, jenes Fremde unnationale Joch abzuschütteln; und es gelingt ihm."

23. BGE, in *Friedrich Nietzsche, Kritische Studienausgabe*, ed. Giorgio Colli and Mazzino Montinari, vol. 5, *Jenseits von Gut und Böse, Zur Genealogie der Moral* (Berlin: de Gruyter, 1999), 193. Dass Deutschland reichlich *genug* Juden hat, dass der deutsche Magen, das deutsche Blut Noth hat (und noch auf lange Noth haben wird), um auch nur mit diesem Quantum "Jude" fertig zu werden—so wie der Italiäner, der Franzose, der Engländer fertig geworden sind, in Folge einer kräftigeren Verdauung—: das ist die deutliche Aussage und Sprache eines allgemeinen Instinktes, auf welchen man hören, nach welchem man handeln muss. "Keine neuen Juden mehr hinein lassen! Und namentlich nach dem Osten (auch nach Österreich) zu die Thore zusperren!"

24. D, in *Friedrich Nietzsche, Kritische Studienausgabe*, ed. Giorgio Colli and Mazzino Montinari, vol. 3, *Morgenröte, Idyllen aus Messina, Die fröhliche Wissenschaft* (Berlin: de Gruyter, 1999), 213–14. *Die Reinigung der Rasse*.—Es giebt wahrscheinlich keine reinen, sondern nur reingewordene Rassen, und diese in grosser Seltenheit. Das Gewöhnliche sind die gekreuzten Rassen, bei denen sich immer, neben der Disharmonie von Körperformen (zum Beispiel wenn Auge und Mund nicht zu einander stimmen), auch Disharmonien der Gewohnheiten und Werthbegriffe finden müssen. (Livingstone hörte Jemand sagen: "Gott schuf weisse und schwarze Menschen, der Teufel aber schuf die Halbrassen.") Gekreuzte Rassen sind stets zugleich auch gekreuzte Culturen, gekreuzte Moralitäten: sie sind meistens böser, grausamer, unruhiger. Die Reinheit ist das letzte Resultat von zahllosen Anpassungen, Einsaugungen und Ausscheidungen, und der Fortschritt zur Reinheit zeigt sich darin, dass die in einer Rasse vorhandene Kraft sich immer mehr auf einzelne ausgewählte Functionen *beschränkt*, während sie vordem zu viel und oft Widersprechendes zu besorgen hatte: eine solche Beschränkung wird sich immer zugleich auch wie eine *Verarmung* ausnehmen und will vorsichtig und zart beurtheilt sein. Endlich aber, wenn der Process der Reinigung gelungen ist, steht alle jene

Kraft, die früher bei dem Kampfe der disharmonischen Eigenschaften daraufgieng, dem ge-sammten Organismus zu Gebote: weshalb reingewordene Rassen immer auch *stärker* und *schöner* geworden sind.—Die Griechen geben uns das Muster einer reingewordenen Rasse und Cultur: und hoffentlich gelingt einmal auch eine reine europäische Rasse und Cultur.

25. GM, in *Nietzsche, Kritische Studienausgabe,* vol. 5, 277. "Diese Träger der niederdrückenden und vergeltungslüsternen Instinkte . . . ."

26. Ibid. die Nachkommen alles europäischen und nichteuropäischen Sklaventums, aller vorarischen Bevölkerung insonderheit—sie stellen den Rückgang der Menschheit dar! Diese "Werkzeuge der Kultur" sind eine Schande des Menschen, und eher ein Verdacht, ein Gegenar-gument gegen "Kultur" überhaupt! Man mag im besten Rechte sein, wenn man vor der blonden Bestie auf dem Grunde aller vornehmen Rassen die Furcht nicht los wird und auf der Hut ist: aber wer möchte nicht hundertmal lieber sich fürchten, wenn er zugleich bewundern darf, als sich nicht fürchten, aber dabei den ekelhaften Anblick des Missratenen, Verkleinerten, Verkümmerten, Vergifteten nicht mehr loswerden können? Und ist das nicht unser Verhängnis?

27. Ibid., 263. " . . . wer steht uns dafür, ob nicht die moderne Demokratie, der noch modernere Anarchismus und namentlich jener Hang zur 'commune,' zur primitivsten Gesells-chafts-Form, der allen Sozialisten Europas jetzt gemeinsam ist, in der Hauptsache einen unge-heuren *Nachschlag* zu bedeuten hat—und daß die Eroberer- und *Herren-Rasse,* die der Arier, auch physiologisch im Unterliegen ist?"

28. Ibid., 277. " . . . dass das Gewürm 'Mensch' im Vordergrunde ist und wimmelt . . . ."

29. Ibid. dass der "zahme Mensch," der Heillos-Mittelmässige und Unerquickliche bereits sich als Ziel und Spitze, als Sinn der Geschichte, als "höheren Menschen" zu fühlen gelernt hat—ja dass er ein gewisses Recht darauf hat, sich so zu fühlen, insofern er sich im Abstande von der Überfülle des Missratenen, Kränklichen, Müden, Verlebten fühlt, nach dem heute Europa zu stinken beginnt, somit als etwas wenigstens relativ Geratenes, wenigstens noch Lebensfähiges, wenigstens zum Leben Ja-sagendes.

30. Ibid., 263. " . . . vielmehr schlägt an diesen Stellen die *vorarische* Bevölkerung Deutsch-lands vor. (Das gleiche gilt beinahe für ganz Europa: im wesentlichen hat die unterworfne Rasse schließlich daselbst wieder die Oberhand bekommen, in Farbe, Kürze des Schädels, vielleicht sogar in den intellektuellen und sozialen Instinkten."

31. Ibid. "Im lateinischen *malus* (dem ich *melas* zur Seite stelle) könnte der gemeine Mann als der Dunkelfarbige, vor allem als der Schwarzhaarige ('hic niger est–') gekennzeichnet sein, als der vorarische Insasse des italischen Bodens, der sich von der herrschend gewordnen blon-den, nämlich arischen Eroberer-Rasse durch die Farbe am deutlichsten abhob . . . ."

32. NF2, in *Friedrich Nietzsche, Kritische Studienausgabe,* ed. Giogio Colli and Mazzino Montinari, vol. 8, *Nachgelassene Fragmente, 1875–1879* (Berlin: de Gruyter, 1988), 444. In den Eigenthümlichkeiten der indogermanischen Sprachen, welche sie gegen die Urmutter-sprache abheben, hat man die zurückgelassenen Spuren der verlorenen Sprachen zu erkennen, welche ursprünglich die Völker hatten, die durch indogermanische Wanderstämme überfallen und besiegt wurden: und so daß die Sprache der Eroberer ebenfalls siegreich wurde und auf die Unterworfenen übergieng. Vielleicht im Accent und dergleichen blieb die alte Gewöhnung noch hängen und gieng auf die neu erlernte Sprache über.

33. Ibid., 453. Die Erfinder der indogermanischen Sprache waren wahrscheinlich der ober-sten Kaste zugehörig und benutzten die vorhandenen geringeren Sprachen. Eine hohe philoso-phische und dichterische Bildung sprach aus ihnen und bildete eine entsprechende Sprache; diese ist ein bewußtes Kunstprodukt; musikalisches dichterisches Genie gehörte dazu. Dann wurde es eine Dichter- und Weisensprache, verbreitete sich später über die nächsten Kasten und wanderte mit den Kriegstämmen aus. Es war das kostbarste Vermächtniß der Heimat, das man zäh festhielt.

34. GM, in *Nietzsche, Kritische Studienausgabe,* vol. 5, 262. "Zwar benennen sie sich vielleicht in den häufigsten Fällen einfach nach ihrer Überlegenheit an Macht (als 'die Mächtigen,' 'die Herren,' 'die Gebietenden') oder nach dem sichtbarsten Abzeichen dieser Überlegenheit, zum Beispiel als 'die Reichen,' 'die Besitzenden' (das ist der Sinn von *arya:* und entsprechend im Eranischen und Slavischen)."

35. My forthcoming work shall treat the important. if neglected. themes of money and visual culture in Hitler's Germany and the time after.

36. NF1, in *Nietzsche, Kritische Studienausgabe*. vol. 7, 106. "Die Religion des Zoroaster hätte. wenn Darius nicht überwunden wäre. Griechenland beherrscht."

37. NF3, in *Friedrich Nietzsche, Kritische Studienausgabe*. vol. 9, 519. "Zarathustra, geboren am See Urmi. verliess im dreissigsten Jahre seine Heimat. gieng in die Provinz Aria und verfasste in den zehn Jahren seiner Einsamkeit im Gebirge den Zend-Avesta."

38. EH, in *Friedrich Nietzsche, Kritische Studienausgabe*. ed. Giorgio Colli and Mazzino Montinari, vol. 6, *Der Fall Wagner, Götzen-Dämmerung, Der Antichrist, Ecce homo, Dionysos-Dithyramben, Nietzsche contra Wagner* (Berlin: de Gruyter, 1999), 314. Man höre den welthistorischen Accent, mit dem auf Seite 30 der Begriff "tragische Gesinnung" eingeführt wird: es sind lauter welthistorische Accente in dieser Schrift. Dies ist die fremdartigste "Objektivität." die es geben kann: die absolute Gewissheit darüber, was ich *bin*, projicirte sich auf irgend eine zufällige Realität.—die Wahrheit über mich redete aus einer schauervollen Tiefe. Auf Seite 71 wird der *Stil* des Zarathustra mit einschneidender Sicherheit beschrieben und vorweggenommen; und niemals wird man einen grossartigeren Ausdruck für das *Ereigniss* Zarathustra, den Akt einer ungeheuren Reinigung und Weihung der Menschheit, finden, als er in den Seiten 43–46 gefunden ist.—

39. NF3, in *Friedrich Nietzsche, Kritische Studienausgabe*. vol. 9, 577. "Das neue Problem: ob nicht *ein Theil der Menschen* auf Kosten des anderen zu einer höheren Rassen zu erziehen ist. Züchtung—"

40. BT, in *Friedrich Nietzsche, Kritische Studienausgabe*. ed. Giorgio Colli and Mazzino Montinari, vol. 1, *Die Geburt der Tragödie, Unzeitgemäße Betrachtungen I–IV, Nachgelassene Schriften 1870–1873* (Berlin: de Gruyter, 1999), 68–69.

41. Ibid.

42. D, in *Nietzsche, Kritische Studienausgabe*. vol. 3, 180. "*Vom Volke Israel.*—Zu den Schauspielen. auf welche uns das nächste Jahrhundert einladet . . . ."

43. Ibid.. 180–81. " . . . gehört die Entscheidung im Schicksale der europäischen Juden. Dass sie ihren Würfel geworfen, ihren Rubikon überschritten haben, greift man jetzt mit beiden Händen: es bleibt ihnen nur noch übrig. entwede die Herren Europa's zu werden oder Europa zu verlieren, so wie sie einst vor langen Zeiten Aegypten verloren, wo sie sich vor ein ähnliches Entweder-Oder gestellt hatten."

44. NF1, in *Nietzsche, Kritische Studienausgabe*. vol. 7, 99. "Wie Oedipus, gelangen wir erst im Hain der Eumeniden zum Frieden."

45. Murrey, *Hölderlin's Dionysiac Poetry*, 2, 2.3, 3.3.

46. Ibid., 9.2, 11.2.

47. EH, in *Nietzsche, Kritische Studienausgabe*. vol. 6, 313. "Jene neue Partei des Lebens, welche die grösste aller Aufgaben, die Höherzüchtung der Menschheit in die Hände nimmt, eingerechnet die schonungslose Vernichtung alles Entartenden und Parasitischen . . . ."

48. Ibid. " . . . wird jenes Zuviel von Leben auf Erden wieder möglich machen, aus dem auch der dionysische Zustand wieder erwachsen muß. Ich verspreche ein *tragisches* Zeitalter: die höchste Kunst im Jasagen zum Leben. die Tragödie. wird wiedergeboren werden, wenn die Menschheit das Bewußtsein der härtesten, aber notwendigsten Kriege hinter sich hat. *ohne daran zu leiden*."

49. UM, in *Nietzsche, Kritische Studienausgabe*. vol. 1, 228. Denn wer sich an der deutschen Sprache versündigt hat, der hat das Mysterium aller unserer Deutschheit entweiht: sie allein hat durch alle die Mischung und den Wechsel von Nationalitäten und Sitten hindurch sich selbst und damit den deutschen Geist wie durch einen metaphysischen Zauber gerettet. Sie allein verbürgt auch diesen Geist für die Zukunft. falls sie nicht selbst unter den ruchlosen Händen der Gegenwart zu Grunde geht. "Aber Di meliora" Fort Pachydermata, fort! Dies ist die deutsche Sprache. in der Menschen sich ausgedrückt, ja, in der grosse Dichter gesungen und grosse Denker geschrieben haben. Zurück mit den Tatzen!

50. Murrey, *Hölderlin's Dionysiac Poetry*, 4.3.

51. GM, in *Nietzsche, Kritische Studienausgabe*. vol. 5, 262. "In Hinsicht auf *unser* Problem. das aus guten Gründen ein *stilles* Problem genannt werden kann und sich wählerisch nur an wenige Ohren wendet. ist es von keinem kleinen Interesse. festzustellen, daß vielfach noch

in jenen Worten und Wurzeln, die 'gut' bezeichnen, die Hauptnuance durchschimmert, auf welche hin die Vornehmen sich eben als Menschen höheren Ranges fühlten."

52. Ibid., 263. Aber auch nach einem *typischen Charakterzuge*: und dies ist der Fall, der uns hier angeht. Sie heißen sich zum Beispiel "die Wahrhaftigen"; voran der griechische Adel, dessen Mundstück der megarische Dichter Theognis ist. Das dafür ausgeprägte Wort *esthlos* bedeutet der Wurzel nach einen, der *ist*, der Realität hat, der wirklich ist, der wahr ist; dann, mit einer subjektiven Wendung, den Wahren als den Wahrhaftigen: in dieser Phase der Begriffs-Verwandlung wird es zum Schlag- und Stichwort des Adels und geht ganz und gar in den Sinn 'adelig' über, zur Abgrenzung vom *lügenhaften* gemeinen Manne, so wie Theognis ihn nimmt und schildert—bis endlich das Wort, nach dem Niedergange des Adels, zur Bezeichnung der seelischen Noblesse übrigbleibt und gleichsam reif und süß wird.

Chapter Ten

Jews/Christians

"The Chosen People among Peoples"

"JEWISH HISTORY"

To complete our discussion of Nietzsche's *proto-National Socialism*, we turn to his relationship with Christianity and Judaism. As we have seen, despite his explicit racism, Nietzsche's understanding of the Jews is not always racist. In fact, his psycho-historical insight into Jewish identity (both early historic and modern) is not without value.

Firstly, Nietzsche accents the trauma that not only ruptured, but also may have generated a modern identity of the Jews: the time when the Jewish ruling class is conquered and removed to Babylon in the sixth century B.C.E. (2.1). Secondly, Nietzsche notes the psychic perversion that inevitably emerges from a traumatic loss of home (community and earth)—that is, when a people are *"no longer* united" (2.1) with their local environment. In particular, Nietzsche trenchantly (if also somewhat unconsciously) brings to light the spirit of *monetized* and *visualized* vengeance that festers within a community that has lost its way. Critical is how one's sense of belonging and claim to uniqueness, given that it is uprooted and no longer in balance with nature, becomes (potentially) unlimited in its illusion of (secret and resentful) superiority. One thinks of the explicit racism that we find in the familiar idea that the Jews are "the chosen people among peoples" (2.1). Communal selection no longer rooted in the earth knows no limit in regard to its (abstract and visual) aggression against others who are (perceived as) foreign.

Thirdly—and lastly—Nietzsche shows that the racial violence that lurks within the heart of this evil strain of (post-Babylonian) Judaism has become more aggressive and consuming of other religions, cultures, and histories in modern time. This is clear in his statement regarding education in Germany in the nineteenth century:

> In our schools Jewish history is presented as sacred: Abraham is more important to us than any person from Greek or German history. And from him that which we feel from David's psalms is so different from than that which excites us when we read Pindar or Petrarch that it seems to be a foreign home. (10.2)

As Nietzsche implies, it is unnatural to force one's religion, culture, and history onto others—and that it is especially perverse when one forces the sacred story of this religion onto those to whom it does not belong.

These three insights raise the question: If Nietzsche is right to criticize the racism that lurks within early historic and modern Jewish identity, then how are we to reconcile this antiracist insight with his anti-Semitic racism? (7–10).

"VENGEFUL-ADDICT INSTINCTS OF AN UNHAPPY PRIEST"

We have also noted Nietzsche's criticism of the *monetized* and *visualized* spirit of Christianity. The (money-driven) crusades—"an elevated form of piracy"—are inseparable from the "physiological evilness" of an uprooted (and hence abstract and *visualized*) "kingdom . . . not of this world" (2.2).

For Nietzsche, Christianity "is *not* a reaction against Jewish instincts," but, instead, it is "their inevitable product."[1] The transfer (and concentration) of a *monetized* and visually evil spirit betrays itself in the Christian "hatred of the senses, of the joy of the senses"—for instance, when "the first Christian order after the banishment of the Moors closed the public baths, of which there were 270 in Cordova alone."[2] The psychosis to which a community succumbs when it faces death and (to preserve even a perverted form of its identity) chooses its imagination over reality is a physical perversion as well. One recalls the "'evil eye,' '*böser Blick*,' 'the poisonous eye of *ressentiment*,' *das Giftauge des Ressentiment*, and 'treacherous eyes,' *verrätersich[e] Augen*" (2.1). When Christianity inherits a strain of (post-Babylonian) Jewish racism, it inherits "a religion that teaches the misunderstanding of the body . . . a holiness that is itself just a series of symptoms of an impoverished, enervated and incurably corrupted body!"[3] That such (spiritual and physical) derangement is an act not only of inter-personal, but also inter-communal violence should be obvious. Such "faith actually moves no mountains, but instead *raises* them up where there were none before: all this is made abundantly clear by a walk through a *lunatic asylum*."[4]

But a powerful strain of Christianity turns the potentially racist spirit that it inherits from Judaism into a weapon that it can use (and not without tragic irony) even against its own historic origin. The concept of the purity of blood that is present in the belief—for instance, in the outlandish fantasy that the Jews are "the chosen people among peoples" (2.1)[5] —becomes precisely that which Christians take up not only to separate themselves from, but also to persecute, torture, and murder Jews. Critical to this reversal (and application) of racial violence is the emergence (and ritual cultivation of) the belief that the Jews are responsible for the murder of God—and thus secretly the children of Satan.[6] This use of an ancient, inhuman spirit lurking within the most unfortunate strain of Judaism by subsequent (evil) Christians to, in turn, eradicate the Jews culminates in the Old Medieval criterion of the purity of blood, *limpieza del sangre* (in German, *Reinheit des Blutes*), that forms the foundation of the Spanish and Portuguese Inquisitions.[7]

Nietzsche is of course critical of Christianity, to say the least, in particular of how it undermined the "excellence instincts" of the Germans. "The German nobility, which in essence is a Viking-nobility," he declares,

> was in its element: the Church knew only too well how one can *have* the German nobility. . . . The German nobility, always the "Swiss Guard" of the Church, always in the service of all the bad instincts of the church,—but *well paid*. . . . That the church carried out its holy war against everything excellent on earth with the help of German swords, German blood and German courage! Here one could raise a mass of embarrassing questions. German nobility is almost *missing* in the history of higher cultures: the reason is obvious enough. . . . Christianity and alcohol—the two great means of corruption.[8]

Nietzsche is even against the German Reformation. In a rare passage about the Dionysian spirit of Catholicism, he writes:

> I see before me a *possibility* of a perfect supernatural magic and excitation of colour:—it seems to me to scintillate with all the shuddering of a refined beauty such that within it is an art at work that is so godlike, so devilishly-divine, that one would search in vain through centuries for another such possibility; I see a spectacle so sensually rich, so simultaneously full of wondrous paradox that all the gods of Olympus would have occasion for an immortal laugh—*Cesare Borgia as pope*.[9]

"What happened?" Nietzsche proceeds. "A German monk, Luther, came to Rome,"[10] he answers.

> This monk with all the vengeful-addict [rachsüchtigen] instincts of an unhappy priest, rebelled against the Renaissance in Rome. . . . Instead of understanding the monstrosity that had occurred with profound thankfulness, the conquering of Christianity at its *capital*, his hatred understood this spectacle in way to stimulate its nourishment. A religious man thinks only of himself.—Luther saw only the depravity of the papacy when exactly the opposite was occurring: the old corruption, the peccatum originale, Christianity *no* longer sat on the papal chair! But instead life! the triumph of life! the great Yes to all high,

beautiful and daring things! . . . And Luther *restored the Church once again*:
he attacked it. [11]

But this brings us back to the urgent question concerning the racist spirit that
neutralizes Nietzsche's "Dionysian philosophy" (4.1). If Western racism
such as Nietzsche's can be traced back to a racist strain of Christianity that,
although appropriated for its immoral holy war against the Jews, has its
origins finally in a racism lurking within the rulers of the early historic
Jewish people, then how are we to understand Nietzsche's anti-Semitic (and
anti-Christian) racism? As we might expect, Nietzsche often appears to be
something like a pan-racist of sorts. This includes, we must note, a racism
against even the productive, non-racist strains of Judaism and Christianity.
"We would prefer 'early Christians' as little as polish Jews for companions,"
he confides, "not that one would need to find an objection to them. . . .
Neither has a pleasant smell." [12]

"IF CHRISTIANITY REMAINS, THE *GERMANS* WILL BE TO BLAME"

To understand Nietzsche's (seemingly contradictory) style of modern racism,
let us return to and continue with the conclusion of his later invective against
Luther. "The Renaissance—an event without meaning, a great *for nothing*!" [13] he writes.

> Ah these Germans, what they have cost us already! For nothing—that was
> always the *work* of Germans.—The Reformation; Leibniz; Kant and the so-
> called German philosophy; the wars of liberation; the *Reich*—each time some-
> thing that was, something *irrecoverable*, is for nothing, . . . They are my
> enemies, I confess it, these Germans: I loathe their style of conceptual- and
> value-uncleanliness, of *cowardice* before every justified yes and no. For al-
> most a thousand years they have tangled and confused everything they touch
> with their fingers, they have all the half-measures—three-eighths-measures!—
> of which Europe is sick on their conscience,—they have the most unclean style
> of Christianity there is, the most incurable, the most indestructible, Protestant-
> ism on the conscience. . . . If Christianity remains, the *Germans* will be to
> blame. [14]

Nietzsche's (unlimited) rage against Christianity combines, significantly,
with a similar (unlimited) self-hatred in regard to the protracted lack of an
authentic religious leader—a true *father*—in modern Germany. Consider another of the many diatribes that the son of Carl Nietzsche (the protestant
pastor who, like Hölderlin's father, dies within the first few years of his son's
life) [15] —willfully ejects:

> Among Germans I am immediately understood when I say that philosophy has
> been spoiled by theology-blood. The protestant pastor is the grandfather of
> German philosophy, Protestantism itself its peccatum originale. Definition of
> Protestantism: the partial paralysis of Christianity—and of reason . . . one has
> only to speak the word "Tübingen Seminary" to be understood. . . . The
> Swabians are the best liars in Germany since they lie innocently. [16]

The (limitless) loathing for Christianity, German philosophy, and the (communal and individual) self is inextricably tied to a psychosis that witnesses an unstable transition from love to hate. For does not Nietzsche's eternal condemnation of the anti-Dionysian spirit of Luther emerge out of the failure of his youthful, Wagnerian love of Luther's "Dionysian luring-call" (8.4) to found a *Vaterland*?

To conclude part II, I suggest that the modern German racism (a mixture of the *proto-National Socialist chronotope* and *language*) into which Nietzsche's *Dionysiac chronotope* and *language* are absorbed emerges from the transfer of a strain of Christian racism (itself an unconscious transference of a strain of Jewish racism after Babylon) to nineteenth-century biology, physiology, and linguistics. Nietzsche's variation of this (rather common) leap of racist thought is admittedly complex, for he turns it even against the everyday, secular spirit of science—that is, another place where racism tends to emerge and fester. The allegory of *The Madman* whose desolate isolation recalls a Dionysian mystic initiand and who thus has the potential to identify, criticize, and transform the destructive power of money and its reckless visual culture (4.1) threatens to degenerate into a lethal and all-too-Christian, anti-Semitic condemnation of the careless (satanic) culprits of Christ's tragic death: "the murders of all murders" (4.1, 11.2).

Nietzsche's criticism of philosophy that has been "spoiled by theology-blood" indeed retrieves the Christian phantasm of *limpiezza del sangre* (11.2). This invites us to rethink his Dionysian "love" of all "*that* which *one* writes with his blood" (6.4). As I have shown, Hölderlin's Hellenic concept of writing—"the silent text" (v 8) that "[f]ollows the fruit, like the dark leaf/ Of the meadow" (v 7–8)—is eclipsed by "[t]he fixed letter" (v 225) of Protestantism—a Christian concept of text that, in turn, reinforces Hölderlin's nationalism. [17]

But how are we to evaluate Nietzsche's celebration of "blood" (including "foreign blood") as "spirit" that secretly pulsates in (authentic) texts—and this means lives on in alphabetic writing (a significant, if ancient and little understood visual media) that remains rooted in that which is (nonvisual) "learned by heart" (6.4)? Is not this Dionysian openness to earth and its communally constructive darkness (tragically) close by when Nietzsche declares war on the new excesses of unclean "Jews . . . that the German stomach and German blood [das deutsche Blut] have trouble" (10.2) digesting in modern time? And is not this perverse (unconscious) complex itself concealed by an all-too-Judeo-Christian concealment that has nothing to do with the spirit of secrecy in mystery-cult? Consider again Nietzsche's proclamation that his texts are "only for a few select ears" (10.3). "Here too the public sphere is missing; hiding, the dark room is Christian."[18]

Although Hölderlin's *Dionysian chronotope* and *language* also dissolve into Christianity,[19] the absorption of Nietzsche's retrieval of Dionysus into its monetized and abstract (and *visualized*) spirit is more threatening. Hidden within his search for an Indo-Germanic *Übermensch*—for "H[e] who is not the God of the Jews alone" (10.1)—is room enough for a trace of he who Müller is careful not to name: the God of Christ. Like all racists—Christian ones included—who bury an experience of the conquered-self within a delusion of superiority, Nietzsche ritualizes an (unlimited) lust for *Sieg und Heil* in his distracting "power-consciousness," *Macht-Bewusstsein* (2.1),[20] that he, like perhaps the corrupt leaders of the ancient Israelis, should have been strong enough to let go.

NOTES

1. AC, in *Friedrich Nietzsche, Kritische Studienausgabe*, ed. Giorgio Colli and Mazzino Montinari, vol. 6, *Der Fall Wagner, Götzen-Dämmerung, Der Antichrist, Ecce homo, Dionysos-Dithyramben, Nietzsche contra Wagner* (Berlin: de Gruyter, 1999), 191. "Ich berühre hier nur das Problem der Entstehung des Christenthums. Der erste Satz zu dessen Lösung heisst: das Christenthum ist einzig aus dem Boden zu verstehen, aus dem es gewachsten ist,—es ist nicht eine Gegenbewegung gegen den jüdischen Instinkt, es ist dessen Folgerichtigkeit selbst, ein Schluss weiter in dessen furchteinflössender Logik. In der Formel des Erlösers: 'das Heil kommt von den Juden.'"

2. Ibid., 188. Hier wird der Leib verachtet, die Hygiene als Sinnlichkeit abgelehnt; die Kirche wehrt sich selbst gegen die Reinlichkeit (—die erste christliche Massregel nach Vertreibung der Mauren war die Schliessung der öffentlichen Bäder, von denen Kordova allein 270 besass). Christlich ist ein gewisser Sinn der Grausamkeit, gegen sich und andre; der Hass gegen die Andersdenkenden; der Wille, zu verfolgen. Düstere und aufregende Vorstellungen sind im Vordergrunde; die höchstbegehrten, mit den höchsten Namen bezeichneten Zustände sind Epilepsoiden; die Diät wird so gewählt, dass sie morbide Erscheinungen begünstigt und die Nerven überreizt: Christlich ist die Todfeindschaft gegen die Herren der Erde, gegen die "Vornehmen"—und zugleich ein versteckter heimlicher Wettbewerb (—man lässt ihnen den "Leib," man will *nur* die "Seele" . . .). Christlich ist der Hass gegen den *Geist*, gegen Stolz, Mut, Freiheit, libertinage des Geistes; christlich ist der Hass gegen die *Sinne*, gegen die Freuden der Sinne, gegen die Freude überhaupt . . . .
See also 60, p. 249.
Das Christentum hat uns um die Ernte der antiken Kultur gebracht, es hat uns später wieder um die Ernte der *Islam*-Kultur gebracht. Die wunderbar maurische Kultur-Welt Spaniens, *uns* im Grunde verwandter, zu Sinn und Geschmack redender als Rom und Griechenland, wurde *niedergetreten*—ich sage nicht von was für Füssen—warum? weil sie vornehmen, weil sie Männer-Instinkten ihre Entstehung verdankte, weil sie zum Leben ja sagte auch noch mit den seltnen und raffinierten Kostbarkeiten des maurischen Lebens! . . .

3. Ibid., 231. Es steht niemandem frei, Christ zu werden: man wird zum Christentum nicht "bekehrt,"—man muss krank genug dazu sein . . . Wir anderen, die wir den *Mut* zur Gesundheit *und* auch zur Verachtung haben, wie dürfen *wir* eine Religion verachten, die den Leib missverstehn lehrte! die den Seelen-Aberglauben nicht loswerden will! die aus der unzureichenden

Ernährung ein "Verdienst" macht! die in der Gesundheit eine Art Feind, Teufel, Versuchung bekämpft! die sich einredete, man könne eine "vollkommne Seele" in einem Kadaver von Leib herumtragen, und dazu nötig hatte, einen neuen Begriff der "Vollkommenheit" sich zurecht-zumachen, ein bleiches, krankhaftes, idiotisch-schwärmerisches Wesen, die sogenannte "Hei-ligkeit,"—Heiligkeit, selbst bloss eine Symptonen-Reihe des verarmten, entnervten, unheilbar verdorbenen Leibes!...

4. Ibid., 230–31. Dass der Glaube unter Umständen selig macht, dass Seligkeit aus einer fixen Idee noch nicht eine *wahre* Idee macht, dass der Glaube keine Berge versetzt, wohl aber Berge *hinsetzt*, wo es keine gibt: ein flüchtiger Gang durch ein *Irrenhaus* klärt zur Genüge darüber auf. *Nicht* freilich einen Priester: denn der leugnet aus Instinkt, dass Krankheit Krank-heit, dass Irrenhaus Irrenhaus ist. Das Christentum hat die Krankheit *nötig*, ungefähr wie das Christentum einen Überschuss von Gesundheit nötig hat,—krank-*machen* ist die eigentliche Hinterabsicht des ganzen Heilsprozeduren-System's der Kirche. Und die Kirche selbst—ist sie nicht das katholische Irrenhaus als letztes Ideal?— Die Erde überhaupt als Irrenhaus?— Der religiöse Mensch, wie ihn die Kirche *will*, ist ein typischer décadent; der Zeitpunkt, wo eine religiöse Krisis über ein Volk Herr wird, ist jedes Mal durch Nerven-Epidemien gekennzeich-net; die "innere Welt" des religiösen Menschen sieht der "inneren Welt" der Überreizten und Erschöpften zum Verwechseln ähnlich; die "höchsten" Zustände, welche das Christentum als Wert aller Werte über die Menschheit aufgehängt hat, sind epileptoide Formen,—die Kirche hat nur Verrückte *oder* grosse Betrüger in majorem dei honorem heilig gesprochen ... Ich habe mir einmal erlaubt, den ganzen christlichen Buss- und Erlösungstraining (den man heute am besten in England studiert) als eine methodisch erzeugte *folie circulaire* zu bezeichnen, wie billig, auf einem bereits dazu vorbereiteten, das heisst gründlich morbiden Boden.

5. We should note that the concept of purity, in particular when it is used in regard to blood, is destructive only when it is appropriated to legitimate the superiority of one commu-nity (blood) over and above another—which of course then leads to (ancient or modern) genocide.

6. This is in the New Testament. See, for example, the Gospels of Matthew, Luke, and John. Melito von Sardes explicitly reprimands Pontius Pilate for the killing of God. See also John 8:43: " ... you have the devil for a father ... he was a murderer from the beginning ...."

7. See, for instance, Yitzhak Baer, *A History of the Jews in Spain*, vol. 2, trans. Louis Schoffman (Philadelphia: The Jewish Publication Society, 1992), 281.

8. AC, in *Nietzsche, Kritische Studienausgabe*, vol. 6, 249–50. Der deutsche Adel, Wiking-er-Adel im Grunde, war damit in seinem Elemente: die Kirche wusste nur zu gut, womit man deutschen Adel *hat* ... Der deutsche Adel, immer die "Schweizer" der Kirche, immer im Dienste aller schlechten Instinkte der Kirche,—aber *gut bezahlt* ... Dass die Kirche gerade mit Hilfe deutscher Schwerter, deutschen Blutes und Mutes ihren Todfeindschafts-Krieg gegen alles Vornehme auf Erden durchgeführt hat! Es gibt an dieser Stelle eine Menge schmerzlicher Fragen. Der deutsche Adel *fehlt* beinahe in der Geschichte der höheren Kultur: man errät den Grund ... Christentum, Alkohol—die beiden *grossen* Mittel der Korruption ...

9. Ibid., 251.Ich sehe eine *Möglichkeit* vor mir von einem vollkommen überirdischen Zau-ber und Farbenreiz:—es scheint mir, dass sie in allen Schaudern raffinierter Schönheit erglänzt, dass eine Kunst in ihr am Werke ist, so göttlich, so teufelsmässig-göttlich, dass man Jahrtau-sende umsonst nach einer zweiten solchen Möglichkeit durchsucht; ich sehe ein Schauspiel, so sinnreich, so wunderbar paradox zugleich, dass alle Gottheiten des Olymps einen Anlass zu einem unsterblichen Gelächter gehabt hätten—*Cesare Borgia als Papst* ...

10. Ibid., "Was geschah? Ein deutscher Mönch, Luther, kam nach Rom."

11. Ibid.Dieser Mönch, mit allen rachsüchtigen Instinkten eines verunglückten Priesters im Leibe, empörte sich in Rom *gegen* die Renaissance. ... Statt mit tiefster Dankbarkeit das Ungeheure zu verstehn, das geschehen war, die Überwindung des Christentums an seinem *Sitz*—, verstand sein Hass aus diesem Schauspiel nur seine Nahrung zu ziehn. Ein religiöser Mensch denkt nur an sich.—Luther sah die *Verderbnis* des Papsttums, während gerade das Gegenteil mit Händen zu greifen war: die alte Verderbnis, das peccatum originale, das Chris-tentum sass *nicht* mehr auf dem Stuhl des Papstes! Sondern das Leben! Sondern der Triumph des Lebens! Sondern das grosse Ja zu allen hohen, schönen, verwegnen Dingen! ... Und Luther *stellte die Kirche wieder her*: er griff sie an ...

12. Ibid., 46, 223. "Wir würden uns 'erste Christen' so wenig wie polnische Juden zum Umgang wählen: nicht daß man gegen sie auch nur einen Einwand nöthig hätte . . . Sie riechen beide nicht gut."

13. Ibid., 251. "Die Renaissance—ein Ereignis ohne Sinn, ein grosses *Umsonst!*"

14. Ibid., 251–52. Ah diese Deutschen, was sie uns schon gekostet haben! Umsonst—das war immer das *Werk* der Deutschen.—Die Reformation; Leibnitz; Kant und die sogenannte deutsche Philosophie; die Freiheits-Kriege; das Reich—jedes Mal ein Umsonst für etwas, das bereits da war, für etwas *Unwiederbringliches.* . . . Es sind *meine* Feinde, ich bekenne es, diese Deutschen: ich verachte in ihnen jede Art von Begriffs- und Wert-Unsauberkeit, von *Feigheit* vor jedem rechtschaffnen Ja und Nein. Sie haben, seit einem Jahrtausend beinahe, Alles verfilzt und verwirrt, woran sie mit ihren Fingern rührten, sie haben alle Halbheiten—Drei-Achtelsheit-en!—auf dem Gewissen, an denen Europa krank ist,—sie haben auch die unsauberste Art Christentum, die es gibt, die unheilbarste, die unwiderlegbarste, den Protestantismus auf dem Gewissen. . . . Wenn man nicht fertig wird mit dem Christentum, die *Deutschen* werden daran schuld sein . . .

15. Lucas Murrey, *Hölderlin's Dionysiac Poetry: The Terrifying-Exciting Mysteries* (Heidelberg, New York, Dordrecht, London: Springer, 2015), Coda.

16. AC, in *Nietzsche, Kritische Studienausgabe*, vol. 6, 176. Unter Deutschen versteht man sofort, wenn ich sage, das die Philosophie durch Theologen-Blut verderbt ist. Der protestantische Pfarrer ist Grossvater der deutschen Philosophie, der Protestantismus selbst ihr peccatum originale. Definition des Protestantismus: die halbseitige Lähmung des Christenthums—und der Vernunft. . . . Man hat nur das Wort 'Tübinger Stift' auszusprechen, um zu begreifen, was die deutsche Philosophie im Grund ist—eine hinterlistige Theologie. . . . Die Schwaben sind die besten Lügner in Deutschland, sie lügen unschuldig . . .

17. Murrey, *Hölderlin's Dionysiac Poetry* (13.3).

18. AC, in *Nietzsche, Kritische Studienausgabe*, vol. 6, 188. "Hier fehlt auch die Öffentlichkeit; der Versteck, der dunkle Raum ist christlich."

19. Murrey, *Hölderlin's Dionysiac Poetry* (13).

20. AC, in *Nietzsche, Kritische Studienausgabe*, vol. 6, 193.

Conclusion

Herakleitean Hyper-Abstractions

"DOUBTFUL EVEN ABOUT HERAKLEITOS"

The almost impenetrable center of Nietzschean thought—which lingers between "Dionysian philosophy" (4.1) and *proto-National Socialism*—is plagued by a contradictory and hyper-abstract (that is, anti-Dionysian) chaos. Consider Nietzsche's relationship to his countrymen. Because he sounds "the first Dionysian luring-call," Luther is one of "our great artists and poets" (8.4). "This monk," nevertheless, "with all the vengeful-addict instincts of an unhappy priest" (7.1), destroyed the secret Dionysian spirit of the pope (11.2). Although "Kant . . . made it possible for the spirit *of German philosophy* to destroy the complacent desire for the existence of scientific Socraticism" and reintroduced "*Dionysian wisdom*" to humankind, he is also an "idiot" (7.1). The secret "Dürer knight" Schopenhauer has also a secret infectious, "cadaverous-bitter perfume" (7.1). Last but not least, Nietzsche's "sublime fore-fighter [Vorkämpfer]" (8.4) Wagner is of course a "musician-problem" (2.2).

Although Germans make up less than one percent of the world's population, they are secretly—somehow?—both the savior and destroyer of all humanity. But while among the *excellent races* in search of "plunder" (9.2, 9.1), they also embody the "*well paid*" (11.2) and "elevated form of piracy" (2.2) that "destroyed Europe's last great cultural harvest" (7.1).

And what about Nietzsche's "excellent races" (9.1)? How is it that their *excellence* succumbs so easily to inferior races seething with revenge? Whereas "*the Jews*" are more responsible for "[e]verything that has been done on earth against 'the excellent ones'" (9.3) than any other less excellent race—for instance, when they destroyed "Greek culture" (8.3)—Nietzsche looks forward joyfully to the time when Jews eradicate other "European people"—and even rejoices with "the old Jewish God."[1] Is there any doubt that Nietzsche is unable to formulate a clear picture of social organization?

Despite the conspicuous inadequacy of his thought, however, one thing must be granted. Before Nietzsche no one had come close to discovering the origin of philosophy. This is not to say that he himself can claim this honor. Instead, this is to say that he is the first philosopher to initiate a (somewhat more) responsible examination of the earliest signs of (historic) thinking in Western civilization.

As we have noted, Nietzsche illuminates the lethal spirit of abstraction concealed in Classical Greek Philosophy. The decadent essence of Socratic "'[r]easonableness' versus instinct" and Plato's "*theoretical man*" are tied, if unconsciously, to the emergence of money—"bourgeois mediocrity" (2.2)—and *monetized seeing* (the *visualized chronotope*), that is, a new historic style of seeing "*no longer* united" with earth: the "'evil eye,'" *'böser Blick,'* "poisonous eye of *ressentiment*," *das Giftauge des Ressentiment*, and "treacherous eyes," *verrätersich[e] Augen* (2.1). As we have also noted, Nietzsche's critique of the abstract (and unlimited) "will to truth," *Wille zur Wahrheit*,[2] that coalesces about the *monetized* and *visualized* spirit of modern thought— "the tyrannical-insanity of powerlessness" that drives the desire "[t]o *make* all beings thinkable" (6.2)—recalls Hölderlin's adaption and critique of Oedipus (9.3).

Anyone familiar with Nietzsche is also familiar with his interest in pre-Socratic philosophy. This is clear in *The Birth of Tragedy*, for instance, in the "downfall, not [the] victory" of "the struggling hero" that "prepares" Dionysus's return (4.2). Such individual death echoes Anaximander's pre-Socratic saying (which is reproduced almost word for word): "We should recognize that everything that comes into existence must be prepared for a suffering downfall" (4.2). Like his *Lieblingsdichter*, Nietzsche is particularly attracted to "the teaching of the great Herakleitos of Ephesus" (8.2).[3]

On the one hand, this attraction is rooted in Nietzsche's retrieval of the *Dionysiac chronotope* and *language*. When he speaks of a "striving for infinity" (that is derived from Dionysus's mystery-cult), he goes on to say that "the winged-beat of longing" (4.2) that

> accompanies the highest desire in clearly perceived reality reminds us that we have to recognise a Dionysian phenomenon in both conditions, that always again it reveals to us from anew the playful construction and destruction of the individual world as the overflow of primal desire, in a similar way, as when Herakleitos the dark one compares the world-creating force to the playing child setting stones here and there and builds hills of sand and throws them down again.[4]

On the other hand, Nietzsche's interest in Herakleitos is related to his application of Greece to create the foundation of his own "Dionysian philosophy." "The teaching of the 'eternal return,'" he explains,

> that is of the absolute and infinite repeating circularity of all things—this teaching of Zarathustra could finally also have been taught by Herakleitos. The Stoics at least, who inherited all their fundamental concepts from Herakleitos, have traces of it.[5]

Less familiar than Nietzsche's attractions to pre-Socratic philosophy are his discontents. This is also something to which we have gestured. Appalled by the absence of "tragic wisdom" in early historic Greece, he confesses: "I have searched in vain for signs of it even among the great Greek philosophers, those of the two centuries before Socrates" (2.2).[6] This tragedy of the loss of real thinking extends even to Nietzsche's favorite pre-Socratic hero. "I remained doubtful even about Herakleitos, in whose presence alone I felt warmer and more at ease than anywhere else."[7]

Least well known is how Nietzsche understands his philosophy not only as transcending even his pre-Socratic heroes, but also as a retrieval of the secret wisdom of Dionysus. This is something to which we have openly referred throughout this study. "Already that Dionysus is a philosopher, and that gods also philosophise," he reflects in what is arguably one of his most profound insights, "appears to me as something new, and which is not unensnaring, that which perhaps arouses suspicion precisely among philosophers" (4.1). Those concerned with Nietzsche as a pre-Socratic (inspired) philosopher have neglected this deeper, more productive layer of thought that is essential to his "Dionysian philosophy." "In this sense I have the right to regard myself as the first *tragic philosopher*," he declares with uncanny self-awareness: "Before me this translation of the Dionysian into a philosophical pathos did not exist: tragic wisdom is lacking" (2.2).[8] "This beginning of mine is remarkable beyond all measure," he says elsewhere:

> In confirmation of my innermost experience I had discovered the only example of this that history has to offer—with this I was the first one to fathom the wonderful phenomenon of the Dionysian.[9]

But this leads us to the still deeper question. What is it, precisely, that Nietzsche saw when he declares: "I was the first to see the actual contrast"?[10]

"ETERNAL CONTRADICTION, FATHER OF ALL THINGS"

We have noted the emergence of philosophy from the limitless essence of money that constructs in the brain an (unconscious) style of thought that, in turn, views the cosmos as ruled by a similarly abstract, singular, and unlimited substance. [11] This is evident in the water of Thales, the air of Anaximenes, and the One of Parmenides. [12] This (imaginary) pre-Socratic projection is further mirrored in the unlimited (apeiron) of Anaximander and the raging light that rules the Herakleitean cosmos—a peculiarly (uprooted) luminous essence that, being exchangeable for all things, the early historic philosopher compares to gold. [13]

Critical to this (psychic) consequence that haunts the introduction of precious metal into human history is the visual culture that initially facilitates this cataclysmic change and then, in turn, is transformed into money's own (self-sustaining) *visualized chronotope*. The abstract and eerie picture of (unlimited) fire that Herakleitos evokes is not only a result of the abstract and limitless essence of money, but also of a new abstract and limitless essence of seeing that, like precious metal, is *"no longer* united" (2.1) with nature. Nietzsche's insights into the monetized "bourgeois mediocrity" (2.2) to which tragedy succumbs and "the poisonous eye of *ressentiment*," *das Giftauge des Ressentiment* (2.1) indeed have their merits.

But the profound problem that Nietzschean philosophy poses to us today is not its so-called mythic deconstruction (or psychological critique) of metaphysics, nor whether such a critique remains Kantian or not, [14] nor whether or not Zarathustra can transcend the Greeks (embodied in the dead tightrope walker) and Wagner (the living jester), nor finally if Nietzsche's concept of art transcends the self-negating (Buddhist) streak in Schopenhauer—to mention just a few of the countless and popular (and distracting) postmodern discussions.

The real problem of Nietzsche's philosophy, instead, is its failure (even despite its impressive historical insights) to uncover and explore the source of the problematic emergence of philosophy itself within a new *visualized* world. Western thinking, as I have argued, arises not from a radically new style of hearing, touching, tasting, or smelling, but from a new abstract (and alienating) style of seeing that, in turn, transforms each of these prehistoric, biological senses (one thinks also of their neurological relation to one another) anew. [15]

The fiery soul of Herakleitos that knows nothing of gods and humans [16] evokes the lethal unlimitedness that the Dionysian spirit of tragedy transcends. Consider the cosmic cycles of Aeschylus's *Orestia* that conquer the limitless (Herakleitean) oppositions through the establishment of a mystic limit. [17] Important is the insatiable desire of the tyrant who resists earthly and communal (Dionysian) limits. The cosmology of pre-Socratic philosophers consists more or less of the thoughts of individuals who (like Pentheus, Kreon, and Oedipus) are no longer mediated by any context or tradition of (social) performance. [18]

Instead of *preparing* for Dionysus to reveal himself, Nietzsche's Anaximandrian "downfall" (12.1) absorbs tragedy into pre-Socratic monetized reflection (of that which "comes into existence"). This mirrors the unlimitedness of money as well as money's narcissistic visual culture.

This *visualized* being recurs in Nietzsche's celebration, for instance, of the unlimited "construction and destruction of the individual world as the overflow of primal desire" and which he associates with "Herakleitos the dark one" (12.1). The *monetized* and *visualized* space-times expectedly lurk within Nietzsche's "eternal recurrence": the "infinite repeating circularity of all things" (12.1), a thought whose hyper-abstraction quickly degenerates into the demonic,[19] that is, an all-too-Christian (hyper-abstract) thought experiment. Consider further the "infinite repeating circularity" of money and images, not only in ancient Greece, but also in Nietzsche's own time—and our own.

To conclude this section, we turn to the more sinister reason why Nietzschean philosophy fails to confront the origin of pre-Socratic thought. By situating "all things" in an unlimited (Herakleitean) "double orbit" (8.2), the philosopher imagines a never-ending "contrast and war," *Gegensatz und Krieg*.[20] This brutality without limit unconsciously sustains, in turn, a timeless and hyper-abstract battle of races. Witness Nietzsche's questionable concept of an "eternal contradiction, Father of all things":[21] an (abysmal) fatherlessness and self-hatred that underwrites Nietzschean racism. Perhaps here one could reflect also upon the (*monetized* and *visualized*) poison of the tarantula (6.2). Like all philosophers before (and after) him, Nietzsche's attempt to deconstruct the philosophical origins of Western civilization leads tragically to just another prison cell of (Herakleitean) hyper-abstraction.

> That battle [Kampf] and inequality are also even in beauty, and war [Krieg] for power and supremacy: that teaches us here with the clearest example.
> How divinely do vault and arch contrast here in their struggle: how they struggle against one another with light and shadow, the divinely-struggling ones—
> Thus surely and beautifully let us also be enemies, my friends! Divinely do we want to struggle *against* each other![22]

But this leads to still another question. If Nietzsche's need for a racist (timeless and hyper-abstract) cosmology deepens his misunderstanding of the origin of (pre-Socratic) philosophers such as Herakleitos—and this in a way that transcends the confusion that we see in Hölderlin's poetics[23]—then how are we to evaluate his analysis of the birth and death of the tragic play?

"THE PRIMAL PROBLEM OF TRAGEDY"

The first problem that plagues Nietzsche's understanding of tragedy is in regard to its birth. This is not to say that his account of the invention of the tragic play is *"for nothing"* (11.3). The appearance of this art form has its source in the opening out of Dionysian ritual to resist the (unlimited) will of the *monetized* and *visualized* mind of the tyrant.[24] Although Nietzsche, like Hölderlin, could perhaps never have identified the world-historical significance of the emergence of money in this transformation, he nevertheless gestures, if unconsciously, to the cataclysmic shift in visual culture that precedes, accompanies, and finally succumbs to money's lethal essence. This is clear in his discussion of "the weaker degrees of Apolline art" (2.2).

For Nietzsche, "the weaker degrees" of "visualising forces" (3.3) are associated with those who historically precede the tragedians, namely the sculptor and epic poet who are "sunk[en] in pure gazing at pictures" (2.2). The visual culture of early historic Greece, what Nietzsche pictures as a world of "actual Apolline artists" (2.2),[25] is predominated by the introduction of visualized "artistic effects" that create an abstract and individualized unconscious (that, in turn, is projected back onto the cosmos)—"that is, the justification of the world of the individuation with this contemplation, which is the high point and essence of Apolline art."[26]

Impressive is Nietzsche's insight into the will of the visual culture of this time as that of a homogenizing social-political force. Consider the implicit description of Homer's epics as a (poetic) form that aggressively institutes *equality* and *regularity*.

> From the perspective of the epos, this unequal and irregular visual world of lyricism is simply to be condemned: and this is precisely what the celebrating epic rhapsodists of Apolline holidays did in the time of Terpander.[27]

Impressive also is how Nietzsche differentiates the earthly and communal (Dionysian) style of seeing that is unique to the "unequal and irregular visual world of lyricism" from that of the homogenized, abstract, and isolated visual culture that is peculiar to the "perspective of the epos."

> In the poetry of the folk song we also see language strained to its extreme *for the sake of imitating music*: therefore with Archilochus a new world of poetry begins that is in the most fundamental way opposed to that of Homeric one.[28]

The difference that Nietzsche sees between the *visualized language* of Homer and the visual experience that accompanies Dionysian poetry (Archilochus) is that whereas the former is visually self-referential (self-isolating), the latter opens out to other (nonvisual) sensations, in particular to that of listening. "With this we have drawn the only possible relationship between poetry and music, word and tone," Nietzsche proceeds: "the word, the image, the concept searches for an expression analogous to music and now suffers the power of music in itself."[29] In contrast to the *visualizing spirit* of Homeric language, *Dionysiac language* is defined by its more rich and nuanced synaesthesia.[30]

> In this way we are able to differentiate the history of Greek language into two main streams, each in regard to imitating either the world of phenomena and images or the world of music.[31]

This brings us back to something we have already noted, namely the ascendency of Dionysus's linguistic spirit in early historic Greece (2.2).

> One has only to reflect profoundly on the linguistic difference of colour, syntactical structure, and vocabulary in Homer and Pindar to comprehend the meaning of this contrast.[32]

At times, Nietzsche even seems aware of the opening out of the language of mystic initiation to confront the alienating *visualized language* of money.[33] In response to the almost incomprehensible "break with the unconscious metaphysics of [this] earlier existence" (2.2), the early Greeks recall that their "gods also philosophize" and turn to "Dionysus" (4.1) whose earthly and communal spirit rises up to rescue humankind by "impos[ing] silence and attentiveness on everything loud and self-conceited" (3.1)—that is, by conquering the *visualized language* of money.

But Nietzsche, like all philosophers still today, never reaches this historical height. Unable to offer a clear account of the birth of tragedy, he leaves us with his all-too-familiar (and immature) formulation of tragedy as the result of "a metaphysical miracle of Hellenic 'will'" that fuses the Dionysian and Apolline "artistic powers" (3.3). As we have seen, the ancient relation of Dionysus and Apollo extends into prehistoric time, perhaps even to the twelfth or thirteenth centuries B.C.E.[34] Although Nietzsche's argument that tragedy emerges from Dionysian and Apolline artistic impulses is (somewhat) tenable, he nevertheless fails to explain why this unprecedented aesthetic synthesis arises at this particular time in history, that is, in the late sixth and early fifth centuries B.C.E. Why not before, according to his style of thought?

The fatal blind spot in Nietzsche's thinking is his unawareness of the now conspicuous, if recent fact that the "beautiful mixture" (3.3) of artistic forces out of which tragedy ascends is a direct result of the harmful visual culture that accompanies the monetization of human life in seventh to early sixth centuries B.C.E.[35] Consider Nietzsche's turn to Hesiod, who struggles with the contradictions of the Homeric universe, for instance, in regard to "the series of cultural ages"[36] that the early Greek poet sought to express in gold, silver and bronze: he knew not how to reconcile the contradiction within the Homeric world with which he was confronted, the beautiful, but at the same time so awful, so violent, other than by making two ages out of one, which he henceforth placed one behind the other—first, the age of heroes and demigods from Troy and Thebes, as this world remained in the memory of excellent races who had found in them their own ancestors; then the bronze age, as that same age appeared to the descendants of those who were conquered, exploited, ill-treated, exiled, and sold: as an age of bronze, as noted, hard, cold, gruesome, without feeling or conscience, crushing everything and bespattered with blood. [37]

Not only does Nietzsche fail to note that Hesiod is speaking not of three ages, but of five races (gold, silver, bronze, heroes, and iron), but more importantly he also fails to notice that Hesiod's imagination of humankind as emerging from (mostly) metallic races is an unconscious prefiguration of the later idea of a person as a coin. [38]

The second problem that plagues Nietzsche's understanding of the tragic play is in regard to its downfall. That he knows that tragedy died and that this tragic death is historically caught up in "bourgeois mediocrity" (2.2) as well as the "'evil eye,'" 'böser Blick,' "the poisonous eye of *ressentiment*," *das Giftauge des Ressentiment*, and "treacherous eyes," *verrätersich[e] Augen*" (2.1) indeed suggests that Nietzsche at least senses the serious problem of money and its visual culture that erupt already in early historic Greece. His notion that "Greek art and especially Greek tragedy delayed" its "suicide" (2.2) further suggests that he is somewhat aware of the opening out of Dionysian ritual as a way of resisting this dangerous new historical threat.

Nevertheless, the claim that "the primal problem of tragedy"[39] has been revealed is outlandish. Whereas Socrates not only has nothing to do with the death of tragedy—one may even argue that Socrates succumbs to the same mortal enemy (the corruption of the earthly spirit of community by *monetized seeing*), the Jews whom Nietzsche accuses of destroying "Greek culture" (8.3)—to give just one example—are nowhere near Athens in the late sixth and early fifth centuries, or soon thereafter. [40]

Because Nietzsche understands neither its birth nor its death, it is hardly expected that he can understand the meaning of the tragic play. As Seaford notes, through its "depolitialisation of the Dionysiac and of tragedy, their transformation into purely metaphysical phenomena," *The Birth of Tragedy* is "a symptom and cause" of the (common) neglect of the "[t]he profound influence of the monetisation on Athenian tragedy."[41] It is not uninteresting how (the Schopenhauerian) Nietzsche introduces the idea of the "Maya"[42] — a Sanskrit word meaning illusion or the power of magic that appears in the Indian Vedanta, where it expresses the power of the world to veil, through the multiplicity of natural phenomena, the unity of the individual with Brahama (absolute soul). The association of the time when we transcend the *prin-*

cipium individuationis with actual performance (and implicitly with mystic initiation), including Dionysian song and dance, brings us closer to the potential sociopolitics of the god (3.3).

But as Seaford also notes, "whereas tragedy speaks only of the king (basileus) or the tyrant (turannos), Nietzsche—like so many other moderns—imports the 'hero.'"[43] The evil spirit of the tyrant is left (disastrously) unquestioned. And coupled with Nietzsche's tendency to exclude the sociopolitics of tragedy, as when he dismisses the idea that the chorus of the tragic play represents the community as opposed to the royal actions on stage,[44] the tyrannical will of the "tragic hero" can, through Herakleitean hyper-abstractions, form a veil that conceals Nietzsche's nationalism and racism.

> But let the liar and hypocrite beware of German music, for among all our cultures, it is the only pure and purifying fire-spirit from which and toward which, as in the teaching of the great Herakleitos of Ephesus, all things move in a double orbit. (8.2)

At the center of Nietzsche's expected historical ignorance of the battle of *Dionysiac* and *monetized/visualized chronotopes* with his (hyper-abstract) concept of "an aesthetic phenomenon" (4.1) is the (limitless) search for a father who would legitimate his own (unlimited), perhaps even tyrannical will. One recalls the "primal contradiction and primal pain"[45] that tragedy signifies for the fatherless youth: Herakleitean "eternal contradiction, Father of all things" (12.2).

Similar to Hölderlin, Nietzsche's analysis of tragedy shipwrecks on the sublime. We have noted the psychosis of sadism (perverse enjoyment of the suffering of the other) that accompanies this modish modern concept—and the inhumanity that such hyper-abstract accompaniment invites (1.1). We have also noted Nietzsche's attraction to the "terror and sublimities [Schrecken und Erhabenheiten] of the recently out-broken war [Krieg]" (8.1) and the celebration of his "sublime for-fighter [erhabener Vorkämpfer]" (8.4) Wagner. The impressionable youth is doubtlessly also influenced by Schopenhauer's concept of the transition from the beautiful to sublime.

But the unnatural spirit of the sublime that plagues Nietzsche's interest in Dionysian Greece persists into his late, more explicitly racist works. This is clear when we consider "the sublime as the artistic binding of the horrific" (4.1) of his youth with the "horrific happiness" (9.2)[46] of the late Nietzsche. Throughout his life, hyper-abstract concepts that damage an understanding of tragedy (such as the sublime) enable racism at the cost of clear thinking. Consider Nietzsche's tragic "art," *Kunst*, that "must above all demand purity [Reinheit] in its sphere" (4.1) alongside his "self-conscious art-product," *Kunstprodukt*, and its darker goal: "[t]he purification of the race," *Die Reinigung der Rasse* (10.2). Whereas he celebrates the Greeks who arise through their mystical battle against tyrants—"the people of tragic mysteries who fight the Persian wars" (3.3)—is it not the "tragic hero," that is, the potential tyrant of Persia, Zarathustra, with whom Nietzsche identifies?

At the core of Nietzsche's ignorance about the historical reality of Greece is his turn away from *Dionysiac language*. This does not mean that he, again similar to Hölderlin, does not sense the danger of a *visualized language* (influenced by money) already in early historic Greece. Whereas Nietzsche compares a linguistic experience that is alienated from nature to degenerate "coins" (2.2)—and describes the birth of evil and abstract concepts that are "an opposition to life" as being "coined" (2.1)—he also notes the *visualized/ linguistic danger* that accompanies, for instance, the time when a mythic people begin "to comprehend themselves historically," and forsake their "native soil."[47]

The aggressive will to homogenization (that is, to *equality* and *regularity*) that Nietzsche associates with Homer is inextricably tied to how the epic poet is "sunk[en] in pure gazing at pictures" (2.2). From here the threat of a *visualized language* emerges rapidly alongside the (unlimited) expansion of Western civilization— and what is perhaps second only to money as its most powerful, if still unrecognized, technology of alphabetic writing. The "Alexandrian man" who "is finally a librarian and corrector of proofs, and wretchedly goes blind from the dust of books and printer's errors" soon gives way to the "literary *decadence*" (2.2) of our fossil-fueled modern time which consists, incidentally, of an (unlimited) mass of "reading idlers" (5.4) with "pointed eyes" (5.3).

This also does not mean that Nietzsche (uncanny again in his likeness to Hölderlin) does not sense the power of the opening out of *Dionysiac language* to resist a new *visualized language*. Whereas Hölderlin speaks even of Dionysian writing—for instance, "the silent text" (V 8) that "[f]ollows the fruit, like the dark leaf / Of the meadow" (V 7–8; 11.3)—Nietzsche explicitly associates his writings with the natural epiphany of "fruit," as when Zarathustra speaks to his disciples of delicious "figs" that "fall from the trees."[48] "I am a north wind to ripe figs," he declares: "Thus, like figs, my teachings fall to you, my friends: now drink their juice and sweet flesh!"[49] As we have noted, Nietzsche conceives of language as "[t]he transformation of neural stimuli in sounds" that are rooted in the spirit of different local landscapes and peoples—that is, in a humble, terrestrial linguistic spirit that manifests itself in "[t]he various languages that exist alongside one another" (2.2).

This concept of linguistic experience as an event that is unique to earthly places and communal localities raises the act of speaking above that of writing. Just as Zarathustra declares that "spirit itself will stink" after "[a]nother century of readers" (5.4), Nietzsche is careful to transmit the secret wisdom "of the god Dionysus," as if in a whisper, "from mouth to mouth" (4.1).

One of the profound paradoxes that haunt Nietzsche's vast canvass of text, if scarcely recognized, is that he is more interested in spoken versus written language. One thinks of the impossible title, *Thus Wrote Zarathustra*. As if intuiting that they not only invented our enduring, contemporary historical problem of a *monetized* and *visualized language*, but also the solution to this danger in the form of an (unfinished) *Dionysiac language*, Nietzsche names the Greeks "the chariot-drivers of every subsequent culture."[50]

But as we have seen, his final concept of language absorbs the democratic (antiracist) spirit of *Dionysiac language* into a *proto-National Socialist language*. Because words arise from "the highest class" of the warlike "Aryan conquering race" (10.2), they are not available to all peoples and places. "That everyone is able to learn to read eventually corrupts not only writing, but also thinking" (5.4).

This betrays a critical, if overlooked, ignorance upon which Nietzschean (and almost all other forms of) thought is tragically built. Like all philosophers before and since him—and despite a productive fascination with the primal powers and artistry of sound and image—Nietzsche never reflects upon the visual media that dominated his entire life and work: alphabetic writing. In other words, the philosopher is expectedly ignorant of the history of Homer's invention.[51] Nietzsche never considers the tense relationship of alphabetic writing to *Dionysiac language* nor its peculiar power and tendency to facilitate a *monetized/visualized language*—nor, we might also note, the (indirect) similarity of alphabetic writing to a Jewish text, namely the Pentateuch, that is significantly invented in Babylon during the sixth century B.C.E. (2.1).[52]

Similar to Hölderlin, Nietzsche's concept of the origin of language is absorbed into hyper-abstractions that threaten to know nothing of earth and community.[53] Unlike Hölderlin, however, Nietzsche transfers the vengeance that lurks within Judeo-Christian phantasms of language to that of nineteenth-century linguistic racism.

"IN THE TEN YEARS OF HIS LONELINESS"

We have gestured to Nietzsche's unconscious abandonment of Dionysian Greece and implicit return to a contradictory style of *monetized* and *visualized* space-times whose affinity to (unlimited) hyper-abstraction reinforce his racism. But alongside this perverse love of (limitless) Herakleitean "contrast and war," *Gegensatz und Krieg* (12.2), is an all-too-philosophical (and Herakleitean) egoism. As we have seen, pre-Socratic philosophy is inseparable from the emergence of individuals who ritualize their individualism. Parmenides, for instance, is often absorbed (like Herakleitos) in an imagination of his uniqueness—*as the philosopher who knows*—above and beyond all others.[54]

Like his pre-Socratic "tragic hero"/tyrant Herakleitos, Nietzsche never misses a chance to heroize himself. While musing on Dionysus's love, he pauses to note: "Who, other than me, knows what Ariadne is!"[55] Speaking of one of the central songs from his supremely "self-conscious art-product" (10.2), *Zarathustra*, Nietzsche mildly reminds us that "[t]he likes of which has never been poeticised, never felt, never *suffered*."[56] And this is just a trace of that which has already been (self-)confirmed.

> This work stands entirely for itself. Let us leave the poets aside: perhaps absolutely nothing has ever been achieved from such an equal overflow of force. My concept "Dionysian" was here the *highest deed*; measured against it, all the rest of human activity appears poor and limited. That a Goethe, a Shakespeare would not know how to breathe in this vast passion and these heights, that Dante, when compared to Zarathustra, is just one more believer and not one who first *created* truth, a *world-governing* spirit, a destiny—, that the poets of the Veda priests are not even worthy of unfastening the shoes of a Zarathustra, that is all that at least can be said and yet still gives no concept of the distance, of the *azure* loneliness, in which this work lives.[57]

Alongside this self-praise is Nietzsche's similarly perverse (if somewhat creative) appropriation of the vengeful spirit of Rome against the Jews: *Ecce homo*—the desperate mythologizing of himself. One recalls his (infamous) essays: *Why I am so wise*, *Why I am so clever*, *Why I write such good books*, and—last but not least—*Why I am a destiny*.[58] Still more than Hölderlin, Nietzsche advertises himself as the prophet of a new German planet.[59] In contrast to his *Lieblingsdichter*, his struggle against the (*monetized* and *visualized*) nihilism of the present culminates in an Aryan "tragic hero"/tyrant, Zarathustra: the prophet of the *Übermensch* (9.3, 11.3). Although Nietzsche declares that he is "the last disciple and initiate of the god Dionysus" (4.1), it is unclear whether the original and true mystics of mystery-cult would have initiated Nietzsche into their secret world. Probably not.

As we should expect, the Herakleitean spirit of Nietzsche's (unlimited) fighting and self-glorification leads to a state of self-isolation. After declaring that *Zarathustra* "stands entirely for itself," that is, in "*azure* loneliness," he proceeds to declare also that his "tragic hero"/tyrant "has an eternal right to say: 'I draw circles and sacred boundaries about myself; fewer and fewer climb with me.'"[60] That which "has never been poeticised, never felt, never *suffered*" is none other than Zarathustra's lonely *Night-song*: "But I live in my own light, I drink back the flames that break forth from me" (6.3). This is the context in which he proclaims himself the only living human on a planet (with something between one and two billion persons) who knows "what Ariadne is!"

The ancient identification of pre-Socratic philosophers (such as Parmenides) with the isolation of the mystic initiand[61] extends to Herakleitos— whose conceptual, fiery soul has no relation to gods and humans (12.2). As I have shown, mystic isolation is adapted to express that of the monetized and visualized tyrant on the Greek stage.[62]

This hyper-abstract, devious, and lonely spirit is present throughout Nietzsche's works. Consider the picture he paints of the "desolate, lonely individual" (7.2) and the "elevated place of lonely observation where he will have few companions" (8.3) in *The Birth of Tragedy*. One thinks also of the Herakleitean (self-isolating) Zarathustra. Although he speaks of abandoning his "loneliness" (6.1), that is, of the time after Zarathustra "went into the Aryan province and composed the *Avesta* in the ten years of his loneliness in the mountains" (10.3), the community to which Nietzsche's "tragic hero"/ tyrant belongs remains unclear.

To conclude this analysis, the (unlimited) battling, self-heroizing, and self-isolating cosmology of pre-Socratics such as Parmenides, Anaximander, and Herakleitos to whom Nietzsche is attracted—which consists largely of the thoughts of individuals who (like Pentheus, Kreon, and Oedipus) are no longer connected to any context or tradition of (social) performance—invites a perverse fascination with death. In a sense, this is not difficult to understand. For does not the spirit of self-hatred that conceals itself in the degradation of the other through "an imaginary vengeance" (2.1)[63] lead to an "eternal recurrence" (12.1) of self-murder? This invites us to rethink Zarathustra's otherwise thoughtful reflections on "the will's teeth-gnashing and most lonely melancholy" when confronted with mortality (6.2).

As I have shown, Hölderlin also betrays a curious obsession with death. *The Dying Fatherland* and the tragic *Oedipus at Kolonus* who willfully embraces his finitude continue in the poet's commentary, for instance, in his notes on *Antigone* where tragedy is understood as a representation "of the god who is present in the shape of death."[64] Consider further the *Todeslust* to which the poet almost surrenders in *Memento*, in particular the third strophe when Hölderlin dreams of how "sweet / It would be to sleep among the shadows" (v 28–29).[65] But for Nietzsche the peculiar love of the "horrific happiness" (9.2) of death is caught up in a new, still more sinister style of redemption.

Although this is not the place to take up the following specific and profound philosophical discussion to which this conclusion points (and which still today has never been truly addressed), it is important to note that by the mid- to late nineteenth century—that is, about the time Nietzsche was active—the *monetized* and *visualized chronotopes* had, by virtue of the historical emergence of still another new energy transition (that is, from coal and steam to oil), begun to threaten human existence on earth in ways that even Hölderlin, despite the genius of his forward-looking poetry, could never have imagined (1). The sociopolitical powerlessness that Nietzsche suffers while adapting Dionysian Greece to confront this inhumanity represents, therefore, a still more dangerous crisis in German identity, among other things.

Because Nietzsche is unable to resolve the historical problems that he uncovers, the protracted, painful spirit of his life and work gradually shade into an essence of irrational, unending suffering. The spirit of rebirth and purity, in other words, becomes perversely fused to the failure to found a true identity—and escape, finally, the painful proximity to death. Dionysus's unique power to cleanse injustice, to release individuals from mortal finitude and open out a glimpse of an earthly and communal paradise to which all living beings (equally) belong—the original "meaning of earth" (5.1)—is neutralized by Nietzsche's need to associate the unlimited (anti-Dionysian) presence of death in pre-Socratic philosophy. This means "the suffering downfall" for which "everything that comes into existence must be prepared" (4.2) and a modern "despicable sequence of murder" that Nietzschean "happy monsters" (9.2) are destined to execute.

NOTES

1. D, in *Friedrich Nietzsche, Kritische Studienausgabe*, ed. Giorgio Colli and Mazzino Montinari, vol. 3, *Morgenröte, Idyllen aus Messina, Die fröhliche Wissenschaft* (Berlin: de Gruyter, 1999), 180. Dann, wenn die Juden auf solche Edelsteine und goldene Gefässe als ihr Werk hinzuweisen haben, wie sie die europäischen Völker kürzerer und weniger tiefer Erfahrung nicht hervorzubringen vermögen und vermochten, wenn Israel seine ewige Rache in eine ewige Segnung Europa's verwandelt haben wird: dann wird jener siebente Tag wieder einmal da sein, an dem der alte Judengott sich seiner selber, seiner Schöpfung und seines auserwählten Volkes *freuen* darf,—und wir Alle, Alle wollen uns mit ihm freun!

2. BGE, in *Friedrich Nietzsche, Kritische Studienausgabe*, ed. G. Colli and M. Montinari, vol. 5, *Jenseits von Gut und Böse, Zur Genealogie der Moral* (Berlin: de Gruyter, 1999), 15. "Der Wille zur Wahrheit, der uns noch zu manchem Wagnisse verführen wird, jene berühmte Wahrhaftigkeit, von der alle Philosophen bisher mit Ehrerbietung geredet haben: was für Fragen hat dieser Wille zur Wahrheit uns schon vorgelegt!"

3. Lucas Murrey, *Hölderlin's Dionysiac Poetry: The Terrifying-Exciting Mysteries* (Heidelberg, New York, Dordrecht, London: Springer, 2015), chapter 14 (14).

4. BT, in *Friedrich Nietzsche, Kritische Studienausgabe*, ed. Giorgio Colli and Mazzino Montinari, vol. 1, *Die Geburt der Tragödie, Unzeitgemäße Betrachtungen I–IV, Nachgelassene Schriften 1870–1873* (Berlin: de Gruyter, 1999), 153. bei der höchsten Lust an der deutlich perzipierten Wirklichkeit, erinnern daran, daß wir in beiden Zuständen ein dionysisches Phänomen zu erkennen haben, das uns immer von neuem wieder das spielende Aufbauen und Zertrümmern der Individualwelt als den Ausfluß einer Urlust offenbart, in einer ähnlichen Weise, wie wenn von Heraklit dem Dunklen die weltbildende Kraft einem Kinde verglichen wird, das spielend Steine hin und her setzt und Sandhaufen aufbaut und wieder einwirft.

5. EH, in *Nietzsche, Kritische Studienausgabe*, Colli and Montinari, vol. 6, *Der Fall Wagner, Götzen-Dämmerung, Der Antichrist, Ecce homo, Dionysos-Dithyramben, Nietzsche contra Wagner* (Berlin: de Gruyter, 1999), 313. "Die Lehre von der 'ewigen Wiederkunft,' das heisst vom unbedingten und unendlich wiederholten Kreislauf aller Dinge—diese Lehre Zarathustra's könnte zuletzt auch schon von Heraklit gelehrt worden sein. Zum Mindesten hat die Stoa, die fast alle ihre grundsätzlichen Vorstellungen von Heraklit geerbt hat, Spuren davon."

6. Ibid., 312.

7. Ibid., "Ein Zweifel blieb mir zurück bei Heraklit, in dessen Nähe überhaupt mir wärmer, mir wohler zu Muthe wird als irgendwo sonst."

8. Ibid., "In diesem Sinne habe ich das Recht, mich selber als den ersten *tragischen Philosophen* zu verstehn—daß heißt den äußersten Gegensatz und Antipoden eines pessimistischen Philosophen."

9. Ibid., 311. "Dieser Anfang ist über alle Maassen merkwürdig. Ich hatte zu meiner innersten Erfahrung das einzige Gleichniss und Seitenstück, das die Geschichte hat, entdeckt,—ich hatte eben damit das wundervolle Phänomen des Dionysischen als der Erste begriffen."

10. Ibid., "Ich sah zuerst den eigentlichen Gegensatz."

11. This thesis has been put forth, at least implicitly, by Richard Seaford since the late 1990s. Seaford, "Tragic Money," *JHS* (1998):119–39. For its (explicit) argument, see Seaford, "Monetisation and the Genesis of Philosophy," *Ordia Prima* (2004): 2. The main work is Seaford, *Money and the Early Greek Mind* (Cambridge: Cambridge University Press, 2004). See also Murrey, *Hölderlin's Dionysiac Poetry*, 5.2.

12. Richard Seaford, *Cosmology and the Polis: The Social Construction of Space and Time in the Tragedies of Aeschylus* (Cambridge: Cambridge University Press, 2012), 59–64, 331.

13. Ibid., 59, 331, 231–65. Herakleitos, Fragment der *Vorsokratiker, Griechisch und Deutsch*, übersetz. v. Hermann Diels, hg. v. Walther Kranz, vol. 1 (Berlin: Weidmann, 2004), 171. See also Fragments 30 and 45, 157–58, 161, respectively. Anaximander's concentration of necessity (chreōn) and debt (chreos), and Herakleitos's saying that "[t]he way up and down is the same" further echo the limitlessness of money in space and time. Seaford, *Cosmology and the Polis*, 59–64, 331. Herakleitos, Fragment B60 and B80, 164 and 169, respectively. See also A22, 144. Seaford, *Cosmology and the Polis*, 58. For a discussion of this argument in regard to Hölderlin, see Murrey, *Hölderlin's Dionysiac Poetry*, 5.2.

14. Nietzsche's so-called true Kantian nature is an issue that arose, in part, from Kaufmann's translation of his essay "Truth and Lies in an Extramoral Sense," which leaves out a reference to Kant's concept of space and time. Murrey, *Hölderlin's Dionysiac Poetry*, 5.2.

15. Murrey, *Hölderlin's Dionysiac Poetry*, 5.2.

16. Herakleitos, Fragment B30, in *Die Fragmente der Vorsokratiker, Griechisch und Deutsch*, vol. 1, 157–58. "[T]he kosmos, the same for all things, was not made by god or man but always was and is and will be an ever-living fire." As Seaford notes, "fire in some way underlies the constant transformation of opposites into each other. The soul, which is composed of cosmic fire, has no spatial limits (B45)." Seaford, *Cosmology and the Polis*, 59.

17. Seaford, *Cosmology and the Polis*, 259.

18. Ibid.

19. GS, in *Nietzsche, Kritische Studienausgabe*, vol. 3, 527–28, 570.

20. EH, in *Nietzsche, Kritische Studienausgabe*, vol. 6, 313.

21. BT, in *Nietzsche, Kritische Studienausgabe*, vol. 1, 39.

22. Z., in *Friedrich Nietzsche, Kritische Studienausgabe*, ed. Giorgio Colli and Mazzino Montinari, vol. 4, *Also sprach Zarathustra. Ein Buch für Alle und Keinen* (Berlin: de Gruyter, 1999), 131. "Daß Kampf und Ungleiches auch noch in der Schönheit sei, und Krieg um Macht und Übermacht: das lehrt er uns hier im deutlichsten Gleichnis./Wie sich göttlich hier Gewölbe und Bogen brechen, im Ringkampfe: wie mit Licht und Schatten sie wider einander streben, die göttlich-Strebenden—/Also sicher und schön laßt uns auch Feinde sein, meine Freunde! Göttlich wollen wir *wider* einander streben!"

23. Murrey, *Hölderlin's Dionysiac Poetry*, 14.

24. Ibid., 3.

25. BT, in *Nietzsche, Kritische Studienausgabe*, vol. 1, 140.

26. Ibid.

27. Ibid., 49. "Vom Standpunkte des Epos ist diese ungleiche und unregelmässige Bilderwelt der Lyrik einfach zu verurtheilen: und dies haben gewiss die feierlichen epischen Rhapsoden der apollinischen Feste im Zeitalter des Terpander gethan."

28. Ibid., "In der Dichtung des Volksliedes sehen wir also die Sprache auf das Stärkste angespannt, *die Musik nachzuahmen*: deshalb beginnt mit Archilochus eine neue Welt der Poesie, die der homerischen in ihrem tiefsten Grunde widerspricht."

29. Ibid., "Hiermit haben wir das einzig mögliche Verhältniss zwischen Poesie und Musik, Wort und Ton bezeichnet: das Wort, das Bild, der Begriff sucht einen der Musik analogen Ausdruck und erleidet jetzt die Gewalt der Musik an sich."
30. Murrey, *Hölderlin's Dionysiac Poetry*, 3.
31. BT, in *Nietzsche, Kritische Studienausgabe*, vol. 1, 49. "In diesem Sinne dürfen wir in der Sprachgeschichte des griechischen Volkes zwei Hauptströmungen unterscheiden, jenachdem die Sprache die Erscheinungs- und Bilderwelt oder die Musikwelt nachahmte."
32. Ibid.
33. Murrey, *Hölderlin's Dionysiac Poetry*, 4.
34. Ibid., 3.2.
35. Ibid., 3.1.
36. GM, in *Nietzsche, Kritische Studienausgabe*, vol. 5, 277. "Ich habe einmal auf die Verlegenheit Hesiods aufmerksam gemacht, als er die Abfolge der Kultur-Zeitalter aussann."
37. Ibid.und sie in Gold, Silber, Erz auszudrücken suchte: er wusste mit dem Widerspruch, den ihm die herrliche, aber ebenfalls so schauerliche, so gewalttätige Welt Homers bot, nicht anders fertig zu werden, als indem er aus einem Zeitalter zwei machte, die er nunmehr hintereinanderstellte—einmal das Zeitalter der Helden und Halbgötter von Troja und Theben, so wie jene Welt im Gedächtnis der vornehmen Geschlechter zurückgeblieben war, die in ihr die eignen Ahnherrn hatten; sodann das eherne Zeitalter, so wie jene gleiche Weit den Nachkommen der Niedergetretenen, Beraubten, Misshandelten, Weggeschleppten, Verkauften erschien: als ein Zeitalter von Erz, wie gesagt, hart, kalt, grausam, gefühl- und gewissenlos, alles zermalmend und mit Blut übertünchend.
38. Seaford, *Money and the Early Greek Mind*, 298.
39. BT, in *Nietzsche, Kritische Studienausgabe*, vol. 1, 104.Nach der Erkenntniss jenes ungeheuren Gegensatzes fühlte ich eine starke Nöthigung, mich dem Wesen der griechischen Tragoedie und damit der tiefsten Offenbarung des hellenischen Genius zu nahen: denn erst jetzt glaubte ich des Zaubers mächtig zu sein, über die Phraseologie unserer ueblichen Aesthetik hinaus, das Urproblem der Tragoedie mir leibhaft vor die Seele stellen zu koennen: wodurch mir ein so befremdlich eigenthuemlicher Blick in das Hellenische vergoennt war, dass es mir scheinen musste, als ob unsre so stolz sich gebaerdende classisch-hellenische Wissenschaft in der Hauptsache bis jetzt nur an Schattenspielen und Aeusserlichkeiten sich zu weiden gewusst habe.
40. Although Nietzsche also at times seems to mean the implicit attack of the Jews on Dionysus through the resentful spirit of Christianity, it is his lack of historical clarity, despite his creative insights, that I question.
41. Richard Seaford, "Hölderlin and the Politics of the Dionysiac," in *Money, Writing and the Wine God*, ed. Lucas Murrey (forthcoming, 2015).
42. BT, *Nietzsche, Kritische Studienausgabe*, vol. 1, 29–30.Und so möchte von Apollo in einem excentrischen Sinne das gelten, was Schopenhauer von dem im Schleier der Maja befangenen Menschen sagt. Welt als Wille und Vorstellung I, S. 416 "Wie auf dem tobenden Meere, das, nach allen Seiten unbegränzt, heulend Wellenberge erhebt und senkt, auf einem Kahn ein Schiffer sitzt, dem schwachen Fahrzeug vertrauend; so sitzt, mitten in einer Welt von Qualen, ruhig der einzelne Mensch, gestützt und vertrauend auf das principium individuationis."
43. Seaford, "Hölderlin and the Politics of the Dionysiac."
44. BT, in *Nietzsche, Kritische Studienausgabe*, vol. 1, 52. "auf die ursprüngliche Formation der Tragödie ist er ohne Einfluss, da von jenen rein religiösen Ursprüngen der ganze Gegensatz von Volk und Fürst, überhaupt jegliche politisch-sociale Sphäre ausgeschlossen ist." As Seaford notes, Nietzsche's distaste for the "political-social sphere" seems directed against Hegel's interpretation of tragedy, to say nothing of sociopolitics of Bismarck's *Norddeutsches Reich*. See Richard Seaford, *Dionysus* (London and New York: Routledge, 2006), 144.
45. BT, in *Nietzsche, Kritische Studienausgabe*, vol. 1, 44. "Seine Subjectivität hat der Künstler bereits in dem dionysischen Prozess aufgegeben: das Bild, das ihm jetzt seine Einheit mit dem Herzen der Welt zeigt, ist eine Traumscene, die jenen Urwiderspruch und Urschmerz, sammt der Urlust des Scheines, versinnlicht."
46. Ibid., 57. GM, in *Nietzsche, Kritische Studienausgabe*, vol. 5, 275.Die vornehmen Rassen sind es, welche den Begriff "Barbar" auf all den Spuren hinterlassen haben, wo sie gegan-

gen sind: noch aus ihrer höchsten Kultur heraus verrät sich ein Bewusstsein davon und ein Stolz selbst darauf (zum Beispiel wenn Perikles seinen Athenern sagt, in jener berühmten Leichenrede, "zu allem Land und Meer hat unsre Kühnheit sich den Weg gebrochen, unvergängliche Denkmale sich überall im Guten und Schlimmen aufrichtend"). Diese "Kühnheit" vornehmer Rassen, toll, absurd, plötzlich, wie sie sich äussert, das Unberechen-bare, das Unwahrscheinliche selbst ihrer Unternehmungen—Perikles hebt die der Athener mit Auszeichnung hervor—, ihre Gleichgültigkeit und Verachtung gegen Sicherheit, Leib, Leben, Behagen, ihre entsetzliche Heiterkeit und Tiefe der Lust in allem Zerstören, in allen Wollüsten des Siegs und der Grausamkeit—alles fasste sich für die, welche daran litten, in das Bild des "Barbaren," des "bösen Feindes," etwa des "Goten," des "Vandalen" zusammen.

47. BT, in *Nietzsche, Kritische Studienausgabe*, vol. 1, 148.Das Gegentheil davon tritt ein, wenn ein Volk anfängt, sich historisch zu begreifen und die mythischen Bollwerke um sich herum zu zertrümmern: womit gewöhnlich eine entschiedene Verweltlichung, ein Bruch mit der unbewussten Metaphysik seines früheren Daseins, in allen ethischen Consequenzen, ver-bunden ist. Die griechische Kunst und vornehmlich die griechische Tragödie hielt vor Allem die Vernichtung des Mythus auf: man musste sie mit vernichten, um, losgelöst von dem heimischen Boden, ungezügelt in der Wildniss des Gedankens, der Sitte und der That leben zu können.

48. Z, in *Nietzsche, Kritische Studienausgabe*, vol. 4, 109. "Die Feigen fallen von den Bäumen, sie sind gut und süss; und indem sie fallen, reisst ihnen die rothe Haut."

49. Ibid., "Ein Nordwind bin ich reifen Feigen./Also, gleich Feigen, fallen euch diese Leh-ren zu, meine Freunde: nun trinkt ihren Saft und ihr süsses Fleisch!"

50. BT, in *Nietzsche, Kritische Studienausgabe*, vol. 1, 97–98.Und so schämt und fürchtet man sich vor den Griechen; es sei denn, dass Einer die Wahrheit über alles achte und so sich auch diese Wahrheit einzugestehn wage, dass die Griechen unsere und jegliche Cultur als Wagenlenker in den Händen haben, dass aber fase immer Wagen und Pferde vor zu geringem Stoffe und der Glorie ihrer Führer unangemessen sind, die dann es für einen Scherz erachten, ein solches Gespann in den Abgrund zu jagen: über den sie selbst, mit dem Sprunge des Achilles, hinwegsetzen.

51. Barry Powell, "Homer and Writing," in *Money, Writing and the Wine God*, ed. Lucas Murrey (forthcoming, 2015).

52. Barry Powell, "The Philologist's Homer," in *Homer: Blackwell Introductions to the Classical World* (Malden, MA: Blackwell, 2004), 18. "Although attributed to Moses, who may have lived in the Late Bronze Age c. 1200 B.C., the Pentateuch is much too late to be attributed to him in any meaningful way. Sometime in the sixth century B.C., Jewish scholars sat in a room with different scrolls before them. Taking now this, now that, these editors combined pre-existing inconsistent texts to create the version we have today. Some called God Yahweh (evidently a volcano spirit from the Sinai), others called him Elohim (Semitic for "gods"). That is why he has both names in Genesis, a thesis about the origins of the Pentateuch on which all modern scholars agree." Murrey, *Hölderlin's Dionysiac Poetry*, 2.1.

That Nietzsche has never been criticized for his conspicuous (and fundamental) ignorance in regard to the invention of and history of writing is doubtlessly caught up in the fact that German philologists of ancient Greece from August Wolf in the eighteenth and early nineteenth centuries to Wolfgang Schadewaldt in the twentieth century have systematically also failed to free themselves of this ignorance—which persists, tragically, still today. In particular, both Wolf and Schadewaldt make the fundamental mistake of believing that Homer's texts arose (like the Pentateuch) from preexisting traces of writing. See Powell, "The Philologist's Homer," 21. Such hyper-abstractions not only reinforce an inauthentic picture of the Greeks and their relation to other (for instance, Jewish) peoples—see *Hellas und Hesperien. Gesam-melten Schriften zur Antike und zur neueren Literatur, Zum 60. Geburtsrag von Wolfgang Schadewaldt am 15 März 1960*, ed. Ernst Zinn (Zürich, Stuttgart: Artemis, 1960)—but also a persistent (and unexplored) strain of *National Socialism* that continues after 1945. This is implicit when Heidegger reaches out to his (old friend and colleague) Alfred Bäumler through Schadewaldt in 1951. Alfred Bäumler, "Kulturmorphologie und Philosophie," in *Spengler-Studien. Festgabe für Manfred Schröter zum 85. Geburtstag* (München: C.H. Beck, 1965), 115–16.

53. Murrey, *Hölderlin's Dionysiac Poetry*, 13–14.

54. Seaford, *Cosmology and the Polis*, 331. See also Murrey, *Hölderlin's Dionysiac Poetry*, 5.2.

55. EH, in *Nietzsche, Kritische Studienausgabe*, vol. 6, 348.

56. Ibid., "Dergleichen ist nie gedichtet, nie gefühlt, nie *gelitten* worden."

57. Ibid., 343.Dieses Werk steht durchaus für sich. Lassen wir die Dichter beiseite: es ist vielleicht überhaupt nie etwas aus einem gleichen Überfluß von Kraft heraus getan worden. Mein Begriff "dionysisch" wurde hier *höchste Tat*; an ihr gemessen erscheint der ganze Rest von menschlichem Tun als arm und bedingt. Daß ein Goethe, ein Shakespeare nicht einen Augenblick in dieser ungeheuren Leidenschaft und Höhe zu atmen wissen würde, daß Dante, gegen Zarathustra gehalten, bloß ein Gläubiger ist und nicht einer, der die Wahrheit erst *schafft*, ein *weltregierender* Geist, ein Schicksal—, daß die Dichter des Veda Priester sind und nicht einmal würdig, die Schuhsohlen eines Zarathustra zu lösen, das ist alles das wenigste und gibt keinen Begriff von der Distanz, von der *azurnen* Einsamkeit, in der dies Werk lebt.

58. Ibid., 264, 278, 298, 365.

59. Murrey, *Hölderlin's Dionysiac Poetry*, 14, Coda.

60. EH, in *Nietzsche, Kritische Studienausgabe*, vol. 6, 343. "Zarathustra hat ein ewiges Recht zu sagen: 'ich schließe Kreise um mich und heilige Grenzen; immer wenigere steigen mit mir auf immer höhere Berge—ich baue ein Gebirge aus immer heiligeren Bergen.'"

61. Seaford, *Cosmology and the Polis*, 331.

62. Murrey, *Hölderlin's Dionysiac Poetry*, 2–3.

63. GM, in *Nietzsche, Kritische Studienausgabe*, vol. 5, 270.

64. Murrey, *Hölderlin's Dionysiac Poetry*, 11, 9.1.

65. Ibid., 9.2.

Coda

THE BORDELLO IN LEIPZIG

As we have seen, Nietzsche (unconsciously) illuminates the Dionysian spirit of Greece—its confrontation with money and a new (self-isolating) style of seeing that supports the monetization of humankind—that the rich men and women of our time ruthlessly repress (2–6). And because the money-leaders of our species are nowhere near the level of intelligence required to glimpse the meaning of a real democratic community in balance with nature, the sounds and images of the earthly eternity to which Nietzsche gestures remain uneasy reminders of that which these obscenely rich individuals continually take from us, the people.

Symptoms of this tragedy include outlandish attempts to portray Nietzsche after 1945 not only as having never been nationalist nor a racist (nor anti-Semitic)—all of which are, of course, conspicuously false (7–10)—but also the no less superficial image of Nietzsche's "Dionysian" madness.

Soon after Nietzsche's meteoric rise within the academy, the publication of his first (untimely) book, *The Birth of Tragedy*, scattered the support of his colleagues in Classical Philology (including his mentor Ritschl). Isolated within his field and plagued with physical ailments, the lonely, if still relatively young, professor resigns from his post at the University of Basel in 1879 at the age of thirty-five. The following decade of (astonishing) lucidity that Nietzsche enjoys comes to an abrupt and tragic end in 1889 when he suffers a mortal collapse that leaves him in a (Hölderlinian) state of insanity until his death in 1900.

Explanations of the medical cause of Nietzsche's madness that soon flower—one thinks of Paul Deussen's *Memories of Friedrich Nietzsche* from 1901—tend to ascribe his final, indisposed state to an outbreak of syphilis that the youthful (and lustful) student acquired, perhaps, while visiting a bordello in Leipzig in 1865. Although this diagnosis has been called into question—Nietzsche's madness has also been seen as a result, for instance, of brain cancer—the modern myth of the genius who succumbs to the seductions of "Dionysian sexuality" and insanity (and there is no lack of evidence that Nietzsche loses his mind) persists in the popular imagination even today. After all, is not "dark madness," *der finstere Wahnsinn*, a sign of "[t]he god who comes," *Der kommende Gott*?[1] And did not Nietzsche himself—he who is acutely aware of the significance of the name—dissolve into that of "[t]he mad god," *Der wahnsinnige Gott*?[2] One recalls the letters scribbled underneath his dedication of *Dionysus-Dithyrambs* that he composes in Turin, Italy, in early January of 1889:

Insofar as I want to prove an unlimited blessing to humankind, I present to it the dithyrambs.
I lay them in the hands of the poet Isoline, the greatest and first satyr, who lives today—and not only today . . .
Dionysus[3]

No less disgraceful than the post-1945 romantic myth that Nietzsche's (German) madness is—somehow?—a function of Dionysian Greece is another absurd story that predominates before 1945. Although this earlier misidentification is doubtlessly related to the unfortunate influence of Nietzsche's sister Elisabeth Förster-Nietzsche—the wife of Bernhard Förster (10.2) and into whose care the philosopher, after his mother's death, comes around 1897 (Elizabeth Förster-Nietzsche who founds and leads the Nietzsche Archive from 1894 until her own death in 1935)—the nature of the falsity of this earlier image is strikingly (and uncomfortably) similar to the various misidentifications of Nietzsche that fester today. This is something that even Butler echoes when she suggests that

> [t]here are signs that the mysterious affinity which had tormented Hölderlin also preoccupied Nietzsche: the resemblance between Dionysus Zagreus, the god torn limb from limb.[4]

Before 1945, the mythic inseparability of Nietzsche (and his madness) with Greece (and Dionysus) reinforces the abstract (and racist) concept that the Germans are the unique inheritors of Greek culture among humankind. As we have seen, by 1927 the classicist Curtius regards Winckelmann as the first modern German humanist who "seeks not simply knowledge, but life; not simply erudition, but the freedom of a new mankind."[5] "German humanism," Curtius proceeds, "took over the Greek world from Winckelmann as an artistic revelation just as much as it took it over as a scientific object" (7.1). Whereas other countries like France and England develop organically in the seventeenth and eighteenth centuries out of the Italian Renaissance, he argues, the Renaissance was stifled in Germany for two hundred years. When it finally makes its epiphany, the Renaissance is different: "with the others, it is Roman; with us, it is Greek."[6]

Still more striking, however, is how Curtius's claim (unconsciously) continues the "Dionysian" mood of one evening in February 1903—just a few years after Nietzsche's death—when the young student of antiquity had to "tear [Alfred] Schuler out of his rapture and lead him off stage [as h]e really felt he was Orphic."[7] The elaborate, tailored costumes of that festive night— their silver helmets and lyres of tortoiseshell and horn (and the Attic landscape crowned with the acropolis into which the Munich court theater had been transformed)[8] —also continue the ahistorical image of (Germanized) Greece that emerges (ironically) with Winckelmann's *The History of the Art of Antiquity* from 1764.[9]

Anyone who doubts that Nietzsche's perversion of Dionysus lends itself to legitimate the mass death of the (non-German) other may consider the 150,000 (durable) copies of *Zarathustra* (alongside the bible) that German soldiers carried into battle during *the First World War*. In regard to whether or not Nietzsche's Dionysus lends itself to legitimate not only the coming of a godlike German being, but also the celebration of masses who are willing to die for a new Aryan *Fürher* may recall a passage from *Zarathustra*'s preface.

> I love those who do not first seek a reason behind the stars for going down and being sacrifices: but instead sacrifice themselves to the earth, that the earth of the *Übermensch* may be.[10]

The final question Nietzsche's philosophy places before us, let us not forget, is whether we will continue to produce an endless series of (absurd and distracting) postmodern Nietzschean myths (more *visualized chronotopes*). In our time of unlimited money that is deviously reinforced by the unlimited visual media-ocracy that seems to have destroyed our ability to remember our natural place in the cosmos, what will Nietzsche finally mean to us?

On the one hand, it is clear that the established academic order seeks to ignore Nietzsche's conspicuous "Dionysian philosophy" and continue to embrace—as did the Nazis—the vision of a time dominated by an excellent, chosen (mostly pro-Israeli/American) race that has no regard for others (7–10). One thinks of recent (fashionable) comparisons of bankers to Vikings in newspapers, for instance, in the *Financial Times*, alongside Nietzsche's insight that "[t]he Latin *bonus* can be interpreted, I believe, as 'the warrior.'"[11] Do not the monetized and visualized tyrants of investment firms who are regularly gifted trillions from various governments from the poorest in the world openly declare, as does Lloyd Blankfein, that they are "doing

God's work"?—that is, declaring that they are secretly executing the will of a vengeful Jewish (and/or Christian) God who knows nothing of earth and community? Consider the son of Angela Merkel's modest Swabian *Hausfrau* who fatally succumbs to a lethal (Wall Street) reflection of himself. [12]

Or will we begin to see past the unproductive, dangerous spirit of Nietzsche's (German) identity crisis and glimpse the golden meadow to which he desperately gestures—and begin to honor those elements in his work worth rescuing?

NOTES

1. Walter Otto, *Dionysos, Mythos und Kultus* (Frankfurt: Klostermann, 2011), 94, 74.
2. Ibid., 121.
3. Friedrich Nietzsche, *Werke, Kritische Gesamtausgabe*, hg. v. Giorgio Colli und Mazzino Montinari, Abteilung 3, vol. 5, *Briefwechsel, Januar 1887–Januar 1889* (Berlin: Walter de Gruyter, 1984), (1235), 571. "Indem ich der Menschheit eine unbegrenzte Wohltat erweisen will, gebe ich ihr die Dithyramben./Ich lege sie die Hände des Dichters der Isoline, des grössten und ersten Satyr, der heute lebt./Nietzsche. Dionysos."
4. Eliza Butler, *The Tyranny of Greece over Germany: A Study of the Influence Exercised by Greek Art and Poetry over the Great German Writers of the Eighteenth, Nineteenth and Twentieth Centuries* (Cambridge: Cambridge University Press, 1958), 315.
5. Lucas Murrey, *Hölderlin's Dionysiac Poetry: The Terrifying-Exciting Mysteries* (Berlin: Springer Verlag, 2015), chapter 6.2.
6. Ibid.
7. Ibid.
8. Ibid.
9. Ibid.
10. Z, in *Friedrich Nietzsche, Kritische Studienausgabe*, ed. Giorgio Colli and Mazzino Montinari, vol. 4, *Also sprach Zarathustra. Ein Buch für Alle und Keinen* (Berlin: de Gruyter, 1999), 17. "Ich liebe Die, welche nicht erst hinter den Sternen einen Grund suchen, unterzugehen und Opfer zu sein: sondern die sich der Erde opfern, dass die Erde einst des Übermenschen werde."
11. GM, in *Nietzsche, Kritische Studienausgabe*, Giorgio Colli and Mazzino Montinari, vol. 5, *Jenseits von Gut und Böse, Zur Genealogie der Moral* (Berlin: de Gruyter, 1999), 263. "Das lateinische *bonus* glaube ich als 'den Krieger' auslegen zu dürfen . . . ."
12. Here I am thinking of Moritz Erhardt's lethal attraction to a picture of himself as "Gordon Gekko." See "Bank of America intern's death puts banks' working culture in spotlight: Death of Moritz Erhardt, a German student working for Merril Lynch, triggers call for inquiry into excessive hours in City." *The Guardian*, 21 August 2013, http://www.theguardian.com/money/2013/aug/21/bank-intern-death-working-hours. In a speech held in Stuttgart during the 2008 financial crisis in America, Merkel suggested: "One only should have simply asked the Swabian housewife who would have briefly told us, as befitting true life-wisdom: One cannot live beyond one's means in the long run. That is the core of the crisis." "Man hätte einfach nur die schwäbische Hausfrau fragen sollen, die uns eine ebenso kurze wie richtige Lebensweisheit gesagt hätte: Man kann nicht auf Dauer über seine Verhältnisse leben. Das ist der Kern der Krise." Soon thereafter Merkel aggressively supported Mario Draghi's *Long Term Refinancing Operation* (LTRO) that, since early 2012 until today, has secretly given (and continues to give) trillions of euros to well over 800 banks. Apparently the Swabian *Hausfrau* (mother to the tragic Erhadt) imagines a picture of herself with unlimited money.

Bibliography

Baer, Yitzhak. *A History of the Jews in Spain*. Vol. 2. Translated by L. Schoffman. Philadelphia: Jewish Publication Society, 1992.

Baudelaire, Charles. *Revue Française, Paris, June 10–July 20 (1859)*. In *Charles Baudelaire, The Mirror of Art*. Translated by J. Mayne Doubleday. Garden City, NY: Anchor, 1956.

Bäumler, Alfred. "Kulturmorphologie und Philosophie." In *Spengler-Studien. Festgabe für Manfed Schröter zum 85. Geburtstag*. München: C. H. Beck, 1965.

Bierl, Anton. *Der Chor in der Alten Komödie. Ritual und Performativität*. Berlin: de Gruyter, 2001.

———. *Dionysos und die griechische Tragödie. Politische und "metatheatralische" Aspekte im Text*. Tübingen: Gunter Narr Verlag, 1991.

———. "Tragödie als Spiel und das Satyrspiel. Die Geburt des griechischen Theaters aus dem Geiste des Chortanzes und seines Gottes Dionysos." In *Aufgang. Jahrbuch für Denken, Dichten, Musik*, edited by J-S. de Murrillo and M. Thurner, vol. 3, *Kind und Spiel*. Stuttgart: Kohlhammer, 2006.

Böschenstein, Bernhard. "Geschehen und Gedächtnis: Hölderlins Hymnen 'Wie wenn am Feiertage . . . ' und 'Andenken'—Ein einführender Vortrag." In *Le pauvre Holterling: Blätter zur Frankfurter Ausgabe*, vol. 7. Franfurt am Main: Stroemfeld, 1984. 7–16.

———. *Frucht des Gewitters. Hölderlins Dionysos als Gott der Revolution*. Frankfurt am Main: Insel Verlag, 1989.

———. "Übersetzungen." In *Hölderlin-Hanbuch. Leben, Werk, Wirkung*, hg. J. B. Metzler. Stuttgart, Weimar: Metzler, 2011.

Burgin, Victor, et al., eds. *Photography/Politics: One*. London: Photography Workshop, 1979.

Bury, Robert, trans. *Plato, Laws, Books VII–XII*. Vol. 11. Cambridge: Harvard University Press, 2011.

Butler, Eliza. *The Tyranny of Greece over Germany: A Study of the Influence Exercised by Greek Art and Poetry over the Great German Writers of the Eighteenth, Nineteenth and Twentieth Centuries*. Cambridge: Cambridge University Press, 1958.

Cancik, Hubert. *Nietzsches Antike, Vorlesung*, 2. Auflage. Stuttgart: J. P. Metzler, 2000.

Carlyle, Thomas. *The Letters of Thomas Carlyle to his Brother Alexander with Related Family Letters*. Cambridge: Belknap, 1968.

Colli, Giorgio, and Mazzino Montinari, eds. *Friedrich Nietzsche, Kritische Gesamtausgabe*, Abt. 3., vol. 5, *Briefwechsel, Januar 1887–Januar 1889*. Berlin: de Gruyter, 1984.

———. *Friedrich Nietzsche, Kritische Studienausgabe*, vol. 1, *Die Geburt der Tragödie, Unzeitgemäße Betrachtungen I–IV, Nachgelassene Schriften 1870–1873*. Berlin: de Gruyter, 1999.

———. *Friedrich Nietzsche, Kritische Studienausgabe*, vol. 1.1, *Jugendschriften—Nachgelassene Aufzeichnungen Anfang 1852/Sommer 1858*. Berlin: de Gruyter, 1995.

———. *Friedrich Nietzsche, Kritische Studienausgabe*, vol. 2, *Menschliches, Allzumenschliches I und II*. Berlin: de Gruyter, 1988.

———. *Friedrich Nietzsche, Kritische Studienausgabe*, vol. 3, *Morgenröte, Idyllen aus Messina, Die fröhliche Wissenschaft*. Berlin: de Gruyter, 1999.

———. *Friedrich Nietzsche, Kritische Studienausgabe*, vol. 4, *Also sprach Zarathustra. Ein Buch für Alle und Keinen*. Berlin: de Gruyter, 1993.

———. *Friedrich Nietzsche, Kritische Studienausgabe*, vol. 5, *Jenseits von Gut und Böse, Zur Genealogie der Moral*. Berlin: de Gruyter, 1999.

———. *Friedrich Nietzsche, Kritische Studienausgabe*, vol. 6, *Der Fall Wagner, Götzen-Dämmerung, Der Antichrist, Ecce homo, Dionysos-Dithyramben, Nietzsche contra Wagner*. Berlin: de Gruyter, 1999.

———. *Friedrich Nietzsche, Kritische Studienausgabe*, vol. 7, *Nachgelassene Fragmente, 1869–1874*. Berlin: de Gruyter, 1988.

———. *Friedrich Nietzsche, Kritische Studienausgabe*, vol. 8, *Nachgelassene Fragmente, 1875–1879*. Berlin: de Gruyter, 1988.

———. *Friedrich Nietzsche, Kritische Studienausgabe*, vol. 9, *Nachgelassene Fragmente, 1880–1882*. Berlin: de Gruyter, 1988.

———. *Friedrich Nietzsche, Kritische Studienausgabe*, vol. 14, *Kommentar zu den Bänden 1–13*. Berlin: de Gruyter, 1988.

Diels, Herman, and Walter Kranz, eds. and trans. *Die Fragmente der Vorsokratiker, Griechisch Deutsche*. Zürich: Weidmann, 2004.

Diggle, James, ed. *Euripides fabulae*, vol. 3, *Helena, Phoenissae, Orestes, Bacchae, Iphigenia, Avlidensis, Rhesus*. Oxford: Oxford University Press, 1994.

Doy, Gen. "The Camera against the Paris Commune." In *Photography/Politics: One*, ed. V. Burgin et al. London: Photography Workshop, 1979.

Drake, Stillman, trans. *Discoveries and Opinions of Galileo*. Garden City, NY: Doubleday, 1957.

English, Donald. *Political Uses of Photography in the Third French Republic 1871–1914*. Ann Arbor, MI: UMI Research Press, 1984.

Feuerbach, Ludwig. *Das Wesen des Christintums*. Stuttgart: Reclam, 1978.

Franklin, Michael. *Selected Poetical and Prose Works*. Cardiff: University of Wales Press, 1995.

Hazlitt, William. *Characters of Shakespeare's Plays*. 3rd ed. London: John Templeman, 1838.

Kaufmann, Walter. *The Portable Nietzsche*. New York: Viking, 1982.

Lloyd-Jones, Hugh, ed. *Sophoclis Fabulae*. Oxford: Clarendon Press, 1990.

Luxenberg, Alisa. "Creating Desastres: Andrieu's Photography of Urban Ruins in the Paris of 1871." *Art Bulletin* 80 (1998): 1.

Marchant, Edgar, trans., Xenophon, *Memorabilia Oeconomicus, Symposium, Apology* Translated by Otis Todd. Cambridge: Harvard University Press, 2002.

Marr, Wilhelm. *Der Sieg des Judenthums ueber das Germanenthum*. Charleston: Nabu Press, 1879, 2010.

Marshall, Peter. *The British Discovery of Hinduism in the Eighteenth Century*. Cambridge: Cambridge University Press, 1970.

Marx, Karl. *Manifest der Kommunistischen Partei*. Stuttgart: Reclam, 1989.

———. *Ökonomisch-philosophische Manuskripte, Heft III*. 3. Frankfurt am Main: Suhrkamp, 2009.

Marx, Karl, and Friedrich Engels. *Werke*, vol. 23, *Das Kapital: Kritik der politischen Ökonomie*, Erster Band, *Buch I: Der Produktionsprozeß des Kapitals*. Berlin: Dietz Verlag, 1983.

Mayne, Johnathan, ed. *The Mirror of Art*. Garden City, NY: Doubleday Anchor, 1956.

McCumber, John. *Time in the Ditch: American Philosophy and the McCarthy Era*. Evanston, IL: Northwestern Press, 2001.

Mendelsohn, Daniel. "Synkeraunô: Dithyrambic Language and Dionysiac Cult." *CJ* 87 (1992): 105–24.

Müller, Max. *History of Ancient Sanskrit Literature*. London: AMS, 1978.

Murrey, Lucas. *Hölderlin's Dionysiac Poetry: The Terrifying-Exciting Mysteries*. Heidelberg, New York, Dordrecht, London: Springer, 2015.

———. ed. *Money, Writing and the Wine God*. Forthcoming, 2015.

———. *Fin-de-siècle Germany and the Trauma of the Great War*. Forthcoming, 2016.

Otto, Walter. *Dionysos, Mythos und Kultus*. Frankfurt: Klostermann, 2011.

Page, Denys, ed. *Aeschyli septem quae supersunt tragoedias*. Oxford: Clarendon Press, 1972.

Pickard-Cambridge, Arthur. *The Dramatic Festivals of Athens*. Oxford: Oxford University Press, 1968.

Powell, Barry. "Homer and Writing." In *Money, Writing and the Wine God*, edited by Lucas Murrey. Forthcoming, 2015.

———. "The Philologist's Homer." In *Homer: Blackwell Introductions to the Classical World*. Malden, MA: Blackwell, 2004.

Powell, Barry, and Ian Morris, eds. "Homer and Writing." In *A New Companion to Homer*. Leiden, New York, Köln: Brill, 1997.

Rackham, Horace, trans. *Aristotle, The Athenian Constitution, The Eudemian Ethics, On Virtues and Vices*. Cambridge: Harvard University Press, 1935.

Rennie, Michael, ed. *Demosthenes, Orationes*. Vol. 3. Oxford: Oxford University Press, 1991.

Römer, Ruth. *Sprachwissenschaft und Rassenideologie in Deutschland*. München: Wilhelm Fink Verlag, 1989.

Schivelbusch, Wolfgang. *Geschichte der Eisenbahnreise: Zur Industrialisierung von Raum und Zeit im 19. Jahrhundert*. München: Wilhelm Fink Verlag, 1989.

Schlegel, Friedrich. *Über die Sprache und Weisheit der Indier, Ein Beitrag zur Begründung der Alterthumskunde*. Heidelberg: Mohr und Zimmer, 1808.

Schmidt, Jochen, ed. *Dichter über Hölderlin*. Frankfurt: Insel Verlag, 1969.

———. *Friedrich Hölderlin, Sämtliche Werke und Briefe*, Bd. 1, *Gedichte*. Frankfurt am Main: Deutscher Klassiker Verlag, 1992.

Schwaner, Wihlhelm. *Germanenbibel. Aus heiligen Schriften germanischer Völker*. Schlachtensee: Volkserzieherverlag, 1904–1905.

Seaford, Richard. *Ancient Greece and Global Warming: The Benefits of a Classical Education, or: Learn from the Past to Live in the Present*. Exeter: Credo Press, 2011.

———. *Dionysus*. London and New York: Routledge, 2006.

———. "Hölderlin and the Politics of the Dionysiac." In *Money, Writing and the Wine God*, edited by Lucas Murrey. Forthcoming, 2015.

———. "Monetisation and the Genesis of Philosophy." *Ordia Prima* (2004): 2.

———. *Money and the Early Greek Mind: Homer, Tragedy, Philosophy*. Cambridge: Cambridge University Press, 2004.

———. "Tragic Money." *JHS* (1998): 118–39.

Sontag, Susan. *On Photography*. London: Penguin, 1977.

Weber, Max. *Gesammelte Aufsätze zur Religionssoziologie II*. Tübingen: J. C. B. Mohr, 1972.

Wu, Duncan. ed. *Selected Writings of William Hazlitt*, vol. 1, *An Essay on the Principles of Human Action, Characters of Shakespeare's Plays*. London: Pickering & Chatto, 1998.

Zinn, Ernst, ed. *Hellas und Hesperien. Gesammelten Schriften zur Antike und zur neueren Literatur, Zum 60. Geburtsrag von Wolfgang Schadewaldt am 15 März 1960*. Zürich, Stuttgart: Artemis, 1960.

Index

cosmic (vertical) axis of language, 22
cosmic (vertical) axis of light, 61
cosmological confusion, xxx, 16, 20
cosmological death-struggle, 92
cosmology of pre-Socratic philosophers, 122
cosmos, 31, 44, 121
counter-Alexanders, 8
counter-point, 8
critical layman, 8
crusades, 8
cult gatherings, 17
cultural and linguistic inheritance, 72
culture, *Kultur*, 40

dance, 17
dancing star, 45
Daniel, 6
death, 15, 137
death-battle, 101
deathless god, 17
"deathly silent clamour", 18, 33, 43
death of Greek tragedy, 7
decadence music, 10, 31
degenerate, 75; art, 10; spirit, 59
degraded and overpowered, 89
Demeter, 15
Descartes, 9, 29
descend, 34
descendants of all European and non-European slavery, 101
descendants of those who were conquered, exploited, ill-treated, exiled, and sold, 126
descending through Greece, 99
destruction, xiv
Deutschland, Deutschland über alles, 10
deux ex machine (god of machines), 7, 27, 48
Digital Revolution, xxix
"dignity of labour", 10
Diotima, xviii
Dionysiac: chronotope, xviii, 21; language, xxvi, xxvii, 7, 21, 124, 128; silence, 43; word, 43
Dionysian, xiv; and Apolline artistic powers, 19, 125; art, 30; chorus, 19; dismemberment, 33; eyes (thawing out), 16; festival procession (from

Greece to India), 16, 77, 84, 97; Greece, 103, 127; mask, 20; music, 16; mystic, 60; myth, 29, 41; paradise, 22, 61; person, 17; philosophy, 29; release, 54; reveler, 17; ritual, 21; rulers, 8; seeing, xvii, 15; space-time, 21; spirit of tragedy, 122; storm and excess, 19; tones, 10; wisdom, 22, 73; wisdom of tragedy, 31
Dionysus, xxiv, xxix, 15, 29; and Apollo, 6; chariot, 16; as the democratic god par excellence, 71; female mystics, 33; gentle whisper, 16; love, 130; as philosopher, 29
Dionysus-Dithyrambs, 31
diseased mind, xxiv
dismembered, dying body, 41
dismembered ears,
dismembered god, 15
dismembered hands and arms and all body-parts, 54
dismemberment of Dionysiac language, 105
dismemberment of monetized and visualized language, 46
dithyramb, 16, 21, 138
dithyrambic artist, 33
dithyrambic dance, 18
drama of words, 22
dramatic mysteries, 17

early 2012 until today, 140n12
early Christians, 114
early Greek poet, 125
early Greeks, 125
early historic and modern Jewish identity, 111, 112
early historic Greece, xxvi, 6, 121, 124, 128
early historic philosopher, 121
earth, xiii, 44, 86, 139
earth (unchained from sun), 31
earthly: and communal (Dionysian) limits, 122; and communal spirit of Dionysus, 95; epiphany, 34; goddesses of revenge, 104; magic of honey, 60; masters, xx; places and communal localities, 128; superabundance, 32
earth's darkness, 10

individual death, 41; language, 16;
myth, 6, 15, 18; play, 123, 126; picture
(of blindness), 21, 31; seeing, 15, 45;
stage, 56; time, 105; wisdom, 7, 29, 121
tragically absorbed, 76
tragically germanified Greek culture, 73
tragic-joyous ecstasy, 63
train, xxi
transcending, 121
transfer (and concentration) of a monetized
and visually evil spirit, 112
transfer of a strain of Christian racism, 115
transfigured, 15; Apolline world, 20
transformation, 124
transformation of neural stimuli in sounds,
48
transformative power, 45
transformed, 122
transforming the Greek transformation of
ritual, 105
translation of the Dionysian into a
philosophical pathos, 29, 121
treacherous eyes, *verrätersiche Augen*, 5,
44
tribe (of tragic mysteries), 17
typewriter, xxvi, 3, 9, 48
tyrannical cry, 82
tyrannical family, 104
tyrannical-insanity of powerlessness, 57,
120
tyrannical towards nature, 27
tyrannical will, 127
tyrannical will of the tragic hero, 127
tyranny of modern Germany, 73
tyranny of self-isolating philosophers, 29
tyrants (conquered), 15

ugly and disharmonic, 18
unaware modern humans, 48
unawareness, 125
uncanny, 29, 128; self-awareness, 121
unchained spirit, 55
unchanging biological identity, 99
unconscious: abandonment of Dionysian
Greece, 129; evocation of precious
metal (Greece in the fifth century
B.C.E. and Europe in the nineteenth
century), 102; imagination, 29;
prefiguration, 126; sense, 74; style of

thought, 121; transference of a strain of
Jewish racism after Babylon, 115
unconsciously continues, 139
unconsciously illuminates, 137
unconsciously sustains, 123
unconsciously (unconsciousness, the
unconscious), 111, 120
underground and birthplace of the word,
22, 105
understanding tragedy, 127
underworld, 34; of darkness and gloom, 19
undestroyed in beautiful health, depth and
Dionysian strength, 82
un-Dionysian spirit, 27
uneasy reminders of that which is
continually taken from us, 137
uneasy consciences, 27, 29, 31, 43
unequal and irregular visual world of
lyricism, 124
unerring judge, Dionysus, 28
unfamiliar blood, 63
(unfinished) Dionysiac language, 129
unfortunate narrowness of modern space-
time and language, 72
un-German, 72
unhappy priest, 113, 119
unique, 124, 128
uniqueness, 32
universal human rights, 95
universal problem of learning, 75
universe, 29
unlearning the spirit of revenge, 60
unlimited: (anti-Dionysian) presence of
death in pre-Socratic philosophy, 132;
(apeiron) of Anaximander, 121;
battling, self-heroizing, and self-
isolating cosmology of pre-Socratics,
131; blessing to humankind, 138;
construction and destruction of the
individual world as the overflow of
primal desire, 123; ego, 18; egoism, 48;
expansion of Western civilization, 128;
exploitation of nature, 40;
(Herakleitean) "double orbit", 123;
images distracting from the lethal
essence of money, 46; language (of
technology, money and visual culture),
xxv; money deviously reinforced by the
unlimited visual media-ocracy, 139;

mass of "reading idlers" with "pointed
eyes", 128; nationalism and racism, 82;
rage against Christianity, 114; self-
hatred, 114; will of the monetized and
visualized mind of the tyrant, 124
unlimitedness of money, 123
unmusical listeners, 8
unnatural, 112
unnatural spirit of the sublime, 127
unprecedented aesthetic synthesis, 125
unprecedented population growth, 98
unproductive, dangerous spirit of
    Nietzsche's (German) identity crisis,
    140
unseeable spectacle, 45
unsettling, 92
un-silence-able, 61
unstable transition from love to hate, 115
unstoppable progress, 32
unsuccessful priest, 72
unsuspecting great dangers to our species,
    48
untouched side, 76
unwritten laws, 17
urbanization, xix

verbal game, xiv, 42, 47
verbal swill, xiv, 42, 47–48, 49, 57, 63
vineyard, 5, 16
visible, 15
visible middle-world, 19
vision, 17
visual: arts, 9; corruption, 45; culture, xiii,
    32, 122, 124; culture of text
    (newspapers, journals, etc.), 48; culture
    (underlying money), 21, 98, 122; desire
    for entertainment, 40; despair, 54;
    emptiness and horror, 44; enrichment,
    19; experience that accompanies
    Dionysian poetry (Archilochus), 124;
    horror, 53; media (of money), xiv;
    perversion, 6; phantasmagoria, 10;
    spectacle, 43; spirit of money, xxi;
    technology, 8; vengeance, 71
visualizations, 7
visualized "artistic effects", 124
visualized being, 123
visualized cosmos, xxiv
visualized chronotope, xxi, xxiii, 5, 21, 44

visualized education (*Bildung*), 44
visualized language, 8, 46, 128
visualized language of Homer, 124
visualized language of money, 125
visualized/monetized tyrant, 45
visualized nature and being, 27
visualized philosophy of modern time, 33
visualized sounds of the crowd, 46
visualized space and time, 44
visualized tragic hero, 20
visualizing forces, 124
visually self-referential (self-isolating),
    124

wailing, 16, 18
wakers-of-the-dead, 9, 73
waking, 16
Wagner, Richard, 4
Wagner (musician problem), 10
Wagner's music, 29
Wagner's nationalizing of Beethoven, 81
wealthy men (and women), xiii
Western civilization, xviii, 7, 30
Western racism, 114
Western thinking, 122
West Semitic Aramaic, 6
wine (Dionysus), 18
word, image and concept, 10
word as a passive tool, 103
words, 8, 10
world-creating force, 120
world-governing spirit, 130
world-historic loss, 7
world-historic significance of Greece, 33
world-historical significance of money,
    124
world of appearance, 19
world of images, 81
world of miseries, 18
world of music, 10
world of phenomena and images, 125
world's population, 119
world-transfiguring power (of music), 10
wreath, 16, 77, 84
writing, xxix

Yahweh, 6

Zagreus, 15, 138

About the Author

Lucas Murrey is from southern California and received his PhD in German studies and philosophy from Yale University. Since 2012, he has been teaching seminars and giving public lectures (mostly in western Europe) at various colleges and universities.

CPSIA information can be obtained at www.ICGtesting.com
Printed in the USA
BVOW05*0122160315

391508BV00003B/4/P